PC Architecture and Peripherals—I

PC Architecture and Peripherals—I

Dinesh Maidasani

B.A., Dip. Comp. Sc.

FIREWALL MEDIA

(An Imprint of Laxmi Publications Pvt. Ltd.)

BANGALORE • CHENNAI • COCHIN • GUWAHATI • HYDERABAD
JALANDHAR • KOLKATA • LUCKNOW • MUMBAI • RANCHI
NEW DELHI • BOSTON, USA

Published by :
FIREWALL MEDIA
(*An Imprint of Laxmi Publications Pvt. Ltd.*)
113, Golden House, Daryaganj,
New Delhi-110002

Phone : 011-43 53 25 00
Fax : 011-43 53 25 28

www.laxmipublications.com
info@laxmipublications.com

Price : **Rs. 125.00** *Only.*

First Edition : 2007
Reprint : 2008

OFFICES

India

© **Bangalore**	080-26 61 15 61
© **Chennai**	044-24 34 47 26
© **Cochin**	0484-239 70 04
© **Guwahati**	0361-254 36 69, 251 38 81
© **Hyderabad**	040-24 65 23 33
© **Jalandhar**	0181-222 12 72
© **Kolkata**	033-22 27 43 84
© **Lucknow**	0522-220 95 78
© **Mumbai**	022-24 91 54 15, 24 92 78 69
© **Ranchi**	0651-221 47 64

USA

Boston
11, Leavitt Street, Hingham,
MA 02043, USA

FPC-2931-125-PC ARCH. AND PERIPH (I)
C—15954/08/06
Typeset at : Kalyani Computer Services, New Delhi.
Printed at : Pack Printers, Delhi

CONTENTS

1. **Introduction to Hardware and Personal Computers** 1
Definition of Personal Computer 1
Personal Computer and its Parts 3
Detailed Block Diagram of Personal Computer 4
The main components of a typical Personal Computer are: 4
Introduction to Microprocessors 5
Peripherals of Personal Computers PC, PC-XT and PC-AT 6
PC XT 7
PC AT 8
RAM and Other Memory Types 9
ROM 9
Introduction to Personal Computers 13
Central Processing Unit 14

2. **Personal Computers Motherboards** 20
Personal Computer Motherboards 20
Various Motherboard Types 21
Intel 4 Processor Family 26
Advancements in Motherboard Technology 27
Chipsets for the Pentium and Beyond 28
Various Cards on the Motherboards 30
Motherboard Problems 37
Diagnostics of the Cards 38
PCI 39
SDRAM 40
DDR2 SDRAM 42
DD3 SDRAM 44

3. Storage Devices **49**

An Introduction to Storage Devices 49

HDD 49

FDD 58

CD-ROM 66

Structure of CD-ROM drive 67

Recordable Disk:Write Once, Read Many (WORM) 73

Erasable Disks: Magneto-Optical Disks 74

DVD 74

Tape Drive 76

Zip Drives 80

SCSI Drive 80

FM 81

MFM 82

4. Computer Serial Devices **87**

Introduction to Serial Devices of Personal Computers 87

Mouse 87

Keyboard 91

Understanding Ports and Their Functions 96

Modem 99

5. Computer Parallel Devices **103**

Introduction to Parallel Devices of Personal Computers 103

Printers 103

Connecting Printer with Computer 109

Scanner 124

Plotters 131

6. USB Devices **135**

Introduction to Parallel Devices of Personal Computers 135

USB Hub 136

USB Flash Drivers 140

USB 2.0 141

Model Test Papers **145**

1 Introduction to Hardware and Personal Computers

Definition of Personal Computer

There is a story that 5 blind men came across an elephant. Each one of them touched the different parts of its body. The one who touched the trunk said that the elephant was like a snake; the one who held the tail, said that it was like a rope. The ones holding other parts of its body said different things.

Like elephant, a computer is made of different parts which when looked at from any user angle will give a different definition. We should just remember that a computer:

1. Cannot think
2. It has vast capabilities of calculations like addition, substraction, etc. and
3. It is totally under the control of the user.

So, we can say that a computer is a machine, totally at the command of the user, which can perform operations at a much higher speed than a human being.

So may times you have seen or heard that a telephone bill or an electricity bill has been wrongly prepared and the amount charged is enormous. It is not because of computer's mistake but it is so since the meter reading given to the computer was wrong, possibly the reading was wrongly taken by the meter reader who had gone to the house to read and record the meter reading.

Therefore, we understand that there is nothing magical about a computer. It is actually a friendly machine which is totally at your command. Do you remember the story Aladdin and the Magic Lamp? Just like the Genie of the magic lamp, a computer will obey your command. If you make a mistake in giving commands to the computer, it will carry out these commands giving wrong results.

Thus, the Computer is a machine which works on the raw Data given to it and gives out meaningful results in the form of Information.

Computer Age

Though the first fully operational electronic computer was introduced to the world in 1946, but the historian assumes the starting of a computer age from 1951, when first commercial computer UNIVAC was introduced. The remarkable thing about the computer age is that so much has happened in so much short time. We have leapfrogged four generations of technology in about 50 years - a span of time whose events are within the memories of many people today. The first three computer generations are pinned to three technological developments:

1. vacuum tube

2. transistor and
3. integrated circuit

Each has drastically changed the nature and size of computers. We define the timing of each generation according to the beginning of commercial delivery of the hardware technology. Defining subsequent generations has become more complicated because the entire industry has become more complicated.

Uses of Computers

There are lots of uses of computers. In fact, in our everyday life it is used in almost every step. Some of the places where it is used is listed below. I have listed them alphabetically.

Airlines booking	Now you can book your ticket for a flight leaving New York while sitting in Melbourne. All the airlines are interconnected through computers. The same goes for Railways but it is restricted to individual countries only.
Banks	Computers in Banks have made it possible that you can get your account information while sitting at home only. For this your bank must be an e-bank, which most of them are. ATMs are another computer applications of banks.
Business	For most of the companies, all the work relating to accounts is now done on computers, for accuracy and speediness. You can even have your correspondence on it.
Cartoons	There are various programs available in computers which allow you to create animations. By learning them you can become an expert animator. You may even make a movie of your own.
Cinema	Now a days most of the film editing is done by computers. You can add and delete film clips at a snap using computers. In fact, some movies are totally made using computers. Films like Toy Story are made using computers.
Defence	America has used the computers in defence for the fullest with pin pointing the position of enemy targets. Most of the missiles these days are computer controlled.
DTP	It has revolutionized how composing for printing used to done. Now every book for printing is composed on computer since it is very easy to edit and read on screen.
Education	Computers can help in teaching too. In fact this books on computers was created using computers. Most of the schools now use computers for accounting, students record management, papers preparation and even results compilation.
Home	At home it has become an additional entertainment media. You can use it for playing games, watching movies, listening to songs,

	writing letters, creating your own database of friends, etc., the options are unlimited.
Library	Maintaining the records in library manually used to be a very cumbersome method. Computers have dramatically changed the way the cataloging is done in libraries.
Medicine	Lots of research in medicine is done using computers. Doctors now a days can see the complete inside of the human beings using the computers.
Space Technology	All the movements of the satellites are controlled using computers.
Weather	Using computers and satellites you can predict the weather for the next few days. In fact, the biggest computer in India is with the Meteorological Department of India, at New Delhi.

Personal Computer and its Parts

If you see, the computer is physically divided into 3 main parts:

Monitor

It is like the TV and all the information is displayed here.

Central Processing Unit

It is the main processing unit where all the processing takes place.

Keyboard

It is like the typewriter and is used to give information to the computer.

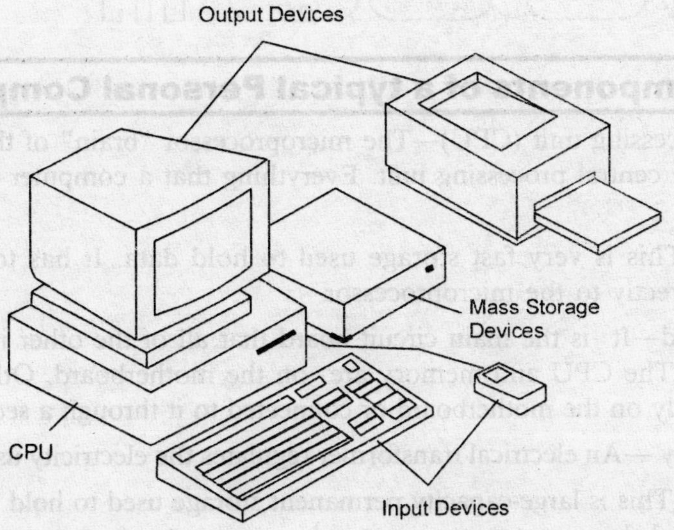

Detailed Block Diagram of Personal Computer

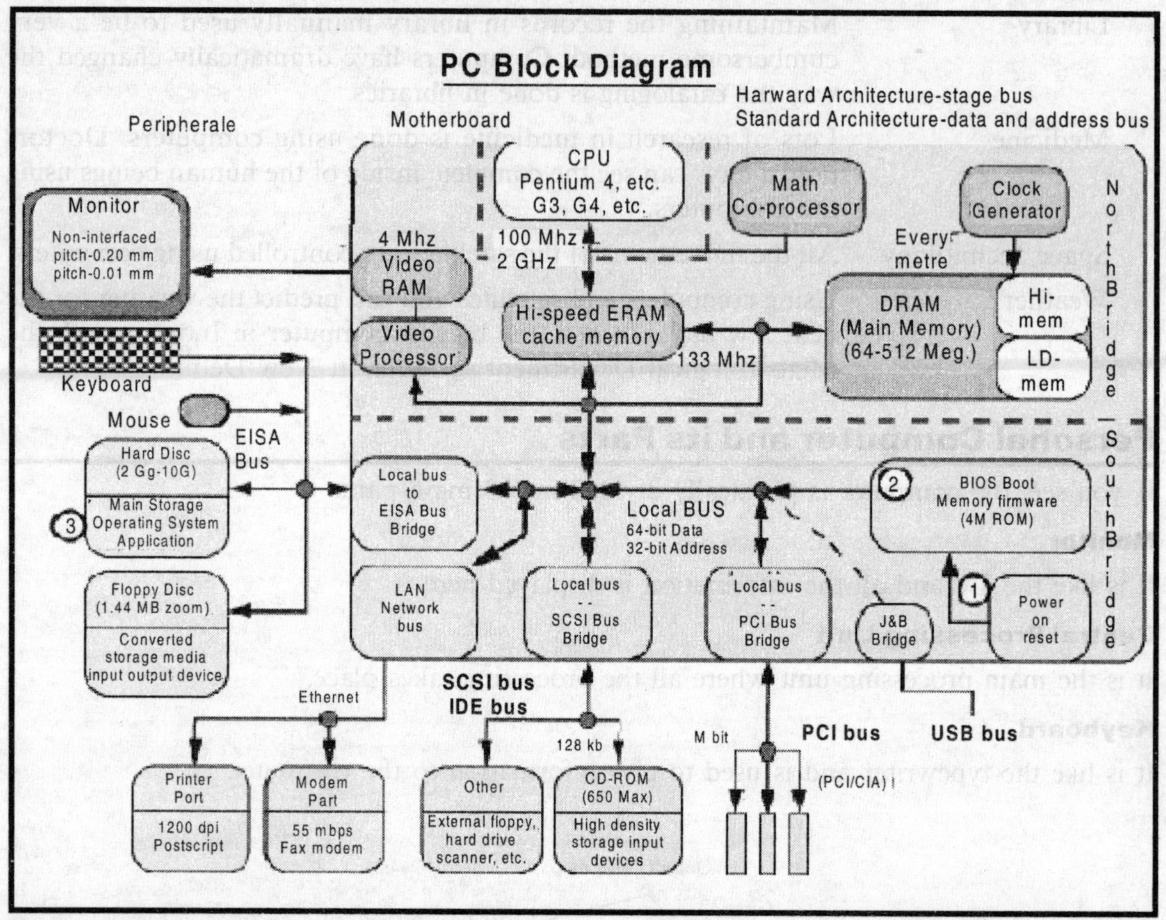

The main components of a typical Personal Computer are:

1. Central processing unit (CPU)—The microprocessor "brain" of the computer system is called the central processing unit. Everything that a computer does is overseen by the CPU.
2. Memory—This is very fast storage used to hold data. It has to be fast because it connects directly to the microprocessor.
3. Motherboard—It is the main circuit board that all of the other internal components connect to. The CPU and memory are on the motherboard. Other systems may be found directly on the motherboard or connected to it through a secondary connection.
4. Power supply —An electrical transformer regulates the electricity used by the computer.
5. Hard disk—This is large-capacity permanent storage used to hold information such as programs and documents.
6. Operating system—This is the basic software that allows the user to interface with the computer.

7. Integrated Drive Electronics (IDE) Controller—This is the primary interface for the hard drive, CD-ROM and floppy disk drive.
8. Peripheral Component Interconnect (PCI) Bus—The most common way to connect additional components to the computer, PCI uses a series of slots on the motherboard that PCI cards plug into.
9. SCSI—The small computer system interface is a method of adding additional devices, such as hard drives or delete, to the computer.
10. AGP—Accelerated Graphics Port is a very high-speed connection used by the graphics card to interface with the computer.
11. Sound card—This is used by the computer to record and play audio by converting analog sound into digital information and back again.
12. Graphics card—This translates image data from the computer into a format that can be displayed by the monitor.

Introduction to Microprocessors

The introduction of the microprocessor in the 1970s significantly affected the design and implementation of CPUs. Since the introduction of the first microprocessor (the Intel 4004) in 1970 and the first widely used microprocessor (the Intel 8080) in 1974, this class of CPUs has almost completely overtaken all other central processing unit implementation methods. Mainframe and minicomputer manufacturers of the time launched proprietary IC development programs to upgrade their older computer architectures, and eventually produced instruction set compatible microprocessors that were backward-compatible with their older hardware and software. Combined with the advent and eventual vast success of the now ubiquitous personal computer, the term "CPU" is now applied almost exclusively to microprocessors.

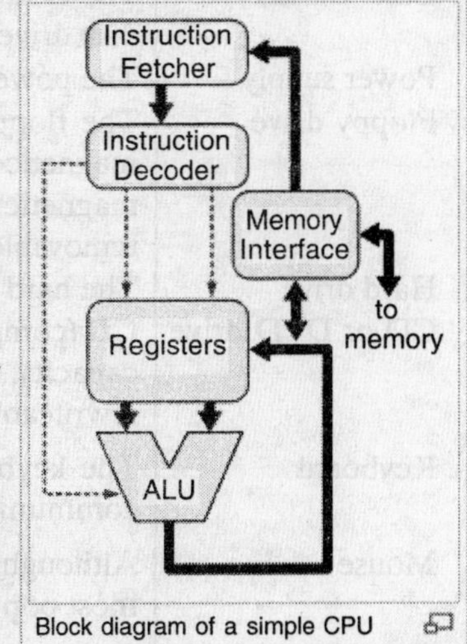

Block diagram of a simple CPU

Previous generations of CPUs were implemented as discrete components and numerous small integrated circuits (ICs) on one or more circuit boards. Microprocessors, on the other hand, are CPUs manufactured on a very small number of ICs; usually just one. The overall smaller CPU size as a result of being implemented on a single die means faster switching time because of physical factors like decreased gate parasitic capacitance. This has allowed synchronous microprocessors to have clock rates ranging from tens of megahertz to several gigahertz. Additionally, as the ability to construct exceedingly small transistors on an IC has increased, the complexity and number of transistors in a single CPU has increased dramatically. This widely observed trend is described by Moore's law, which has proven to be a fairly accurate predictor of the growth of CPU (and other IC) complexity to date.

While the complexity, size, construction, and general form of CPUs have changed drastically over the past sixty years, it is notable that the basic design and function has not changed much at all. Almost all common CPUs today can be very accurately described as von Neumann stored-program machines.

As the aforementioned Moore's law continues to hold true, concerns have arisen about the limits of integrated circuit transistor technology. Extreme miniaturization of electronic gates is causing the effects of phenomena like electromigration and subthreshold leakage to become much more significant. These newer concerns are among the many factors causing researchers to investigate new methods of computing such as the quantum computer, as well as to expand the usage of parallelism and other methods that extend the usefulness of the classical von Neumann model.

Peripherals of Personal Computers PC, PC-XT and PC-AT

There are three type of peripherals in use for the computers. These can be classified as Input, Output and Storage. Various types of peripherals can be listed below.

Table: Peripherals of PC,PC-XT,PC-AT

Component	Description
Motherboard	The motherboard is the core of the system. It really is the PC; everything else is connected to it, and it controls everything in the system.
Processor	The processor is often thought of as the "engine" of the computer. It's also called the CPU (central processing unit).
Memory (RAM)	The system memory is often called RAM (for random access memory). This is the primary memory, which holds all the programs and data the processor is using at a given time.
Case/chassis	The case is the frame or chassis that houses the motherboard, power supply, disk drives, adapter cards, and any other physical components in the system.
Power supply	The power supply feeds electrical power to every single part in the PC.
Floppy drive	The floppy drive is a simple, inexpensive, low-capacity, removable-media, magnetic-storage device. Many recent systems use other types of removable magnetic or USB-based flash memory devices instead of floppy drives for removable storage.
Hard drive	The hard disk is the primary archival storage memory for the system.
CD or DVD drive	CD (compact disc) and DVD (digital versatile disc) drives are relatively high-capacity, removable media, optical drives; many recent systems include a rewriteable CD (CD-RW) along with or combined with a DVD-ROM drive.
Keyboard	The keyboard is the primary device on a PC that is used by a human to communicate with and control a system.
Mouse	Although many types of pointing devices are on the market today, the first and most popular device for this purpose is the mouse.
Video card	The video card controls the information you see on the monitor.
Monitor	Monitors is the visual display unit that displays the result.
Sound card	It enables the PC to generate complex sounds.
Modem	Most prebuilt PCs ship with a modem (generally an internal modem).

PC XT

The IBM Personal Computer XT, often shortened to the PC XT or simply XT, was IBM's successor to the original IBM PC. It was released as IBM product number 5160 on March 8, 1983, and was one of the first computers to come standard with a hard drive. It was based on essentially the same architecture as the original PC, with only incremental improvements; a new 16-bit bus architecture would follow in the AT. The system was largely intended for business users, and a corresponding 3270 PC featuring 3270 terminal emulation was released later in October 1983. XT stands for eXtended Technology.

The XT originally came with 128 KiB of memory, a 360 kB double-sided 5 1/4" full-height floppy disk drive, and a 10 MB hard drive, a serial port, eight 8-bit ISA expansion slots, and an Intel 8088 microprocessor running at 4.77 MHz (with a socket for an 8087 math coprocessor); the operating system usually sold with it was PC-DOS 2.0. The eight slots were an increase over the five in the IBM PC, although three were taken up by the floppy drive adapter, the hard drive adapter, and the serial card. Later models came with 256 KiB of memory standard, and eventually models with 640 KiB and a 20 MB hard drive were sold.

The XT originally came only in a standard configuration with the hard disk. It was not until 1985 that a model without the hard drive became available. Other models came with two half-height floppy drives as well as the hard drive.

IBM PC/XT (model 5160)	
Type	Personal computer
Released	March 8, 1983
Discontinued	1987
Processor	Intel 8088 @ 4.77 MHz
Memory	128 KiB ~ 640 KiB
OS	IBM BASIC / PC-DOS 2.0

In 1986, the XT/286 (IBM 5162) with a 6 MHz Intel 80286 processor was introduced. This system actually turned out to be faster than the ATs of the time using 8 MHz 286 processors due to the fact that it had zero wait state RAM that could move data more quickly.

Like the original PC, the XT came with a BASIC interpreter in ROM. Since this interpreter was meant to be used with a cassette drive (which wasn't offered on the XT), the only ways to access it were by disconnecting the hard drive and leaving the floppy drive empty, using the BASICA program, included on a floppy disk, which added extensions for using the disk drives, or invoking a BIOS call manually using a debugger.

PC and XT keyboards are not compatible with more modern PCs (IBM AT or newer), even with DIN to PS/2 mini-DIN plug adapters, because PC/XT keyboards use different keyboard scan codes. An XT to AT signal adapter is needed to create compatibility with modern computers. Also, the 'parkbd' driver can be used under linux in order to support either sort of keyboard via a simple adapter through the parallel port.

PC AT

The IBM Personal Computer/AT, more commonly known as the IBM AT and also sometimes called the PC AT or PC/AT, was IBM's second-generation PC, designed around the Intel 80286 microprocessor running at 6 MHz and released in 1984 as model number 5170. Because the AT used various technologies that were new at the time in personal computers, the name AT originally stood for Advanced Technology, and indeed, the Intel 80286 processor used in the AT supported Protected mode. Later, IBM released a version of the AT running at 8 MHz.

Features of AT

- AT-Bus — The AT motherboard had a 16-bit data bus and 24-bit address bus that was backward compatible with PC-style expansion cards (which were 8-bit data, 20-bit address).
- 15 IRQs and 7 DMA channels, expanded from 8 IRQs and 4 DMA channels for the PC. IRQ 8–15 are cascaded through IRQ 2, which leaves 15 active instead of 16. Similarly, DMA channel 4 is reserved for cascading 0–3 leaving 7 channels active.
- Over 15 MiB maximum memory (because of the 24-bit address bus of the 286), compared to the PC's 640 KiB
- Battery backed Real-time clock on motherboard with 50 bytes CMOS memory available for power-off storage of BIOS parameters. (the basic PC had required either manual setting of its software clock using Time and Date commands, or the addition of an accessory expansion card with real-time clock, to avoid the default 01-01-80 file date)
- 84-key AT keyboard layout — the "84th key" being, *i.e.*, System Request; numerical keypad now clearly separated from main key group; also added indicator LEDs for Caps lock/Scroll lock/Num lock. The AT keyboard uses the same 5-pin DIN connector as the PC keyboard, and is electrically compatible with it, but it generates different keyboard scan codes.
- 1.2 MB 5 1/4 inch floppy disk drive (15 sectors of 512 bytes, 80 tracks, 2 sides) stored over three times as much data as the 360 kiB PC floppy disk (9 sectors of 512 bytes, 40 tracks, 2 sides)
- 20 MB hard disk drive was twice as fast (about 40 msec) as the PC XT's 10 MB drive, although the early drives manufactured by Computer Memories (CMI) had a 25–

IBM PC/AT (model 5170)	
Type	Personal Computer
Released	1984
Discontinued	1987
Processor	Intel 80286 @ 6 and 8 MHz
Memory	256 KiB ~ 16 MiB
OS	PC-DOS 3.0+, OS/2 1.x

30% failure rate after one year. This was attributed partly due to failure to automatically retract the read/write heads when the computer was powered off, and partly due to a bug in the DOS 3.0 FAT algorithm.

- Optional Enhanced Graphics Adapter with 16 display colors from a 64 color palette on a 640 x 350 pixel resolution screen
- Optional Professional Graphics Controller with 256 colors from a 4096 color palette and 640 x 480 resolution and accelerated 2D and 3D display functions for Computer Aided Design (CAD) applications
- PC-DOS 3.0 was released to support the new AT features
- The AT was equipped with a lock and key that could be used to prevent access to the computer.

RAM and Other Memory Types

So far at every stage we have said that computer cannot think on its own and cannot remember anything unless we store in hard disk with save. While working all the information is stored in what is called the memory of the computer till we press the button to save it. Till that point all the information and results are stored in memory. So usually a big memory means a faster and more useful computer.

A PC's memory is made up of electronic components in which the PC temporarily stores data and instructions. Technically, any device that stores data or instructions on the PC can be called memory, including the hard disk, floppy disks, ROM, CMOS, RAM and cache. However, what is commonly referred to as memory on the PC is its primary storage, which is also known as system memory, temporary storage or RAM. With the exception of ROM, the other forms of storage (hard disk, floppy disk, CD-ROM and the like) are known as secondary storage.

ROM

It's logical then that data stored on read-only memory (ROM) cannot be changed, as its name implies. ROM also has the added feature of being nonvolatile, which means that it can keep its contents even without a power source. This makes it ideal for storing the PC's startup instructions and system BIOS (Basic Input/Output System). While virtually all ROM chips are packed in a DIP (dual inline packaging) form, there are three types of ROM used in a PC:

PROM (programmable read-only memory)

This type of ROM chip is programmed using a special type of programming device called a RPOM burner (a.k.a. PROM programmer), which permanently stores machine language (binary instructions) code on the PROM chip. A PROM chips is also referred to as OTP (One Time Programmable) memory.

EPROM (erasable programmable read-only memory)

This type of ROM, pronounced "e-prom," is erasable and can be reprogrammed. Unlike a

PROM chip that cannot be reused and can only be thrown out when it becomes obsolete, an EPROM chip can be reprogrammed and reused. An EPROM has a quartz window on the face of the chip that exposes the chip's interior circuits. When ultraviolet (UV) light is shined through this window, it causes a chemical reaction that erases the EPROM. In order to reprogram an EPROM, it must be removed from the computer, erased with UV light and then reprogrammed on a PROM programmer.

EEPROM (electronically erasable programmable read-only memory)

Most newer PCs now include an EEPROM (pronounced "e-e-prom") that can be reprogrammed like an EPROM, but unlike the EPROM doesn't need to be removed from the CP to be reprogrammed. An EEPROM can be reprogrammed, a process called flashing, using specialized software that runs on your PC. An EEPROM is also referred to as flash ROM. Flashing lets you upgrade your computer's BIOS easily without removing and replacing the ROM chip. One thing that all DIP chips suffer from including removable and replaceable PROMs and EPROMs is a condition called chip creep. DIP chips are inserted into what are called through-hole sockets and can and do squirm out of their sockets. Should a ROM chip creep out of its socket, it can cause startup problems. If you have an older motherboard that includes removable DIP ROM or memory chips, you should check them occasionally for creep.

CMOS

Because of the initial cost of Complementary Metal Oxide Semiconductor (CMOS) technology, memory, transistors and large parts of most microprocessors were once reserved for storing the startup configuration of the PC. With technology advances and lower costs, however, CMOS technology is now used throughout the PC. CMOS memory requires only about one-millionth of an amp to hold any data stored on it. Using only a lithium battery, CMOS memory is able to store the startup configuration of a PC for many years. The term CMOS is still synonymous with the PC's startup configuration data.

RAM

RAM or random access memory, is used in the PC for its primary memory. RAM is where all active programs and data are stored so that they are readily available and easily accessed by the CPU and other components of the CPU. When you execute a program on your PC, a copy of the program is copied into RAM from whatever secondary storage it is on, usually the hard disk. Once it is in RAM, the instructions that make up the program are passed one at a time to the CPU for execution. Any data the program accepts or reads from a disk is also stored in RAM. There are several reasons that RAM is used in a PC but perhaps the most important is that RAM can transfer data to and from the CPU much faster than all secondary storage devices. Without RAM, all programs instructions and data would be read from the disk drive, slowing the computer to a crawl. With RAM speeds as fast, if not faster, than the speed of the CPU, the entire PC operates much more efficiently.

RAM is a group of integrated circuits (ICs or chips) that contain small electronic components (called capacitors) that store binary 1s and 0s. A variety of memory chips can be used for RAM, but some are better suited to storing large amounts of data, fit better in the space available in the PC and are less expensive. However, not all memory applications in the PC need to store a large amount of data, so most PCs use three different layers of memory: primary memory, level 1 (l1) cache and level 2 (l2) cache. RAM in its common usage refers to the primary memory layer of the PC's memory.

Uses of RAM

The key benefit of RAM over types of storage which require physical movement is that retrieval times are short and consistent. Short because no physical movement is necessary, and consistent because the time taken to retrieve a piece of data does not depend on its current distance from a physical head; it costs practically the same time to access any piece of data stored in a RAM chip.

Because of this speed and consistency, RAM is used as 'main memory' or primary storage: the working area used for loading, displaying and manipulating applications and data. In most personal computers, the RAM is not an integral part of the motherboard or CPU—it comes in the easily upgraded form of modules called memory sticks or RAM sticks about the size of a few sticks of chewing gum, which can be quickly removed and replaced when they become damaged or too small for current purposes. A smaller amount of random-access memory is also integrated with the CPU, but this is usually referred to as "cache" memory, rather than RAM.

The disadvantage of RAM over physically moving media is cost, and the loss of data when power is turned off. For these reasons, nearly all PCs have disc storage as "secondary storage". Small PDAs and music players (up to 8 GiB in Jan 2007) may dispense with disks, but rely on flash memory, to maintain data between sessions of use.

Recent developments

Currently, several types of non-volatile RAM are under development, which will preserve data while powered down. The technologies used include carbon nanotubes and the magnetic tunnel effect. In summer 2003, a 128 KiB magnetic RAM chip was introduced, which was manufactured with 0.18 μm technology. The core technology of MRAM is based on the magnetic tunnel effect. In June of 2004, Infineon Technologies unveiled a 16 MiB prototype again based on 0.18 μm technology.

As for carbon nanotube memory, Nantero built a functioning prototype 10 GiB array in 2004. In 2006 Solid state memory came of age, especially when implemented as Solid State Disks capacities for these have now exceeded 150 gigabytes with speeds far exceeding traditional disks. This development has started to blur the definition between traditional random access memory and disks, dramatically narrowing the performance differential.

DRAM

For economical reasons, the large (main) memories found in personal computers, workstations, and non-handheld game-consoles (such as Playstation and Xbox) normally consists of dynamic RAM (DRAM). Other parts of the computer, such as cache memories and data buffers in hard disks, normally use static RAM (SRAM).

General DRAM packaging formats

Dynamic random access memory (DRAM) is produced as integrated circuits (ICs) bonded and mounted into plastic packages with metal pins for connection to control signals and buses. Today, these DRAM packages are in turn often assembled into plug-in modules for easier handling. Some standard module types are:

- DRAM chip (Integrated Circuit or IC)
- Dual in-line Package (DIP)
- DRAM (memory) modules
- Single In-line Pin Package (SIPP)
- Single In-line Memory Module (SIMM)
- Dual In-line Memory Module (DIMM)
- Rambus In-line Memory Module (RIMM), technically DIMMs but called RIMMs due to their proprietary slot.
- Small outline DIMM (SO-DIMM). Smaller version of the DIMM, used in laptops. Comes in versions with:
- 72 pins (32-bit)
- 144 pins (64-bit)
- 200 pins (72-bit)
- Small outline RIMM (SO-RIMM). Smaller version of the RIMM, used in laptops.
- Stacked v. non-stacked RAM modules
- Stacked RAM chips use two RAM wafers that are stacked on top of each other. This allows large module (like a 512mb or 1Gig SO-DIMM) to be manufactured using cheaper low density wafers. Stacked chip modules draw more power.

Common DRAM packages

Common DRAM packages as illustrated to the right, from top to bottom:

1. DIP 18-pin (DRAM chip, usually pre-FPRAM)
2. SIPP (usually FPRAM)
3. SIMM 30-pin (usually FPRAM)
4. SIMM 72-pin (so-called "PS/2 SIMM", usually EDO RAM)
5. DIMM 168-pin (SDRAM)
6. DIMM 184-pin (DDR SDRAM)

Common DRAM packages

7. DIMM 240-pin (DDR2 SDRAM)—(not in picture)

Introduction to Personal Computers

A computer can be judged by various factor, among them are:

Speed

Computers provide the processing speed essential to our fast-paced society. The quick service we have come to expect-for bank withdrawals, telephone calls, and travel reservations, to name a few-is made possible by computers. Businesses depend on the speedy processing computers to handle high volume activities such as balancing ledgers and designing products.

The smallest unit of time in the human experience is, realistically, the second. Computer operations—for example, the execution of an instruction, such as multiplying pay—rate with numbers of hours worked-are measured in milliseconds, microsecond, nanoseconds and picoseconds (one thousandth, one millionth, one billionth, and one trillionth of a second respectively).

Although all computers are fast, but there is a wide diversity of computer speeds. The execution of an instruction on a very slow computer may be measured in less than a millisecond. Most computer can execute an instruction measured in microseconds range, but still to be broken in the picosecond barrier.

A computer speed is generally expressed in megahertz (MHz), millions of machine cycles per second. Thus a PC (Personal Computer) listed at 100 MHz has a processor capable of handling 100 million machine cycles per second. Another measure of computer speed is MIPS (one million instructions per second). MIPS is often a more accurate measure than clock speed, because some computers can use each tick of the clock more efficiently than others.

A third measure of speed is the megaflops (MFLOPS), which stands for one million floating point operations per second. It measures the ability of the computer to perform complex mathematical operations.

Reliability

Computers are extremely reliable. Where reliability is the measurement of the performance of a computer, measured against some predetermined standard for operation without the failure of it.

Reliability Of Computer = Serviceable Time/Serviceable Time + Down Time

where serviceable time is the total time during which a computer is in a state where it can operate normally, including time when the computer is idle, but not the time when it is unattended. Down time is the time when a computer is inoperable due to a machine fault. Computer systems are particularly adept at repetitive tasks. They don't take sick leave and tea breaks, and they seldom complain anything below 99.9% serviceable time, the time when the computer system is in operation, is usually unacceptable. For some companies, any down time is unacceptable. These companies provide backup computers that take over automatically if the main computer fails.

Accuracy

Errors do occur in computer based information systems, but precious few can be directly attributed to the computer system itself. The vast majority can be traced to a program logic error, a procedural error, or erroneous data. These are human errors. High accuracy implies small error, but accuracy is contrasted with precision, *e.g.*, three places of decimals properly computed are less precise but more accurate than four places of decimals containing an error. The accuracy of the results obtained from computer mainly depends on the method of programming and the way the results are interpreted.

Central Processing Unit

It is actually the main brain of the computer system. It is here that the whole processing takes place. It consists of 4 main units:

Primary Storage

Arithmetic Logic Unit

Control Unit

Output Unit

Let us read about them one by one.

Primary Storage Unit

This is main storage area, which is also called the main memory area. Its main functions are listed below:

1. Holding the data in its memory till it is required to be processed.
2. Holding the result of the processed data.
3. Holding program instructions which are required for processing.

Arithmetic Logic Unit

This is used for the most of the logical processing, for example, for calculations or comparisons. The arithmetic operations like, +, –, *, and / are performed here. The logical operations like, <, >, =, <=, >=, and <> are also performed here. In most of the arithmetical operations the result is in numerical form while in the case of logical operations the result can be YES/NO or TRUE/FALSE.

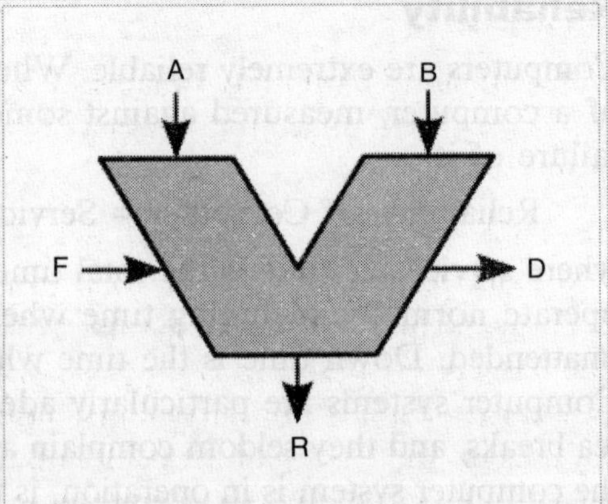

A typical schematic symbol for an ALU: A & B are operands; R is the output; F is the input from the Control Unit; D is an output status

The arithmetic logic unit (ALU) is a digital circuit that calculates an arithmetic operation (like an addition, subtraction, etc.) and logic operations (like an Exclusive Or) between two numbers. The ALU is a fundamental building block of the central processing unit of a computer. Many types of electronic circuits need to perform some type of arithmetic operation, so even the circuit inside a digital watch will have a tiny ALU that keeps adding 1 to the current time, and keeps checking if it should beep the timer, etc...

By far, the most complex electronic circuits are those that are built inside the chip of modern microprocessors like the Pentium. Therefore, these processors have inside them a powerful and very complex ALU. In fact, a modern microprocessor (or mainframe) may have multiple cores, each core with multiple execution units, each with multiple ALUs.

Many other circuits may contain ALUs inside: GPUs like the ones in NVidia and ATI graphic cards, FPUs like the old 80387 co-processor, and digital signal processor like the ones found in Sound Blaster sound cards, CD players and High-Definition TVs. All of these have several powerful and complex ALUs inside

Control Unit

This unit controls the flow and manipulation of data and information. It also controls the flow of data from input devices to memory and from memory to output devices.

Output Unit

The output unit consists of the output devices attached to the computer. These devices take machine-coded output results from the processor and convert them into a form that can be understood by the user.

Generation of Computers

Development of computer over the ages can be divided into 5 generations. These are listed below with the year when they have been around and what was the main storing method:

First Generation	This was based on Thermionic Valve or so called Vacuum Tube	1949
Second Generation	This was based on Transistors	1956
Third Generation	Integrated Circuits or ICs	1966
Fourth Generation	Microprocessors Chips	1975
Fifth Generation	Large Scale Integration Systems	1980

Personal Computers

In 1981, IBM introduced the first Personal Computer. Since then, IBM has brought out different versions/models with variations of floppy disks, hard disks, chips, etc., making them faster and faster.

The various versions of IBM PC compatible computers. The latest being Pentium V computer based on Pentium V chip.

Classification of Computers

If we classify the computers by their sizes, we would have the following classification:

- Super Computers
- Mainframe Computers
- Super Mini Computers

- Mini Computers
- Micro Computers or Personal Computers

Let us read about each one of them in brief.

Super Computers

A supercomputer contains a number of processing units which operate in parallel to make it faster. They are in fact, very large computers and are thus used for bigger applications. In India, there is only one such computer which is used by the Metrological department in weather forecasting.

Mainframe Computers

It is again a large computer but where it differs from super computer is that it can be connected to various computers to share facilities. For example, a System/370 can be attached to several personal computers so that they can share programs and data. Mainframe computers are used in research organizations, large industrial banks, airlines, and railway reservations where large data base is required.

Super Mini Computers

These are cross between minicomputers and super computers. They are commonly used as dedicated computers, for one processing function at a time.

Mini Computers

They are inferior to mainframe computers both in speed and storage. They can also support various terminals. In fact, they can support upto 100 terminals. Minicomputers have operating systems with multitasking and network capabilities enabling them to serve more than one user.

Laptops

In recent years design changes have reduced the size of some microcomputers, making computer technology portable and affordable. Laptop computers are roughly the size of a large notebook. Their power source, a battery is completely self-contained yet can be recharged from an electrical outlet. Laptops sometimes called notebook computers, can contain more than 20 GB of hard disk memory, 64 MB of RAM, CD Drive, mouse, keyboard and a colour display.

Power adapters can be used to plug into any electrical outlet throughout the world. It can be connected with an additional battery or serial port, a network or fax equipment. Laptops are not as inexpensive as their size may suggest, many carry a prize tag equivalent to full-size personal computer for business.

Revision

1. A computer: cannot think, it has vast capabilities of calculations like addition, substraction, etc. and It is totally under the control of the user.
2. Though the first fully operational electronic computer was introduced to the world in 1946, but the historian assumes the starting of a computer age from 1951, when first commercial computer UNIVAC was introduced.
3. Computer is vastly used for Airlines booking, Banking business, Professional Business, Cartoons creations, Cinema editing, Defence applications, Desk Top Publishing, Education books and teaching, Home videos and games, Library management of books, Medicine records, Space Technology and Weather reporting.
4. The main parts of the computer are: Monitor, Central Processing Unit and Keyboard.
5. The block diagram shows all the parts of the computer.
6. Over the years personal computers have gone through various changes and have been named as XT, AT, etc.
7. There are various types of memories which are used by computers.
8. RAM, Random Access Memory and ROM, Read Only Memory are the most common.
9. ROM can be of the type: PROM, EPROM, and EEPROM.
10. Personal computers are known for their speed, reliability and accuracy.
11. The Central Processing Unit has: Primary Storage Unit, Arithmetic Logic Unit, Control Unit and Output Unit.
12. The development of computers have been classified in the form of generations.
13. There are five generation of computers.
14. Computers can of various types: Super Computers, Mainframe Computers, Super Mini Computers and Mini Computers.
15. Laptop computers are also very popular these days.

Multiple Choice Questions

1. RAM stands for:
   (a) Random Allowed Memory (b) Ready Access Memory
   (c) Random Access Memory
2. RAM consists of binary numbers 1s and :
   (a) 0s (b) 2s
   (c) 3s
3. CPU contains Primary Storage, Arithmetic Logic Unit and
   (a) Control Unit (b) Data Unit
   (c) Alpha Unit
4. Data stored in ROM cannot be changed:
   (a) Yes (b) No
5. A copy of the current instruction is stored in:
   (a) Instruction Register (b) Working Register
   (c) General Register

6. Computers are classified into ______ generations:
   (a) 7 (b) 3
   (c) 5
7. The three main units of computer are: Keyboard, Central Processing Unit and :
   (a) Monitor (b) Mouse
   (c) Motherboard
8. Which of the following does not belong to the Intel's Processor's series:
   (a) 8086 (b) 80186
   (c) 80486 (d) 8051

True/False Questions

1. The main parts of the computer are: Mouse, Central Processing Unit and Keyboard.
2. The block diagram shows all the parts of the computer.
3. Over the years personal computers have gone through various changes and have been named as XT, AT, etc.
4. There are various types of memories which are used by computers.
5. RAM is Random Access Memory .
6. ROM is Read Over Memory.
7. ROM can be of the type: PROM, EPROM, and EEPROM.
8. Personal computers are known for their speed, reliability and accuracy.
9. The Central Processing Unit has: Primary Storage Unit, Arithmetic Logic Unit, Control Unit and Output Unit.
10. The development of computers have been classified in the form of generations.
11. There are seven generation of computers.
12. Laptop computers are also very popular these days.
13. Microprocessor is a semiconductor chip consist billions of transistors.
14. 80287 processor is used on PC-AT.
15. DRAM is a type of primary memory.

Short Answer Type Questions

1. What is Random Access Memory? Explain its construction.
2. What is BIOS?
3. Describe the personal computer.
4. Which are the main parts of computers?
5. What is Central Processing Unit?

Descriptive Questions

1. What changes have been brought about in computer over the ages?
2. Describe the various peripherals used in PC, PC-XT and PC-AT.
3. Which type of memories are used by personal computers?
4. Describe the various generations of computers.

5. Describe the various classifications of computers.
6. Draw the block diagram of computer and give its working.
7. Give difference between ROM and RAM.
8. What is microprocosser? Explain its working?

Answers to Objective Type Questions

Multiple Choice Questions

1. c	2. a	3. a	4. b
5. a	6. c	7. a	8. d

True False Questions

1. F	2. T	3. T	4. T
5. T	6. F	7. T	8. T
9. T	10. T	11. F	12. T
13. T	14. F	15. T	

2 Personal Computers Motherboards

Personal Computer Motherboards

Motherboard is the main component inside the main system unit. This is the biggest electronic circuit board inside the computer system, on which many other board are attached. The boards that attach to the motherboard are known as daughterboard or expansion board.

The motherboard contains following:

1. **Processor Support:** The motherboard dictates directly your choice of processor for use in the system.
2. **Peripheral Support:** The motherboard determines, what types of peripherals you can use in your PC.
3. **Performance:** The motherboard is a major determining factor in system's performance, the motherboard determines what types of processors, memory, system buses, and hard disk interface speed your system can have, and these components dictate directly your system's performance.
4. **Upgradability:** The capabilities of motherboard dictate to what extent you will be able to upgrade your machine.

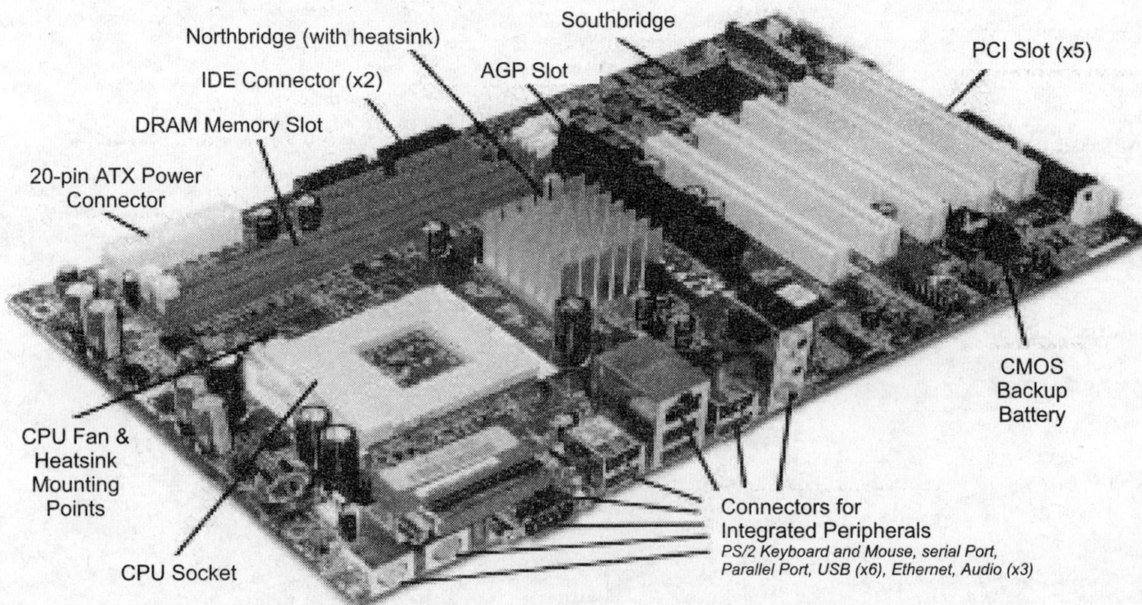

5. **Organization:** The way that the motherboard is designed and laid out dictates how the entire computer is going to be organized.
6. **Control:** The motherboard contains the chipset and BIOS program, which control most of the data flow within the computer.
7. **Communication:** All communication between the PC and its peripherals, other PCs, and user, goes through the motherboard.

Various Motherboard Types

PC/XT

It is series of personal computers based on the Intel 8088 processor, introduced by IBM in 1983. XT stands for eXtended Technology.The PC/XT was the first personal computer to offer a built-in hard disk and the capability to expand memory 640K on the motherboard. The original PC/XT used an Intel 8088 running at a clock speed of 4.77 MHz . The system was largely intended for business users. It came with 128 kB of memory, a 360 kB double-sided 5 1/4" full-height floppy disk drive, and a 10 MB hard drive, a serial port, eight 8-bit

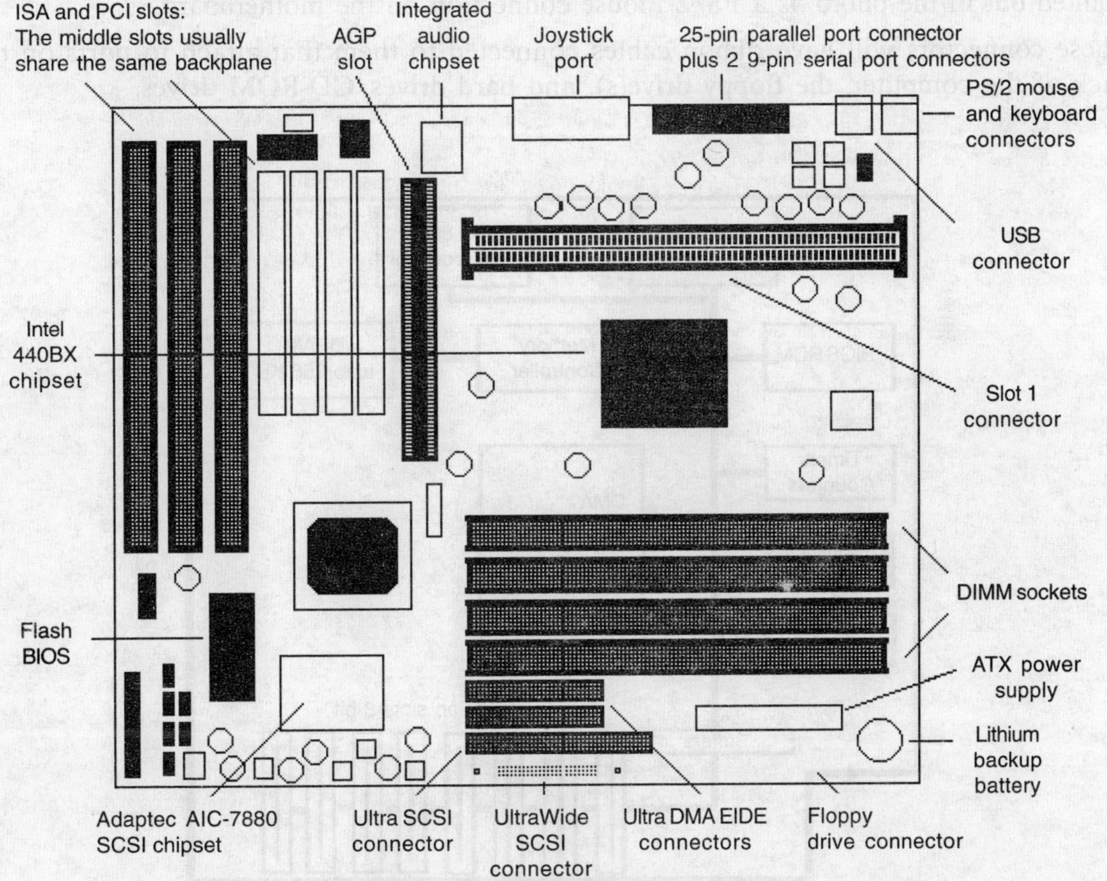

PC-XT Motherboard

ISA expansion slots, and an Intel 8088 microprocessor running at 4.77 MHz. The eight slots were an increase over the five in the IBM PC, although three were taken up by the floppy drive adapter, the hard drive adapter, and the serial card. Like the original PC, the XT came with a BASIC interpreter in PC and XT keyboards are not compatible with more modern PC.

PC AT

PC/AT, was IBM's second-generation PC, designed around the Intel 80286 microprocessor running at 6 MHz and released in 1984. AT originally stood for Advanced Technology .The AT represented a significant performance increase over previous computers, up to 75 percent faster than the PC/XT, and the AT bus standard is used in many clones or IBM compatible computers.

It was the most advanced machine in the PC line and featured a new keyboard, a higher-capacity 5.25" floppy (1.2MB) and a 16-bit data bus. AT-class machines ran considerably faster than the earlier 8088-based XT PCs. The motherboard includes connectors for two serial ports, a parallel port, floppy drive, and two IDE chains (for IDE devices such as hard disks and CD-ROM drives). Located just to the left of the keyboard connector, but not pointed out in the photo, is a PS/2 mouse connection on the motherboard.

These connectors will have ribbon cables connected to them that attach to ports on the back of the computer, the floppy drive(s), and hard drives/CD-ROM drives.

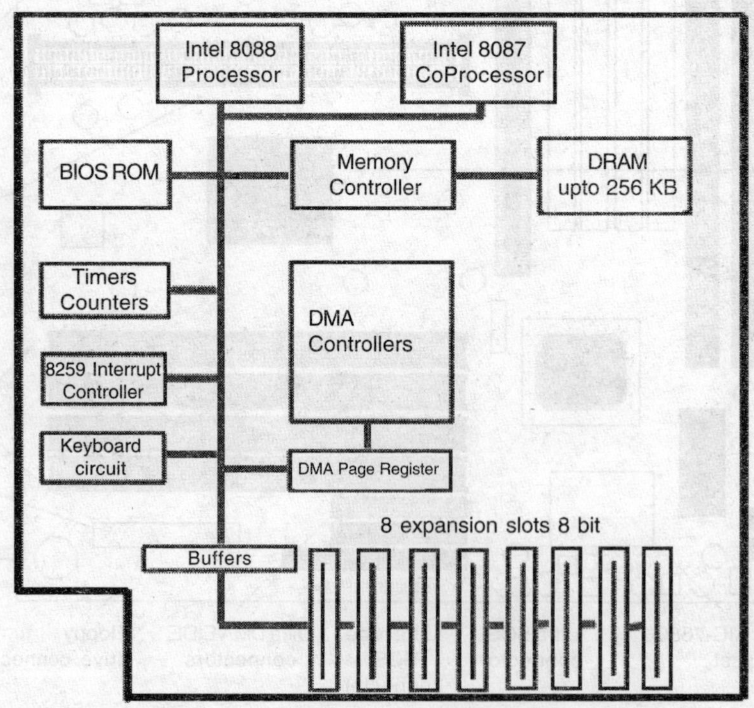

PC-XT Block Diagram

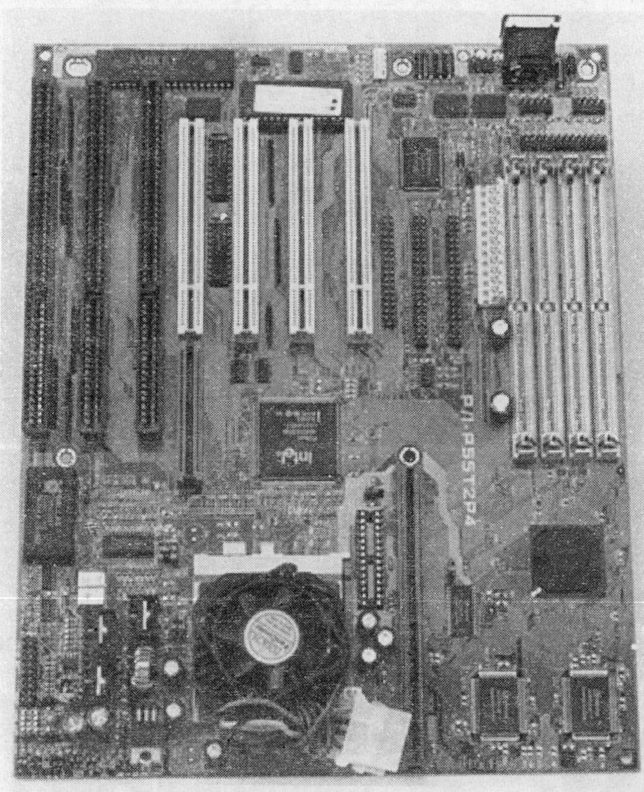

PC-AT Motherboard

Differences Between PC/XT and AT Systems

System Attributes	(8-Bit) PC/XT Type	(16/32/64-Bit) AT Type
Supported processors	All x86 or x88	286 or higher
Processor modes	Real	Real/Protected/Virtual Real
Software supported	16-bit only	16- or 32-bit
Bus slot width	8-bit	16/32/64-bit
Slot type	ISA only	ISA, EISA, MCA, PC-Card, Cardbus, VL-Bus, PCI, and AGP
Hardware interrupts	8 (6 usable)	16
DMA channels	4 (3 usable)	8
Maximum RAM	1MB	16MB/4GB or more
Floppy controller speed	250Kbps	250/300/500/1,000 Kbps
Standard boot drive	360KB or 720KB	1.2MB/1.44MB/2.88MB
Keyboard interface	Unidirectional	Bidirectional
CMOS memory/clock	None standard	MC146818-compatible
Serial-port UART	8250B	16450/16550A or greater

Fig. Pentium Motherboard

ATX motherboard

Intel, the primary manufacturer of PC CPUs, has proposed a new motherboard layout called the ATX.

Fig. ATX Motherboard

The bus slots are parallel to the short side of the motherboard. Instead of the long side of the motherboard running front to back in the PC, the short side runs front to back. The bus slots are located in the same general location, and the adapters still install in these slots and mount to the back of the computer's chassis. The serial, parallel, keyboard, and mouse connectors are built right onto the motherboard and stick out the back of the chassis when the motherboard is installed. One of the main reasons for the ATX design is to move the

CPU closer to the power supply fan for better cooling, which means the CPU will last longer and suffer fewer faults.

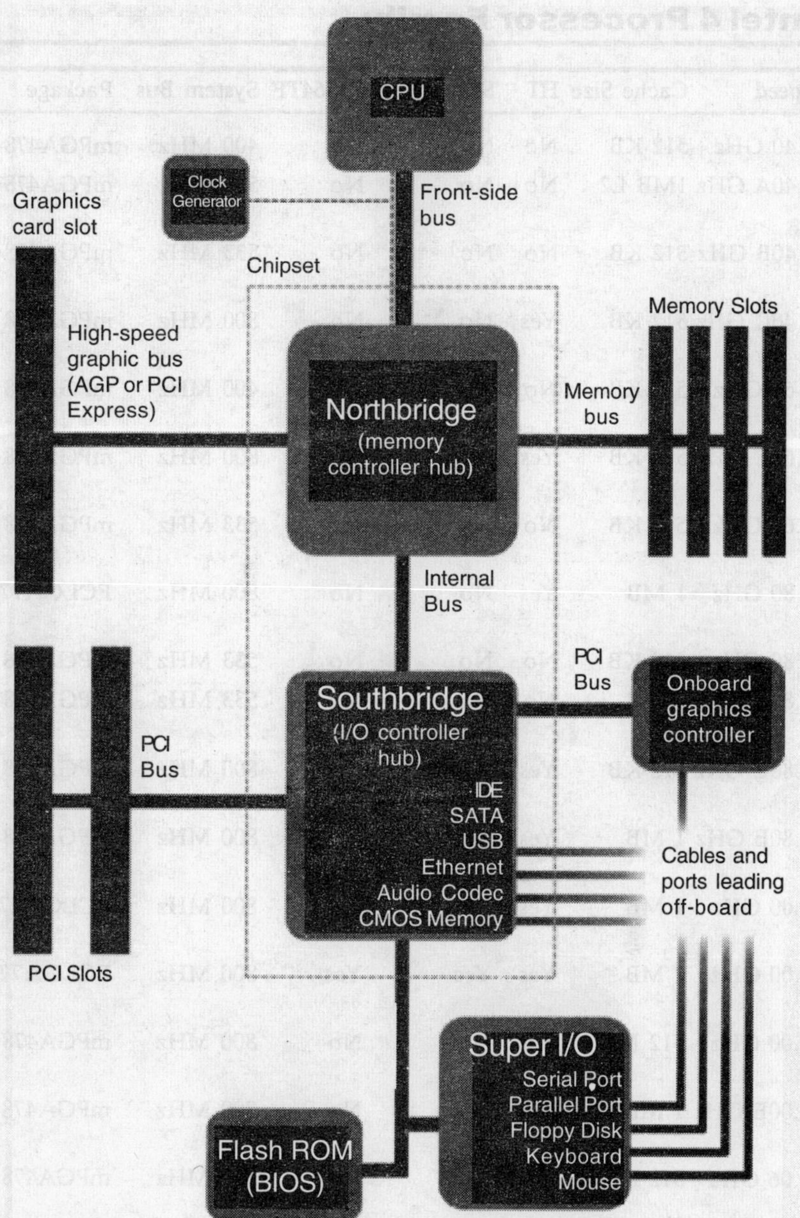

LPX motherboard

It is Low-Profile Extended motherboard introduced in 1997 by Western Digital. Unlike boards for desktop and tower cases that hold the expansion cards perpendicular to the board, cards plug into a riser card on the LPX and are parallel with the board. The LPX form factor is not a standard one but a non-standard proprietary one sometimes found in desktop computer models. This form factor is characterized by an expansion board that runs parallel to the motherboard. A riser card arrangement is used for expansion cards thereby allowing for smaller cases. LPX motherboards are typically integrated and most have the video and sound components built-in.

NLX motherboard

It is New Low-Profile Extended motherboard introduced in 1987. Unlike boards for desktop and tower cases that hold the expansion cards perpendicular to the board, cards plug into a riser card on the NLX and are parallel with the board. NLX has been a form factor in use with desktops for quite some time. It is a compact form factor, often referred to as a "low-profile application". NLX motherboards are easily distinguished by the riser card to which the expansion cards connect. The riser cards allow from two to four expansion cards to be plugged in. These expansion cards sit parallel to the motherboard. The benefit of the NLX form factor is that the bulk of a traditional server is reduced to a space-saving smaller server.

Intel 4 Processor Family

Speed	Cache Size	HT	Speed Step	EM64TF	System Bus	Package	Product Name
2.40 GHz	512 KB	No	No	No	400 MHz	mPGA478	Pentium 4 orocessor 2.40 GHz
2.40A GHz	1MB L2	No	No	No	533 MHz	mPGA478	Pentium 4 processor 2.40A GHz
2.40B GHz	512 KB	No	No	No	533 MHz	mPGA478	Pentium 4 processor 2.40B GHz
2.40C GHz	512 KB	Yes	No	No	800 MHz	mPGA478	Pentium 4 processor with 2.40C GHz
2.60 GHz	512 KB	No	No	No	400 MHz	mPGA478	Pentium 4 processor with 2.60 GHz
2.60C GHz	512 KB	Yes	No	No	800 MHz	mPGA478	Pentium 4 processor with HT 2.60C GHz
2.66 GHz	512 KB	No	No	No	533 MHz	mPGA478	Pentium 4 processor with 2.66 GHz
2.80 GHz	1 MB	Yes	No	No	800 MHz	FCLGA775	Pentium 4 processor 520 GHz with HT
2.80 GHz	512 KB	No	No	No	533 MHz	mPGA478	Pentium 4 processor 2.80 GHz
2.80A GHz	1 MB	No	No	No	533 MHz	mPGA478	Pentium 4 processor 2.80A GHz
2.80C GHz	512 KB	Yes	No	No	800 MHz	mPGA478	Pentium 4 processor with HT 2.80 GHz
2.80E GHz	1 MB	Yes	No	No	800 MHz	mPGA478	Pentium 4 processor with HT 2.80 GHz
3.00 GHz	1 MB	Yes	No	No	800 MHz	FCLGA775	Pentium 4 processor 530 with HT
3.00 GHz	2 MB	Yes	Yes	Yes	800 MHz	FCLGA775	Pentium 4 processor 630 with HT
3.00 GHz	512 MB	Yes	No	No	800 MHz	mPGA478	Pentium 4 processor with HT 3 GHz
3.00E GHz	1 MB	Yes	No	No	800 MHz	mPGA478	Pentium 4 processor with HT 3E GHz
3.06 GHz	512 KB	Yes	No	No	533 MHz	mPGA478	Pentium 4 processor with HT 3.06 GHz
3.20 GHz	1 MB	Yes	No	No	800 MHz	FCLGA775	Pentium 4 processor 540 with HT
3.20 GHz	2 MB	Yes	Yes	Yes	800 MHz	FCLGA775	Pentium 4 processor 640 with HT
3.20 GHz	512 KB	Yes	No	No	800 MHz	mPG [illegible]78	Pentium 4 processor with HT 3.20 GHz
3.20E GHz	1 MB	Yes	No	No	800 MHz	mPGA [illegible]78	Pentium 4 processor with HT 3.20E GHz
3.40 GHz	1 MB	Yes	No	No	800 MHz	FCLGA775	Pentium 4 processor 550 with HT

3.40 GHz	2 MB	Yes	Yes	Yes	800 MHz	FCLGA775	Pentium 4 processor 650 with HT
3.40 GHz	512 KB	Yes	No	Yes	800 MHz	mPGA478	Pentium 4 processor with HT 3.40 GHz
3.40 GHz	512 KB L2 cache 2 MB L3 cache	Yes	No	No	800 MHz	FCLGA775	Pentium 4 processor with HT Extreme Edition 3.40 GHz
3.40E GHz	1 MB	Yes	No	Yes	800 MHz	mPGA478	Pentium 4 processor with HT 3.40E GHz
3.46 GHz	512 KB L2 cache 2 MB L3 cache	Yes	No	No	1066 MHz	FCLGA775	Pentium 4 processor with HT Extreme Edition 3.46 GHz
3.60 GHz	1 MB	Yes	No	No	800 MHz	FCLGA775	Pentium 4 processor 560 with HT
3.60 GHz	2 MB	Yes	Yes	Yes	800 MHz	FCLGA775	Pentium 4 processor 660 with HT
3.73 GHz	2 MB	Yes	No	Yes	1066 MHz	FCLGA775	Pentium 4 processor with HT Extreme Edition 3.73 GHz
3.80 GHz	1 MB	Yes	No	No	800 MHz	FCLGA775	Pentium 4 processor 570 with HT

Advancements in Motherboard Technology

Intel NetBurst microarchitecture delivers a number of innovative features including Hyper-Threading Technology, hyper-pipelined technology, 1066, 800, 533 or 400 MHz system bus, and Execution Trace Cache. It also provides a number of enhanced feature such as Advanced Trnaster Cache, Advanced Dynamic Execution, enhanced floating-point and multimedia unit, and Streaming SIMD Extension, enhanced loating-point and mutimedia unit, and Streaming SIMD Extensions 2 (SSE2). Further enhancements in the 90 nm process-based Pentium 4 processor include Steaming SIMD Extension 3 (SSE3).

Many of these innovations and advances were made possible with improvements in processor technology, process technology, and circuit design and could not previously be implemented in high-volume, manufacturable solutions.

The features and resulting benefits of the microarchitecture are defined below:

Hyper-Threading Technology

Hyper-Threading Technology (HT Technology) is a groundbreaking technology to improve processor performance. It allows software programs to "see" two processors and work more efficiently.

This new technology enables the processor to execute two series, or threads, of instructions at the same time, thereby improving performance and system responsiveness. Hyper-Threading Technology requires a computer system with an Intel Pentium 4 processor supporting HT Technology and a HT Technology enabled chipset, BIOS and operating system.

Hyper-Pipelined Technology

The hyper-pipelined technolgy of the Intel NetBurst microarchitecutre increases the pipeline depth delivering increased performance, frequency and scalability of the processor.

Intel Enhanced Memory 64 Technology (Intel EM64T)

Intel EM^$T provides an enhancement to the Intel's 32-bit architecture by enabling the desktop processor platform to access larger amounts of memory. With appropriate 64-bit supporting hardware and software, platforms based on an Intel processor supporting Intel EM64T can enable use of extended virtual and physical memory. EM64T requrires a computer system with a processor, chiset, BIOS, operating system, device drivers and applications enabled for Intel EM64T, Processor will not operate (including 32-bit operation) without an Intel EM64T enabled BIOS.

Integrated 2MB Level 3 Cache on Intel Pentium 4 Processor Extreme Edition 3.46 GHz

The 2-MB L3 cache is available only with the Pentium 4 processor Extreme Edition. The additional third level of cache is located on the processor die and is designed specifically to meet the computer needs of high-end gamers and other power users. The Integrated L3 cache is available in 2 MB and when coupled with either the 1066 MHz or 800 MHz system bus provides a high bandwidth path to memory. The efficient design of the integrated L3 cache proveds a faster path to large data sets stored in cache on the processor. This results in reduced average memory latency and increased throughput for larger workloads.

Integrated 2MB Level 2 Cache on Intel Pentium 4 Processor Extreme Edition 3.73 GHz and 6xx

The 2-MB Advanced Transfer Cache (on-die, full speed Level 2 cache) with 8-way associative and Error Correcting Code (ESS) can improve overall performance by allowing the processor to have faster access to a larger amount of the most often used data.

Advanced Dynamic Execution

The Advance Dynamic Execution engine is a very deep, out-of-order speculative execution engine that keeps the execution units executing instructions. It also includes an enhanced branch prediction algorithm that has the net effect of reducing the number of branch mis-predictions.

Chipsets for the Pentium and Beyond

Pentium chipsets (referred to as fifth-generation chipsets) were more closely tied to the design of the processor than were the 486 chipsets. When Intel created the Pentium processor, it also developed the PCI bus and a chipset to support and integrate the capabilities of these two developments. This PCIset, as it became known, was developed as an exact match for the Pentium processor. Intel chipsets are designated in numbered series: the 420 for 486 chipsets, the 430 for Pentium chipsets, the 440 series for Pentium II and the 450 series for Pentium Pr chipsets (along with the 400FX). The newer 460 and 800 series chipsets just being announced are designed to support the IA-64 (Intel Architecture – 64 bits) processors, such as the Itanium, now emerging.

Here are some of the more common Intel Pentium and above chipsets:

430LX (Mercury): The 430LX was the first Pentium chipset developed to support the 60MHz and 66MHz 5V processors. The Mercury chipset included the PCI bus and supported up to 128MB of RAM. This chipset was made absolute by the chipsets that supported the 90MHz and 100MHz 3.3V processors.

430NX (Neptune): The 430NX was developed to support Intel's second generation Pentium chips. It supported Pentium processors running at 90MHz to 133MHz. Some of the improvements offered over he 430LX chipset are support for dual processors, 512MB of RAM and 512KB of L2 cache.

430FX (Triton I): This was first of the Triton chipsets. It featured support for EDO RAM pipelined burst and synchronous cache, Plug-and-Play and PCI level 2.0 compliance. However, it only supported 128MB of RAM (down from the 512MB supported by the Neptune chipset) and did not have dual processor capabilities.

430MX (Mobile Triton): This is a version of the 430FX designed for laptop, notebook and other portable PCs.

430HX (Triton II): This chipset supported EDO RAM and concurrent PCI buses and was designed for use in business-level servers. It was the next generation of the 430NX and included support for 512MB of RAM and L2 cache.

430VX (Triton III): This chipset was developed to support the home PC market. It featured support for USB, SDRAM and PCI interfaces.

430TX: With this chipset, Intel dropped the Triton label for its chipsets. The 430TX was adaptable for both desktop and mobile use and provided CPI, USB, DMMA and other interfaces.

440LX: Designed for the Pentium II, this AGPset chipset provides support for the LS-120 "superdisk," Ultra DMA, AGP, USB, SDRAM, ECC RAM and the PC97 power management specification. Figure 5-5 shows this chipset.

440LXR: A low-end version of the 440LX chipset.

440BX: Another Pentium II chipset that supports 100MHz bus, dual processors, FireWire and up to 1GB of RAM.

440GX: This chipset is designed for midrange workstations and supports dual CPU and up to 2GB of SDRAM along with dual AGP interfaces. This is an AGPset.

440FX (Natoma): This chipset supported both the Pentium II and the Pentium Pro processors with USB, EDO RAM, ECC memory, dual processors and PCI.

450GX (Orion server): The 450GX chipset and the 450KX share the same basic design. However, the GX version is optimized for the Pentium Pro and supports four processors and 8GB of RAM but FPM memory only.

450KX (Orion workstation): The workstation version of the Orion chipset supports dual processors and 1GB of RAM.

450NX: This is a high-powered chipset designed for Xeon workstations and servers. It supports up to four CPUs, 2MB of L2 cache, 8GB of EDO memory & two 32-bit or one 64-bit PCI interface.

460GX (Merced): This chipset supports very high-end servers and workstations with supports for four CPUs and other high-performance features. You will see this chipset linked to the new high powered Itanium processor.

810: This chipset is designed for value-priced PCs. It includes support for integrated 3-D graphics (AGP) with MPEG-2, 100MHz system bus, two USB ports and the Intel Accelerated Hub, which features a 266MB per second bus speed between memory and peripherals.

810e: This chipset is an extended version of the 810 chipset based on the 440BX chipset and intended for home market and office PCs. Its features are the same as the 9\810 chipset, with added support for 133MHz system bus and the ATA-66 interface.

815: The Intel 815 chipset is specifically designed to work with the Pentium III processor, but it also provides backward compatibility to other Intel processors.

820: Another extension of the 810 chipset designed to support high-end desktops and workstations.

850: The Intel 850 chipset was designed in tandem with the Pentium 4 processor and supports, among many high-performance innovations and features, a 400 MHz system bus that provides over 3 times the bandwidth of previous chipset and processor technologies.

Various Cards on the Motherboards

As we have seen and studied in this chapter, so far, motherboard has various cards. Let us now go through the various cards and their functioning.

1. **A Display /video card,** is card in computer whose function is to generate and output images to a display. The term is usually used to refer to a separate, dedicated expansion card that is plugged into a slot on the computer's motherboard. A video card consists of a printed circuit board on which the components are mounted. These include:

(i) **The GPU**: It is a microprocessor dedicated to manipulating and rendering graphics according to the instructions received from the computer's operating system and the software being used. At their

Video Cards over the Years

	Year	Text Mode	Graphics Mode	Colors	Memory
MDA	1981	80*25	-	1	4 KB
CGA	1981	80*25	640*200	16	16 KB
HGC	1982	80*25	720*348	1	64 KB
EGA	1984	80*25	640*350	16	256 KB
IBM 8514	1987	80*25	1024*768	256	-
MCGA	1987	80*25	320*200	256	-
VGA	1987	720*400	640*480	256	256 KB
SVGA	1989	80*25	1024*768	256	2 MB
XGA	1990	80*25	1024*768	65,536	1 MB

simplest level, GPUs include functions for manipulating two-dimensional graphics, such as blitting. Modern and more advanced GPUs also include functions for generating and manipulating three-dimensional graphics elements, rendering objects with shading, lighting, texture mapping and other visual effects.

Type	Clock rate (MHz)	Bandwidth (GB/s)
DDR	166 - 950	1.2 - 30.4
DDR2	533 - 1000	8.5 - 16
GDDR3	700 - 1800	5.6 - 54.4
GDDR4	1600 - 2400	64 - 86.4

(*ii*) **Video Memory**: Unlike integrated video controllers, which usually share memory with the rest of the computer, most video cards have their own separate onboard memory, referred to as video RAM (VRAM). If the video card is integrated in the motherboard, it will use the computer RAM memory (lower throughput). If it is not integrated, the video card will have its own video memory which is called Video RAM or VRAM. The VRAM capacity of most modern video cards range from 128 to 768 MB. In 2006, the VRAM was based on DDR technology, standing out DDR2, GDDR3 and GDDR4. The memory clock rate is between 400 MHz and 1.6 GHz. A very important element of the video memory is the Z-buffer, which manages the depth coordinates in 3D graphics.

Pin No.	Function
1	Red Video
2	Green Video
3	Blue Video
4	Monitor ID bit-2
5	Ground
6	Red Return (Ground)
7	Green Retrun (Ground)
8	Blue Return (Ground)
9	Composite Sync.
10	Sync. Return (Ground)
11	Monitor ID bit-0
12	Monitor ID bit-1
13	Horiz. Sync.
14	Vert. Sync.
15	Reserverd

Fig. Display Card

(*iii*) **Video BIOS** chip is a chip that contains the basic program that governs the video card's operations and provides the instructions that allow the computer and software to interface with the card. The video BIOS or firmware chip is a chip that contains the basic program that governs the video card's operations and provides the instructions that allow the computer and software to interface with the card. It contains information on the memory timing, operating speeds and voltages of the processor and ram and other information. It is possible to re-flash a bios although this is typically only done by video card overclockers.

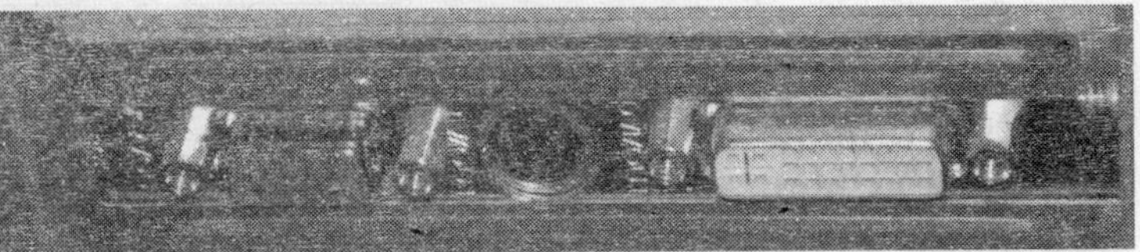

(*iv*) **PCI Express** is the newest slot that most new cards fit into. It comes in a variety of speeds which vary in size proportionate to the speed. Depending on what speed interface used, PCI Express video cards may have a higher speed interface than AGP, leading to increased performance on the high end cards. PCI Express may be up to twice the speed of the AGP interface.

2. A sound card is a computer expansion card that can input and output sound under control of computer programs. Typical uses of sound cards include providing the audio component for multimedia applications such as music composition, editing video or audio, presentation/ education, and entertainment (games). Many computers have sound capabilities built in, while others require these expansion cards if audio capability is desired. Typical sound card includes a sound chip, usually featuring a digital-to-analog converter, that converts recorded or generated digital waveforms of sound into an analog format. This signal is led to a (typically 1/8-inch earphone-type) connector where an amplifier, headphones, or similar

Fig. Sound card

sound destination can be plugged in. More advanced designs usually include more than one sound chip to separate duties between digital sound production and synthesized sounds (usually for real-time generation of music and sound effects utilizing little data and CPU time.

Digital sound reproduction is usually achieved by multi-channel DACs, able to play multiple digital samples at different pitches and volumes, optionally applying real-time effects like filtering or distortion. Multi-channel digital sound playback can also be used for music synthesis if used with a digitized instrument bank of some sort, typically a small amount of ROM or Flash memory containing samples corresponding to the standard MIDI instruments. (A contrasting way to synthesize sound on a PC uses "audio codecs", which rely heavily on software for music synthesis, MIDI compliance and even multiple-channel emulation. This approach has become common as manufacturers seek to simplify the design and the cost of the sound card itself most sound cards have a **line in** connector where the sound signal from a cassette tape recorder or similar sound source can be input. The sound card can digitize this signal and store it (controlled by the corresponding computer software) on the computer's hard disk for editing or further reproduction. Another typical external connector is the **microphone** connector, for connecting to a microphone or other input device that generates a relatively lower voltage than the **line in** connector. Input through a microphone jack is typically used by speech recognition software or Voice over IP applications.

Connections

Most sound cards since 1999 conform to Microsoft's PC 99 standard for color coding the external connectors as follows:

Color	Function
Pink	Analog microphone input.
Light blue	Analog line level input.
Lime green	Analog line level output for the main stereo signal (front speakers or headphones).
Black	Analog line level output for rear speakers.
Silver	Analog line level output for side speakers.
Orange	S/PDIF digital output (sometimes used as an analog line output for a center speaker and subwoofer instead)

3. A network card, **network adapter** or **NIC** (network interface controller) is a piece of computer hardware designed to allow computers to communicate over a computer network. It is both an OSI layer 1 (physical layer) and layer 2 (data link layer) device, as it provides physical access to a networking medium and provides a low-level addressing system through the use of MAC addresses. It allows users to connect to each other either by using cables or wirelessly. Every network card has a unique 48-bit serial number called a MAC address, which is stored in ROM carried on the card. Every computer on a network must have a card with a unique MAC address. No two cards ever manufactured share the same address. This is accomplished by the Institute of Electrical and Electronics Engineers (IEEE), which is responsible for assigning unique MAC addresses to the vendors of network interface controllers.

Whereas network cards used to be expansion cards that plug into a computer bus, the low cost and ubiquity of the Ethernet standard means that most newer computers have a network interface built into the motherboard. These motherboards either have Ethernet capabilities integrated into the motherboard chipset, or implemented via a low cost dedicated Ethernet chip, connected through the PCI (or the newer PCI express bus).

A separate network card is not required unless multiple interfaces are needed or some other type of network is used. Newer motherboards may even have dual network (Ethernet) interfaces built-in.

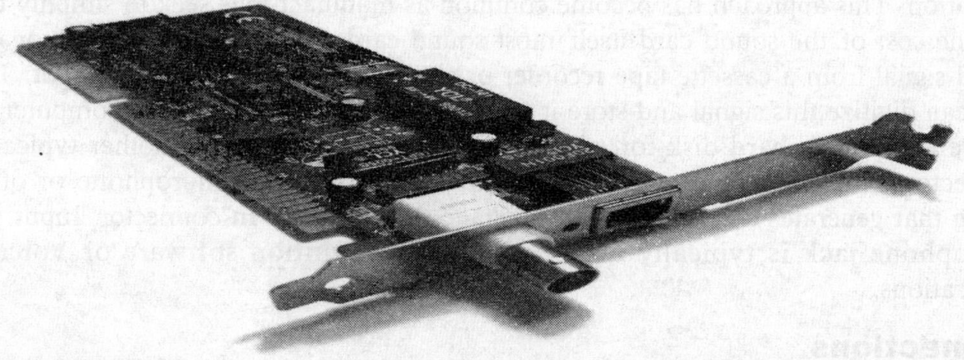

Fig. Network Card

The card implements the electronic circuitry required to communicate using a specific physical layer and data link layer standard such as Ethernet or token ring. This provides a network card typically has a twisted pair, BNC, or AUI socket where the network cable is connected, and a few LEDs to inform the user of whether the network is active, and whether or not there is data being transmitted on it. The Network Cards are typically available in 10/100/1000 Mbits/s(Mbps).

4. A modem (from **mod**ulate and **dem**odulate) is a device that modulates an analogue carrier signal to encode digital information, and also demodulates such a carrier signal to decode the transmitted information. The goal is to produce a signal that can be transmitted easily and decoded to reproduce the original digital data. Modems can be used over any means of transmitting analog signals, from driven diodes to radio. Experiments have even been

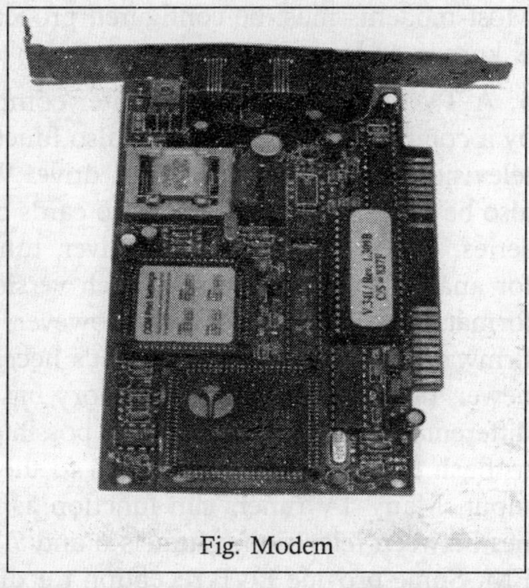
Fig. Modem

performed in the use of modems over the medium of two cans connected by a string. The most familiar example is a voiceband modem that turns the digital '1s and 0s' of a personal computer into sounds that can be transmitted over the telephone lines of Piain Old Telephone Systems (POTS), and once received on the other side, converts those sounds back into 1s and 0s. Modems are generally classified by the amount of data they can send in a given time, normally measured in bits per second, or "bps".Faster modems are used by Internet users every day, notably cable modems and ADSL modems. In telecommunications, "radio modems" transmit repeating frames of data at very high data rates over microwave radio links. Some microwave modems transmit more than a hundred million bits per second. Optical modems transmit data over optic fibers. Most intercontinental data links now use optic modems transmitting over undersea optical fibers. Optical modems routinely have data rates in excess of a billion ($1x10^9$) bits per second.

Broadband

ADSL modems, a more recent development, are not limited to the telephone's "voiceband" audio frequencies. Some ADSL modems use coded orthogonal frequency division modulation (DMT). Cable modems use a range of frequencies originally intended to carry RF television channels. Multiple cable modems attached to a single cable can use the same frequency band, using a low-level media access protocol to allow them to work together within the same channel. Typically, 'up' and 'down' signals are kept separate using frequency division multiple access.

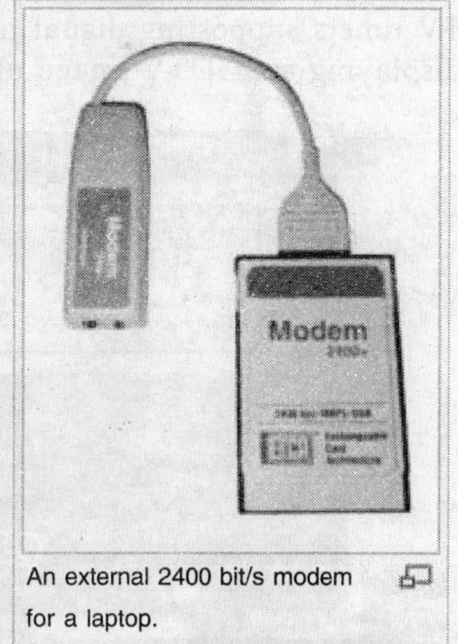

An external 2400 bit/s modem for a laptop.

New types of broadband modems are beginning to appear, such as doubleway satellite and powerline modems. Broadband modems should still be classed as modems, since they do utilise analog/digital conversion. They are more advanced devices than traditional telephone modems as they are capable of modulating/demodulating hundreds of channels simultaneously.

Many broadband "modems" include the functions of a router (with Ethernet and WiFi ports) and other features such as DHCP, NAT and firewall features. When broadband technology was introduced, networking and routers were unfamiliar to consumers. However, many people knew what a modem was as most internet access was through dialup. Due to this familiarity, companies started selling broadband modems using the familiar term "modem" rather than vaguer ones like "adapter" or "transceiver".

Most modems must be configured properly before they can use a router. This configuration is known as bridge mode

5. A TV tuner card is a computer component that allows television signals to be received by a computer. Most TV tuners also function as video capture cards, allowing them to record television programs onto a hard drive. While typically a PCI-bus expansion card, they can also be a USB device. Some video cards double as TV tuners, notably the ATI All-In-Wonder series. The card contains a receiver, tuner, demodulator, and a analog-to-digital converter for analog TV. Like TV sets, each version is designed for the radio frequencies and video formats used in each country. However, many TV tuners used in computers use DSP, so a firmware upgrade is often all that's necessary to change the supported video format. Many newer TV tuners have flash memory big enough to hold the firmwares for decoding several different video formats, making it possible to use the tuner in many countries without having to flash the firmware. In addition to the frequency tuner, many include a composite video input. Many TV tuners can function as FM radios: this is because the FM radio spectrum lies between television channels 6 and 7, and the DSP can be easily programmed to decode FM. Some provide DVB reception for digital radio, television or data signals (either with or without hardware MPEG decoding capability); these may be used to receive satellite broadcasts but normally provide no analogue input capability. Most internal tuners do all the low level demodulation needed to convert a radio signal into an on-screen image using a hardware DSP chip or ASIC; some also have hardware MPEG encoders and use DMA to bypass the CPU entirely. Some cheaper tuners don't have much in the way of onboard signal processing and rely on the system's CPU for that task. External tuners may convert the signal into either a video stream suitable for display on the screen, or to an intermediate format such as MPEG; in either case, the CPU is needed to direct the image onto the screen. TV tuners supporting digital television broadcasts eventually became available; a tuner displaying an HDTV image on a computer monitor is typically much cheaper than a

Fig. TV Tuner Card

dedicated high-definition television system, but with a smaller physical screen. Broadcasts can also be digitally recorded by the computer for later replay, or distribution (illegal in many countries) to other computer users. There is one more PCI card which will act as television receiver (a.k.a Set-top box)- This will be based on DVB and can deliver MPEG-1, MPEG-2, MPEG-4 or DivX content. This is also known as Digital television adapter. Some call this satellite card.

6. IDE Card: Integrated Drive Electronics (IDE) interface is a standard way for a storage device to connect to a computer. IDE is actually not the true technical name for the interface standard. The original name, AT Attachment (ATA), signified that the interface was initially developed for the IBM AT computer.

Fig. IDE Interface

Most motherboards come with an IDE interface. The interface is actually a host adapter, meaning that it provides a way to connect a complete device to the computer (host). The actual controller is on a circuit board attached to the hard drive. That's the reason it's called Integrated Drive Electronics. While the IDE interface was originally developed for connecting hard drives, it has evolved into the universal interface for connecting internal floppy drives, CD-ROM drives and even some tape backup drives.

Motherboard Problems

When switched on, if the system produces error beeps or shows error messages.

- Check for perfect seating of socketed chips such as Memory chips, SIMM modules, BIOS and keyboard controller, CPU, etc.
- Temporarily remove nonessential cards from the Motherboard.
- If the problem is solved, replace cards one by one and each time check for correct operation, this will help to locate the actual faulty device.

- If there is intermittent crashing/stopping of system, determine the circumstances and check whether the crashing of system occurs only when a specific software is executed.
- Remove unnecessary memory resident programs and device drivers.
- Check for various card conflicts like IRQs, input/output ports, DMA channels and memory locations. Reconfigure in case any such conflict is located.
- Remove and reseat expansion cards and interconnecting cables.
- Run diagnostic utilities for identifying any hardware problem.
- Try reducing the speed of processor or the bus clock.

Diagnostics of the Cards

For diagnostics, a tool is used which is called POST card. It is plugged into ISA bus. It decodes the various signals and displays them either on a set of LEDs or a seven-segment numeric display.

Card Diagnosis

A useful diagnostic tool is a POST card. PCs send their POST results out on a particular I/O port-most use port 80, while Compaqs may use port 84 and IBMs use 300. The POST card, which plugs into the ISA bus, decodes these signals and displays them either on a set of LEDs or a seven-segment numeric display. A list of POST codes is needed, and can be used to identify the results being produced by the self-test routine.

If the POST card shows FF, an oscilloscope can be used to see if the processor is accessing the BIOS, looking for clock signals, the address and data strobes on the CPU, and for resets.

Diagnosis requires logical reasoning, which in itself requires that the person doing the diagnosis understand the system events that are supposed to occur, and in which order. Further, many of the clues that might be available require specialized diagnostic equipment that the average user does not possess.

POST automatically runs when your computer is turned on and tests several components of your PC.

The Processor-if the test fails for the CPU, the system stops usually with no error code.

ROMs-POST checks the BIOS ROMs. If there is a problem, the system will stop, usually with no error code.

DMA Controller-if there are any problems with the DMA controller, the system will stop.

Interrupt Controller-if POST detects problems with the Interrupt Controller the system will give an audible error signal of one long beep then one short beep then the system stops.

System Timing Chip-this chip provides timing signals for the bus and processor. Any errors will produce an audible error signal of one long beep and one short beep then the system stops.

Video Card-if the Video Card fails, there will be one long beep then two short beeps then the system halts.

RAM-any RAM errors will generate a "201: Memory Error" message on the screen. Any error codes beginning with 2 indicate a memory error.

Keyboard-a problem with the keyboard will result in a "301: Keyboard Failure" error message followed by a short beep. System may halt or may ignore the error.

Floppy Drives-any problems will result in a "601: Floppy Disk" error code appearing on the screen.

Other Devices-POST checks the other ports and components of the computer, beeps, then continues. It also checks the Master Boot Record (MBR) on the hard drive. If it cannot find the MBR, it will freeze and not continue loading, otherwise it hands control over to the MBR (or DOS Boot Record (DBR) if it is booting from a floppy).

Error Code	Problem Description
1xx	System Board problem
161	CMOS Battery Failure
164	Memory System Size error
2xx	Memory related problem
3xx	Keyboard problem
4xx	Monochrome video problem
5xx	Color video problems
6xx	Floppy Disk problem
17xx	Hard disk problem

Fig. Summary of POST error codes

PCI

The Peripheral Component Interconnect, or PCI Standard (in practice almost always shortened to PCI) specifies a computer bus for attaching peripheral devices to a computer motherboard. These devices can take any one of the following forms:

- An integrated circuit fitted onto the motherboard itself, called a planar device in the PCI specification.
- An expansion card that fits into a socket.

The PCI bus is common in modern PCs, where it has displaced ISA and VESA Local Bus as the standard expansion bus, but it also appears in many other computer types. The bus will eventually be succeeded by PCI Express, which is standard in most new computers, and other technologies.

The PCI specification covers the physical size of the bus (including wire spacing), electrical characteristics, bus timing, and protocols. The specification can be purchased from the PCI Special Interest Group (PCISIG).

Conventional hardware specifications

A typical 32-bit PCI card, in this case a SCSI adapter from Adaptec

These specifications represent the most common version of PCI used in normal PCs.

- 33.33 MHz clock with synchronous transfers
- peak transfer rate of 133 MB per second for 32-bit bus width (33.33 MHz × 32 bits × (1 byte ÷ 8 bits) = 133 MB/s)
- peak transfer rate of 266 MB/s for 64-bit bus width
- 32-bit or 64-bit bus width
- 32-bit address space (4 gigabytes)
- 32-bit port space (now deprecated)
- 256-byte configuration space
- 5-volt signaling
- reflected-wave switching

Conventional

- Later versions of PCI allow (and in the latest versions require) 3.3V slots (keyed differently) on motherboards and allow for cards that are either double keyed for both voltages or even 3.3V only.
- PCI 2.2 allows for 66 MHz signalling (requires 3.3 volt signalling) (peak transfer rate of 533 MB/s)
- PCI 2.3 permits use of 3.3 volt and universal keying, but does not allow 5 volt keyed add in cards.
- PCI 3.0 is the final official standard of the bus, completely removing 5-volt capability.
- PCI-X doubles the width to 64-bit, revises the protocol, and increases the maximum signaling frequency to 133 MHz (peak transfer rate of 1014 MB/s)
- PCI-X 2.0 permits a 266 MHz rate (peak transfer rate of 2035 MB/s) and also 533 MHz rate, expands the configuration space to 4096 bytes, adds a 16-bit bus variant and allows for 1.5 volt signaling
- Mini PCI is a new form factor of PCI 2.2 for use mainly inside laptops
- CardBus is a PCMCIA form factor for 32-bit, 33 MHz PCI
- CompactPCI, uses Eurocard-sized modules plugged into a PCI backplane.
- PC/104-Plus is an industrial bus that uses the PCI signal lines with different connectors.

SDRAM

DDR SDRAM or double-data-rate synchronous dynamic random access memory is a class of memory integrated circuit used in computers. It achieves greater bandwidth than the preceding single-data-rate SDRAM by transferring data on the rising and falling edges of the clock signal (double pumped). Effectively, it nearly doubles the transfer rate without increasing the frequency of the front side bus. Thus a 100 MHz DDR system has an effective clock rate of 200 MHz when compared to equivalent SDR SDRAM, the "SDR" being a retrospective designation.

With data being transferred 64 bits at a time DDR RAM gives a transfer rate of [mbcr x 2 x 64] / 8; annotated it looks like this: (memory bus clock rate) × 2 (for dual rate) × 64 (number of bits transferred) / 8 (number of bits/byte). Thus with a bus frequency of 100 MHz, DDR-SDRAM gives a max transfer rate of 1600 MB/s.

JEDEC has set standards for speeds of DDR SDRAM, divided into two parts: The first specification is for memory chips and the second is for memory modules.

As DDR is superseded by the newer DDR2, the older version is often now referred to as DDR1.

Chip specification

- DDR-200: DDR-SDRAM memory chips specified to operate at 100 MHz
- DDR-266: DDR-SDRAM memory chips specified to operate at 133 MHz
- DDR-333: DDR-SDRAM memory chips specified to operate at 166 MHz
- DDR-400: DDR-SDRAM memory chips specified to operate at 200 MHz

Chip characteristics

- DRAM density. Size of the chip in mebibits. Example: 256 Mibit — 32 MiB chip.
- DRAM organization. Written in the form of 64M x 4, where 64M is a number of storage units (64 million), x4 (pronounced «by 4») — number of bits per chip, which equals the number of bits per storage unit. There are x4 and x8 DDR chips. The former allows the use of advanced error correction features like Chipkill, memory scrubbing and Intel SDDC, while the latter chips are somewhat more expensive.

Stick/module specification

- PC-1600: DDR-SDRAM memory module specified to operate at 100 MHz using DDR-200 chips, 1.600 GB/s bandwidth
- PC-2100: DDR-SDRAM memory module specified to operate at 133 MHz using DDR-266 chips, 2.133 GB/s bandwidth

- PC-2700: DDR-SDRAM memory module specified to operate at 166 MHz using DDR-333 chips, 2.667 GB/s bandwidth
- PC-3200: DDR-SDRAM memory module specified to operate at 200 MHz using DDR-400 chips, 3.200 GB/s bandwidth

Note: All RAM speeds in-between or above these listed specifications are not standardized by JEDEC — most often they are simply manufacturer optimizations using higher-tolerance or overvolted chips.

The package sizes in which DDR SDRAM is manufactured are also standardised by JEDEC.

There is no architectural difference between DDR SDRAM designed for different clock frequencies, e.g. PC-1600 (designed to run at 100 MHz) and PC-2100 (designed to run at 133 MHz). The number simply designates the speed that the chip is guaranteed to run at. Hence DDR SDRAM can be run at lower clock speeds than it was made for (underclocking) or higher clock speeds than it was made for (overclocking).

DDR SDRAM DIMMs have 184 pins (as opposed to 168 pins on SDR SDRAM, or, 240 pins on DDR-2), and can be differentiated from SDRAM DIMMs by the number of notches (DDR SDRAM has one, SDR SDRAM has two). DDR operates at a voltage of 2.5 V, compared to 3.3 V for SDR SDRAM. This can significantly reduce power usage.

Many new chipsets use these memory types in dual-channel or even quad channel configurations, which doubles or quadruples the effective bandwidth.

Variations of 1 GiB PC2100 Registered DDR SDRAM module

Module size	Number of chips	Chip size	Chip organization	Number of rows (ranks)
1 GiB	36	256 Mibit	64M x 4	2
1 GiB	18	512 Mibit	64M x 8	2
1 GiB	18	512 Mibit	128M x 4	1

DDR2 SDRAM

In electronic engineering, DDR2 SDRAM or double-data-rate two synchronous dynamic random access memory is a random access memory technology used for high speed storage of the working data of a computer or other digital electronic device.

It is a part of the SDRAM (synchronous dynamic random access memory) family of technologies, which is one of many DRAM (dynamic random access memory) implementations, and is an evolutionary improvement over its predecessor, DDR SDRAM (double-data-rate synchronous dynamic random access memory).

Its primary benefit is the ability to run its bus at twice the speed of the memory cells it contains, thus enabling faster bus speeds and higher p k throughputs than earlier technologies. This is achieved at the cost of higher latency.

Like all SDRAM implementations, DDR2 stores memory in r. emory cells that are activated with the use of a clock signal to synchronize their operation with an external data bus. Like DDR before it, DDR2 cells transfer data both on the rising and falling edge of the clock (a technique called double pumping). The key difference between DDR and DDR2 is that in DDR2 the bus is clocked at twice the speed of the memory cells, so four words of data can be transferred per memory cell cycle. Thus, without speeding up the memory cells themselves, DDR2 can effectively operate at twice the bus speed of DDR.

DDR2's bus frequency is boosted by electrical interface improvements, on-die termination, prefetch buffers and off-chip drivers. However, latency is greatly increased as a trade-off. The DDR2 prefetch buffer is 4 bits deep, whereas it is 2 bits deep for DDR and 8 bits deep for DDR3. While DDR SDRAM has typical read latencies of between 2 and 3 bus cycles, DDR2 may have read latencies between 3 and 9 cycles. Because of this higher latency, DDR SDRAM running at the same bus speed as DDR2 is generally considered superior; DDR2 is, however, able to run at substantially higher bus speeds which equates to an overall increase in throughput. Another cost of the increased speed is the requirement that the chips are packaged in a more expensive and more difficult to assemble BGA package as compared to the TSSOP package of the previous memory generations such as DDR and SDRAM. This packaging change was necessary to maintain signal integrity at higher speeds.

Power savings are achieved primarily due to an improved manufacturing process through die shrinkage, resulting in a drop in operating voltage (1.8 V compared to DDR's 2.5 V). The lower memory clock frequency may also enable power reductions in applications that do not require the highest available speed.

Specification standards

Chips

Standard name	Memory clock	I/O Bus clock	Data transfers per second
DDR2-400	100 MHz	200 MHz	400 Million
DDR2-533	133 MHz	266 MHz	533 Million
DDR2-667	166 MHz	333 MHz	667 Million
DDR2-800	200 MHz	400 MHz	800 Million
DDR2-1066	266 MHz	533 MHz	1066 Million

Modules

For use in PCs, DDR2 SDRAM is supplied in DIMMs with 240 pins and a single locating notch. DIMMs are identified by their peak transfer capacity (often called bandwidth).

Module name	Bus clock	Chip type	Peak transfer rate
PC2-3200	200 MHz	DDR2-400	3.200 GB/s
PC2-4200	266 MHz	DDR2-533	4.264 GB/s
PC2-5300	333 MHz	DDR2-667	5.336 GB/s[1]
PC2-6400	400 MHz	DDR2-800	6.400 GB/s
PC2-8500 (planned)	533 MHz	DDR2-1066	8.500 GB/s

DDR2-xxx (or DDR-xxx) denotes effective clockspeed, whereas PC2-xxxx (or PC-xxxx) denotes theoretical bandwidth (though it is often rounded up or down). Bandwidth is calculated by taking transfers per second and multiplying by eight. This is because DDR2 memory modules transfer data on a bus that is 64 data bits wide, and since a byte is comprised of 8 bits, this equates to 8 bytes of data per transfer.

Optionally implement ECC, which is an extra data byte lane used for correcting minor errors and detecting major errors for better reliability. Modules with ECC are identified by an additional ECC in their designation. PC2-4200 ECC is a PC2-4200 module with ECC.

Be "registered", which improves signal integrity (and hence potentially clock speed) by electrically buffering the signals at a cost of an extra clock of increased latency. Those modules are identified by an additional R in their designation, PC2-4200R is a registered PC2-4200 module, PC2-4200R ECC is the same module but with additional ECC.

DD3 SDRAM

DDR3 SDRAM or double-data-rate three synchronous dynamic random access memory is the name of the new DDR memory standard that is being developed as the successor to DDR2 SDRAM.

The memory comes with a promise of a power consumption reduction of 40% compared to current commercial DDR2 modules, due to DDR3's 90 nm fabrication technology, allowing for lower operating currents and voltages (1.5 V, compared to DDR2's 1.8 V or DDR's 2.5 V). "Dual-gate" transistors will be used to reduce leakage of current.

DDR3's prefetch buffer width is 8 bit, whereas DDR2's is 4 bit, and DDR's is 2 bit.

Theoretically, these modules could transfer data at the effective clockrate of 800-1600MHz (for a single clock bandwidth of 400-800MHz), compared to DDR2's current range of 400-1066 MHz (200-533 MHz) or DDR's range of 200-600 MHz (100-300 MHz). To date, such bandwidth requirements have been mainly on the graphics market, where fast transfer of information between framebuffers is required.

DDR3 sticks maintain the 240-pin DIMM interface of DDR2, allowing DDR3 compatible chipsets to host DDR2 modules (though not both types at once). [1]

Prototypes were announced in early 2005, while the DDR3 specification is expected to be publicly available in mid-2007. Supposedly, Intel has preliminarily announced that they expect to be able to offer support for it in mid 2007 with a version of their upcoming Bearlake chipset. AMD's roadmap indicates their own adoption of DDR3 to come in 2008.

The GDDR3 memory, with a similar name but an entirely dissimilar technology, has been in use for several years in high-end graphic cards such as ones from NVIDIA or ATI Technologies, and as main system memory on the Xbox 360. It is sometimes incorrectly referred to as "DDR3".

Spec standards

Chips

- DDR3-800 : DDR3-SDRAM memory chips specified to run at 100 MHz, I/O clock at 400 MHz
- DDR3-1066: DDR3-SDRAM memory chips specified to run at 133 MHz, I/O clock at 533 MHz
- DDR3-1333: DDR3-SDRAM memory chips specified to run at 166 MHz, I/O clock at 667 MHz
- DDR3-1600: DDR3-SDRAM memory chips specified to run at 200 MHz, I/O clock at 800 MHz

Sticks/Modules

- PC3-6400: DDR3-SDRAM memory stick specified to run at 400 MHz using DDR3-800 chips, 6.40 GB/s bandwidth
- PC3-8500: DDR3-SDRAM memory stick specified to run at 533 MHz using DDR3-1066 chips, 8.53 GB/s bandwidth
- PC3-10600: DDR3-SDRAM memory stick specified to run at 667 MHz using DDR3-1333 chips, 10.67 GB/s bandwidth
- PC3-12800: DDR3-SDRAM memory stick specified to run at 800 MHz using DDR3-1600 chips, 12.80 GB/s bandwidth

Features

DDR3 SDRAM Components:

- Introduction of asynchronous RESET pin
- Support of system level flight time compensation
- On-DIMM Mirror friendly DRAM ballout
- Introduction of CWL (CAS Write Latency) per speed bin
- On-die IO calibration engine
- READ and WRITE calibration

DDR3 Modules:

- Fly-by command/address/control bus with On-DIMM termination
- High precision calibration resistors

Advantages compared to DDR2

- Higher bandwidth (up to 1600 MHz)

- Performance increase at low power
- Longer battery life in laptops
- Enhanced low power features and thermal design

Disadvantages compared to DDR2

- Commonly higher CAS Latency
- Lower MFIBS per Quad Cycle

Revision

1. Motherboard is the main component inside the main system unit.
2. It is used for the following: Processor Support, Peripheral Support, Performace, Upgradability, Organization, Contol and Communication.
3. The original PC/XT used an Intel 8088 processor running at a speed of 4.77 MHz.
4. PC/AT, known as Advanced Technology of Personal Computer, used Intel 80286 microprocessor.
5. Among the features of AT were: 16-bit ISA bus, 15 IRQs and 7 DMA channels.
6. It supported 16 MB of memory at the most.
7. ATX motherboard had better cooling capacity.
8. LPX, known as Low Profile Extended, motherboard, has video and sound components built-in.
9. NLX. known as New Low Profile Extended, motherboard has been a form factor in use with desktops for quite some time.
10. Display card generates and sends output images to a display.
11. A Sound card can input and output sound under control of computer programs.
12. A Network card allows computers to communicate over a computer network.
13. Modem is a device that modulates an analogue carrier signal to encode digital information and also demodulates such a carrier signal to decode the transmitted information.
14. A TV Tuner card is a computer component that allows television signals to be received by a computer.
15. IDE Card interface is a standard way for a storage device to connect to a computer.
16. POST card is used to diagnose the cards of the computer.
17. Devices which POST checks are: The Processor, ROMs, DMA Controller, Interrupt Controller, System Timing Chip, Video Card, RAM, Keyboard, Floppy Drives and Other Drives.

Multiple Choice Questions

1. LPX stands for:

   (a) Low Profile Extended (b) Low Period Extended

   (c) Low Profile Extra

2. PC-ATs full form of:

   (a) Personal Computer Area Technology

   (b) Personal Computer Advanced Technology

   (c) Personal Computer Advanced Techniques

3. PC XT ran on Intel ____ processor.
   (a) 8086 (b) 80286
   (c) 8088
4. Maximum memory in PC AT could be ___ MB:
   (a) 8 (b) 16
   (c) 32
5. Display card generates:
   (a) Text (b) Sound
   (c) Graphics
6. Program which checks for errors on the various cards is called:
   (a) POST (b) POP
   (c) MAIL
7. Video Output for monitor is obtained from .... card.
   (a) Sound card (b) Network card
   (c) Display card

True/False Questions

1. The original PC/XT used an Intel 8088 processor running at a speed of 4.77 MHz.
2. PC/AT, known as Advanced Technology of Personal Computer, used Intel 8088 microprocessor.
3. It supported 16 MB of memory at the most.
4. ATX motherboard had better cooling capacity.
5. NLX. known as New Low Profile Extended, motherboard has been a form factor in use with desktops for quite some time.
6. Display card generates and sends sound to a output.
7. A Sound card can input and output sound under control of computer programs.
8. A Network card allows computers to communicate over a computer network.
9. A TV Tuner card is a computer component that allows television signals to be received by a computer.
10. POST card is used to diagnose the cards of the computer.
11. EISA slots are available on Intel's 845 GVSR motherboard.

Short Answer Type Questions

1. What is POST?
2. What all POST checks?

Descriptive Questions

1. Describe the various components inside the main computer system.
2. Describe the various uses of the motherboard.
3. How did PC XT worked?
4. Describe the working of PC AT.

5. What all was there on PC AT motherboard?
6. Describe the following: ATX, LPX and NLX motherboards.
7. What do the following cards do: Display card, Sound card, Network card, TV Tuner card, and IDE card?
8. What types of jumper setting are there on Motherboard?

Answers to Objective Type Questions

Multiple Choice Questions

1. a	2. b	3. c	4. b
5. c	6. a	7. c	

True False Questions

1. T	2. T	3. T	4. T
5. T	6. F	7. T	8. T
9. T	10. T	11. T	

3 Storage Devices

An Introduction to Storage Devices

Memory is not the only place where you store the data or program, since it is volatile. So you need to have storage devices which can store your data and programs permanently. For this we use so called storage units. These can be used for storing the data and then, may be, transferring it to another computer or storage media.

HDD

It is also called as mass-storage device. Like floppy disks, hard disks store data in tracks that are divided into sectors. A hard disk is a stack of metal platters that spin on one spindle, like a stack of rigid floppy disks. Each platter is coated with iron oxide and the entire unit is encased in a sealed chamber to make it free from dust and other contamination.

The hard disks are sealed inside an airtight vacuum chamber. This allows the heads of the hard disk to fly much closer to the surface of the disk, also allowing much greater precision. In fact, the heads of hard disks fly so close to the surface of the disk that if a dust particle, a human hair or even a fingerprint were placed on the disk it would bridge the gap between the heads and the disk, causing the heads to crash. A head crash, in which the head touches the disk destroys the data stored in the area of the crash and can destroy a read/write head as well.

Because materials such as hair, fingerprints, and dust or smoke particles are much thicker than the gap between the disk and the read/write head, they can cause the head to crash. The increased surface areas provided by multiple platters is the main reasons that hard disk can store so much more data than floppy disks. Waving a magnet past an electric coil like the one in a drive's read/write head causes a current to flow through the coil. The interesting thing is that the faster you move a magnet, the larger the current it generates in the coil. Conversely, the more current you apply to the magnet the stronger its magnetic field becomes.

Hard disk spins at around 3600 RPM instead of a floppy disk's 300 RPM. Some hard drives spin as fast as 5400 RPM. As the hard disk spins faster, the drive's heads can use a lower-intensity current to polarize a spot on the disk. When the drive head reads data from the surface of the disk the fast speed of the disk amplifies the intensity of the current induced in the read head.

Some hard-disk drives hold as many as 12 disks but both sides of disks are not always used. With hard disk, the number of sides that the disk uses in specified by the number of heads. For example, a particular harddisk drive might have six disk platters (12 sides) but only 10 heads, indicating that two sides are not used to store data. Often these are the top side of the top disk and the bottom side of bottom disk.

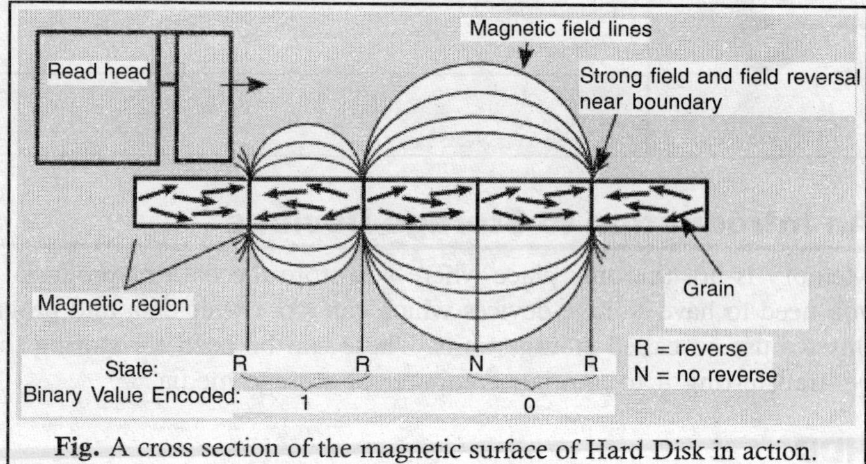

Fig. A cross section of the magnetic surface of Hard Disk in action.

As hard disks are actually a stack of platters, we use new term cylinder to refer to the same track across all the disk sides. Hard disks generally store 512 bytes of data in a sector, but because of their higher tolerance hard disk can have more sectors per track-54, 63 or more.

When reading from or writing to a hard disk, all access arms are moved to the appropriate cylinder. Although the addressing schemes vary considerably between disks, the address normally will include the cylinder (or track), the recording surface, and the sector number. PC users, who never seem to have enough hard disk storage space, may turn to a removable hard disk cartridge. Once full, a removable hard disk cartridge can be replaced with a fresh one. In effect, a removable cartridge is as portable as a diskette, but the disk cartridge holds much more data.

A concept of using several small disks that work together as a unit is called a redundant array of inexpensive disks or simply RAID. The group of connected disks operates as if it were just one large disk, but it speeds up reading and writing by having multiple access paths. The data file for, say automobile factory tools, may be spread across several disks, thus if the computer is used to look up tools for several workers, the computer need not read the data in turn but instead read them at the same time in parallel.

Working of Hard Disk

Disks are rotated continuously so that read/write heads mounted on movable or fixed arms can read or write programs or data to and from the disk. The Hard Disk Drive can be classified into two sections Mechanical Section and Electronic Section. The Mechanical Section consists of the followings which are explained accordingly.

Spindle Motor: One part of a hard disk, around which the platters rotate.

Disk drive: The motor that actually rotates the disk, plus the read/write heads and associated mechanisms, usually in a mountable housing. Sometimes, it is used synonymously to mean the entire disk subsystem

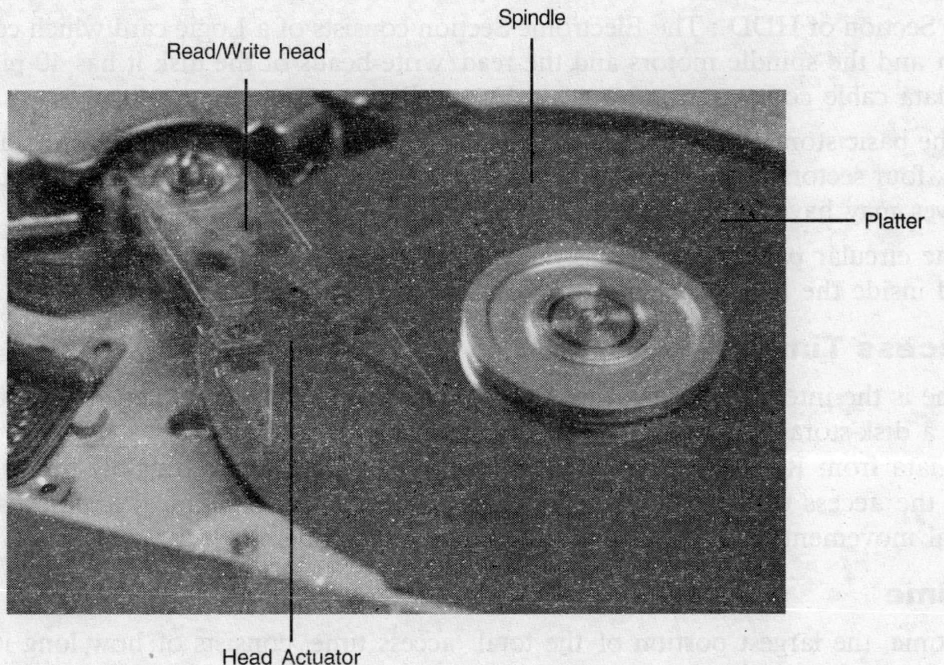

HDD Showing Platters and R/W Heads

Platters: The platters are no. of disks made of aluminum or plastic coated with a magnetic material. The data is stored on the platter.

Read/Write Head: The part of the hard disk which writes data to or reads data from a platter It functions like a coiled wire that reacts to a changing magnetic field by producing a minute current that can be detected and amplified by the electronics of the disk drive.

Head Actuator: In a disk drive, the mechanism which moves the read/write head radially across the surface of the platter of the disk drive.

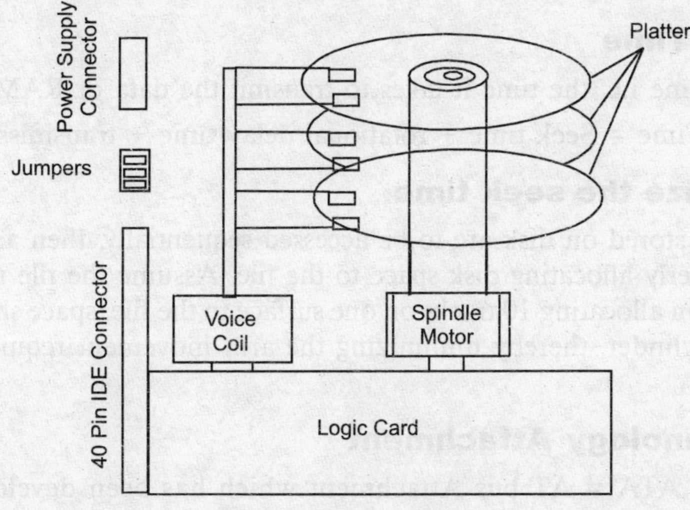

Block Diagram of HDD

Electronic Section of HDD : The Electronic Section consists of a Logic card which controls the stepper and the spindle motors and the read/write heads of the disk it has 40 pin IDE interface data cable connector and a 4 pin D-type Power supply connector.

Sector : The basic storage unit on a hard disk. On most modern hard disks, sectors are 512 bytes each, four sectors make up a cluster, and there are 17 to 34 sectors in a track although newer drives may have a different number of sectors.

Track : The circular path traced across the spinning surface of a disk platter by the read/ write head inside the hard-disk drive. The track consists of one or more clusters.

Disk Access Time

Access time is the interval between the instant a computer makes a request for transfer of data from a disk-storage device to RAM and the instant this operation is completed. The access of data from RAM is performed at electronic speeds-approximately the speed of light. But the access of data from disk storage depends on mechanical apparatus. Any mechanical movement significantly increases the access time.

Seek Time

The seek time, the largest portion of the total access time, consists of how long it takes the access arm (mechanical) to move the read/write head to the desired track or cylinder. Some hard disk drives have two sets of access arms, one for reading and writing on the inside tracks and another for the outside tracks.

Two independent sets of access arms significantly reduce the average seek time because they have a shorter distance to move and can move while the other is reading or writing.

Rotational Delay Time

The rotational delay time is the time it takes for the appropriate data to be positioned under the read/write head. On the average, it would be half the time it takes for one revolution of the disk or about 8 msec for a hard disk spinning at 3600 rpm.

Transmission Time

The transmission time i.e; the time it takes to transmit the data or RAM, is negligible.

Disk Access Time = Seek time + rotational delay time + transmission time

How to minimize the seek time

If records of a file stored on disk are to be accessed sequentially, then access time can be minimized by properly allocating disk space to the file. Assume the file requires 10 tracks of space. Rather than allocating 10 tracks on one surface to the file, space should be allocated to tracks on one cylinder, thereby minimizing the arm movement required to access the records.

Advance Technology Attachment

Shown next is the ATA = AT bus Attachment which has been developed by Western Digital, Conner, Seagate and Quantum.

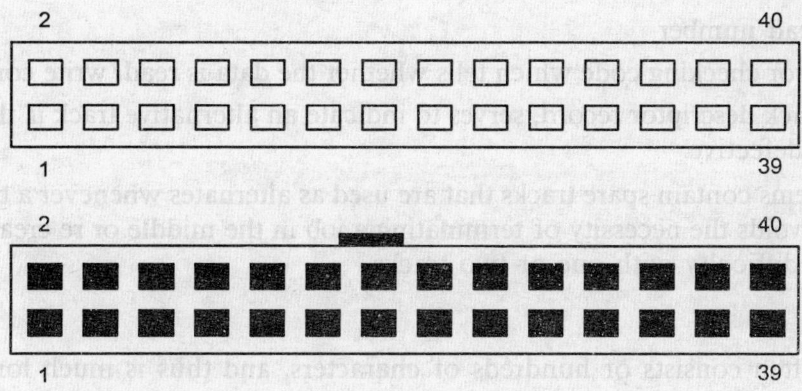

40 PIN MALE and FEMALE at the controller and peripherals.

Average Access Time

The time (in milliseconds) that a disk drive takes to find the right track in response to a request (the seek time), plus the time it takes to get to the right place on the track (the latency).

Arial Density

The amount of data which can be stored in one area of a Hard Disk or Floppy.

Interleaving

A hard-disk term which describes a method of arranging disk sectors to compensate for relatively slow computers Spreads sectors apart instead of arranging them consecutively. For example, 3:1 interleaving means your system reads one out of every three tracks on one rotation. The time required for the extra spin lets the read/write head catch up with the disk drive, which might otherwise outrun the head's ability to read the data

Cluster

A cluster is the minimum amount of space used to store a file. If the cluster size for operating system is 256 bytes even a 1-byte file takes up 256 bytes worth of space.

Recording Data on Disk

Data can be recorded on disk tracks with or without the use of keys. A key is a label that is used to identify a particular record. A key is required whenever the location of the record can't be specified exactly. Layout of the fields on a track in disk storage when data is recorded without the use of keys can be as given below:

BT: beginning of track

G: fields are separated by a gap

HA: home address consists of 4 fields

TC: track condition signals as to whether the track is operative or defective

CY: cylinder number

HD: Head number

EC: Error checking code which tells whether the data is read/write correctly or not.

TDR: Track descriptor record, serves to indicate an alternative track if the given track is defective.

Many disk systems contain spare tracks that are used as alternates whenever a track becomes defective; this avoids the necessity of terminating a job in the middle or re creating an entire file because of difficulty with one or two tracks.

Record

The data are often consists of hundreds of characters, and thus is much longer than the identification and control fields which preceded it on the track. Data is recorded with associated keys. In many disk systems the length of the key is limited to 255 bytes. Key field makes it possible to check the identification of a record in the disk control unit before it is transferred to the central processor, thus conserving central processor time.

Installation of HDD

The following procedure outlines the installation of a hard disk.

1. Disconnect the power to the computer.
2. Configure the appropriate master/slave settings or SCSI ID for the drive.
3. Insert the drive into an available drive bay. If the drive is too small for the bay, you will need a mounting kit.
4. Screw in the 4 screws - 2 on each side of the bay.
5. If the drive is an IDE disk, connect the IDE cable to the drive. There should be a stripe along 1 edge of the cable. This stripe denotes pin 1. Pin 1 on the drive is usually closest to the power connector on the drive, however, you should consult the manufacturers documentation. Then connect the signal cable to the motherboard ID1 or ID2 interface making sure to note the pin 1 orientation there as well. If the drive is a SCSI drive, a SCSI cable would be connected from the drive to a SCSI controller card.
6. Connect one of the power supply's power connectors to the drive.

Once the drive has been installed it must be configured for use in the following steps:

1. CMOS configuration-Newer BIOSes autodetection features will do this automatically. Otherwise, enter the setup utility during boot up and configure the drive.
2. Certain older drives types must be low-level formatted. Do not do this on IDE drives!
3. Partition the drive-Using the DOS utility FDISK, the drive can be partitioned into logical drives. The disk must contain an active primary partition that will be the C drive. An extended partition may also be created if desired. In Windows NT, the Disk Administrator program is used instead of FDISK. The size of the partitions can be set to a desired size, however, note the following:
   - Windows 95 Rev A(FAT16) only supported partitions up to 2GB in size.
   - Windows 95/98 OSR2(FAT32) supported drives up to 8GB.

- Even if the OS supports larger partition sizes, the BIOS must also support logical block addressing (LBA) or the maximum partition that you will be able to create will be either 504 or 528 MB.

4. Once the disk has been partitioned, it must then be formatted. This can be done using the DOS format utility.

Due to the magnetic nature of hard disks, they should remain clear of magnetic fields.

Troubleshooting Hard Disk Drives

Symptoms associated with hard disk drive failures include the following:

1. An Invalid Media Type message appears, indicating the controller cannot find a recognizable track/sector pattern on the drive.
2. A No Boot Record Found, a Nonsystem Disk or Disk Error, or an Invalid System Disk message appears, indicating that the system boot files are not located in the root directory of the drive.
3. The video display is active, but the HDD's activity light remains on and no bootup occurs, indicating that the HDD's CMOS configuration information is incorrect.
4. The front panel indicator lights are visible, and the display is present on the monitor screen, but there is no disk drive action and no bootup.
5. The computer boots up to a system disk in the A drive, but not to the hard drive, indicating that the system files on the hard disk drive (HDD) are missing or have become corrupt.
6. The computer does not boot up when turned on.
7. An IBM-compatible 17xx error code is produced on the display.
8. No motor sounds are produced by the HDD while the computer is running.
9. A HDD Controller Failure message appears, indicating a failure to verify hard disk setup by system configuration file error.
10. A C: or D: Fixed Disk Drive error message appears, indicating a hard disk CMOS setup failure.
11. An Out of Disk Space message appears.
12. A Missing Operating System or a Hard Drive Boot Failure message appears.
13. A Current Drive No Longer Valid message appears, indicating that the HDD's CMOS configuration information is incorrect or has become corrupt.

Hard Disk Enhancements

Hard disk drives are accessed over one of a number of bus types, including ATA (IDE, EIDE), Serial ATA (SATA), SCSI, SAS, and Fibre Channel. Bridge circuitry is sometimes used to connect hard disk drives to busses that they cannot communicate with natively, such as IEEE 1394 and USB. Back in the days of the ST-506 interface, the data encoding scheme was also important. The first ST-506 disks used Modified Frequency Modulation (MFM) encoding, and transferred data at a rate of 5 megabits per second. Later on, controllers using 2,7 RLL (or just "RLL") encoding increased the transfer rate by fifty percent, to 7.5 megabits per second; it also increased disk capacity by fifty percent.

Many ST-506 interface disk drives were only specified by the manufacturer to run at the lower MFM data rate, while other models (usually more expensive versions of the same basic disk drive) were specified to run at the higher RLL data rate. In some cases, a disk drive had sufficient margin to allow the MFM specified model to run at the faster RLL data rate; however, this was often unreliable and was not recommended. (An RLL-certified disk drive could run on a MFM controller, but with 1/3 less data capacity and speed.) Enhanced Small Disk Interface (ESDI) also supported multiple data rates (ESDI disks always used 2,7 RLL, but at 10, 15 or 20 megabits per second), but this was usually negotiated automatically by the disk drive and controller; most of the time, however, 15 or 20 megabit ESDI disk drives weren't downward compatible (i.e. a 15 or 20 megabit disk drive wouldn't run on a 10 megabit controller). ESDI disk drives typically also had jumpers to set the number of sectors per track and (in some cases) sector size.

SCSI originally had just one speed, 5 MHz (for a maximum data rate of 5 megabytes per second), but later this was increased dramatically. The SCSI bus speed had no bearing on the disk's internal speed because of buffering between the SCSI bus and the disk drive's internal data bus; however, many early disk drives had very small buffers, and thus had to be reformatted to a different interleave (just like ST-506 disks) when used on slow computers, such as early IBM PC compatibles and early Apple Macintoshes. ATA disks have typically had no problems with interleave or data rate, due to their controller design, but many early models were incompatible with each other and couldn't run in a master/slave setup (two disks on the same cable). This was mostly remedied by the mid-1990s, when ATA's specification was standardised and the details began to be cleaned up, but still causes problems occasionally (especially with CD-ROM and DVD-ROM disks, and when mixing Ultra DMA and non-UDMA devices).

Serial ATA does away with master/slave setups entirely, placing each disk on its own channel (with its own set of I/O ports) instead. FireWire/IEEE 1394 and USB(1.0/2.0) hard disks are external units containing generally ATA or SCSI disks with ports on the back allowing very simple and effective expansion and mobility. Most FireWire/IEEE 1394 models are able to daisy-chain in order to continue adding peripherals without requiring additional ports on the computer itself.

Acronym	Meaning	Description
SASI	Shugart Associates System Interface	Predecessor to SCSI
SCSI	Small Computer System Interface	Bus oriented that handles concurrent operations.
ST-506		Seagate interface
ST-412		Seagate interface (minor improvement over ST-506)
ESDI	Enhanced Small Disk Interface	Faster and more integrated than ST-412/506, but still backwards compatible
ATA	Advanced Technology Attachment	Successor to ST-412/506/ESDI by integrating the disk controller completely onto the device. Incapable of concurrent operations.

eSATA

Standardized in mid-2004, eSATA defined separate cables, connectors, and revised electrical requirements for external applications:

- Minimum transmit potential increased: Range is 500–600 mV instead of 400–600 mV.
- Minimum receive potential decreased: Range is 240–600 mV instead of 325–600 mV.
- Identical protocol and logical signaling (link/transport-layer and above), allowing native SATA devices to be deployed in external enclosures with minimal modification
- Maximum cable length of 2 m (USB and FireWire allow longer distances.)

Aimed at the consumer market, eSATA enters an external storage market already served by the USB and FireWire interfaces. Most external hard disk drive cases with FireWire or USB interfaces use either PATA or SATA drives and "bridges" to translate between the drives' interfaces and the enclosures' external ports, and this bridging incurs some inefficiency. In the case of USB 2.0, protocol overhead limits the maximum effective bandwidth to a fraction of USB's physical signalling rate. With modern hard disk drives, USB's transfer rate is a bottleneck.

FireWire, with its isochronous transfer mode, is more efficient, such that even in its slower variant, FireWire 400 (IEEE 1394a), the effective transfer rate is significantly faster than that of USB 2.0, but this can still be a bottleneck for fast drives or RAIDs. Some single disks can transfer well over 70 MB/s during real use, well in excess of USB 2.0's or the older FireWire 400's abilities. Finally, some low-level drive features, such as S.M.A.R.T., are not usable through USB or FireWire bridging. eSATA does not suffer from these issues.

eSATA will likely co-exist alongside USB 2.0 and FireWire storage for several reasons. The ubiquity of USB ports on all mass-market computers, and FireWire ports on many consumer electronic appliances, guarantee a large market for USB and FireWire storage. For small form-factor devices (such as external 2.5" disks), a PC-hosted USB or FireWire link supplies sufficient power to operate the device. Where a PC-hosted port is concerned, eSATA connectors cannot supply power, and would therefore be more cumbersome to use.

As of 2007, few computer motherboards have eSATA connectors. Non-equipped desktops can be upgraded with the installation of an eSATA host bus adapter (HBA), while notebooks can be upgraded with Cardbus or ExpressCard versions of an eSATA HBA. Also available are passive eSATA-to-SATA bracket/cable-adapters.

With passive-adapters, the maximum cable length is reduced to 1 meter, due to the absence of compliant eSATA signal levels. Full SATA speed for external disks (115 MB/s) have been measured with external RAID enclosures.

eSATA is likely to be ignored by the enterprise and server market, which has already standardized on the separately-developed Serial Attached SCSI (SAS) interface, which has extra features for remote management, link redundancy, and link monitoring.

eSATA compared to other buses							
	eSATA	SATA 300	PATA 133	FireWire 800	FireWire 400	USB 2.0	Ultra-320 SCSI
Speed (Mbit/s)	2400	2400	1064	786	400	480 (burst)	2560
Max. cable length (m)	2	1	0.46	4.5 (16 cables can be daisy chained up to 72 m)	4.5 (16 cables can be daisy chained up to 72 m)	5 (USB hubs can be daisy chained up to 25 m)	12
Power provided	No	No	No	Yes (12-25 V, 15 W	Yes (12-25 V, 15 W)	Yes (5 V, 2.5 W)	No
Devices per Channel	1 (15 with port multiplier)	1 per line	2	63	63	127	16

SATA vs SCSI

SCSI currently offers transfer rates higher than SATA, but is a more complex bus usually resulting in higher manufacturing cost. Some drive manufacturers offer longer warranties for SCSI devices, however, indicating a possibly higher manufacturing quality control of SCSI devices compared to PATA/SATA devices. SCSI buses also allow connection of several drives (using multiple channels, 7 or 15 on each channel) whereas SATA only allows one per channel.

SATA 3.0 Gbit/s offers a maximum bandwidth of 300 MB/s per device compared to SCSI with a maximum of 320 MB/s. Also, SCSI drives provide greater sustained throughput than SATA drives because of disconnect-reconnect and aggregating performance. SATA devices are generally compatible with SAS enclosures and adapters, while SCSI devices cannot be directly connected to a SATA bus.

SCSI hardware is used in enterprises for server purposes, partially due to higher cost of drives and adapters, and partially due to market reasons. The MTBF of SATA drives is usually about 150,000 hours, while SCSI drives are rated for upwards of 1,500,000 hours.

FDD

There are two kinds of floppies, 3½" and 5¼" in sizes. These floppies are made of vinyl material and have a plastic coated jacket over them. The vinyl material has a coating of magnetic oxide so that data can be stored on it. Floppy disk can be used both as an input device and an output device meaning that you can both write on it and read from it.

Floppy disk is used for the storage of data which is encoded by electromagnetic means on to tracks on the disk surface. A floppy disk is made of flexible material usually a kind of plastic which has magnetizable particles upon its surface. Floppy disks are supplied within special envelopes which have holes set in them for the drive aft and read/write heads of the disk drives which are used to operate with the disks. The d s are designed to be handled within the envelope which protects the recording surface.

Floppy disks are used with word processing systems and with PCs and their popularity is related to the ease with which they can be handled and stored off line. They are classed as exchangeable disks. It is also known as diskette.

Types of Floppy Disks

Floppies come in two physical sizes:

5 1/4 inch and

3 1/2 inch.

The size refers to the diameter of the disk, not to the capacity.

The 5 1/4" type is encased in a flexible vinyl envelope with an oval cutout that allows the read/write head to access the disk.

The density of the disk is a measure of the quantity of the disk surface: the higher the density, the more closely the iron-oxide particles are packed and the more data the disk can store. The disk itself is made of soft flexible mylar plastic with a magnetically sensitive iron oxide coating. The coating is present on both sides, even for single-sided disks that are intended to be recorded on only one side. The second side of a single-sided disk may not have its second side finished, polished and tested but it still has the same coating.

These days 5.25 inch disks (1.2 MB capacity) are used primarily in older computers although some people buy optional 5.25" disk drives for their new PCs to be able to read and write to the old disks. 3.5 inch type is encased in a hard plastic shell with a sliding metal cover. When the disk is inserted into the drive, the cover slides back to expose the disk to the read/write head. The term floppy disk refers to the disk inside, not to the square plastic protector.

The 3.5 inch size floppy disk come in three capacities:

1. double density
2. high density and
3. very high density

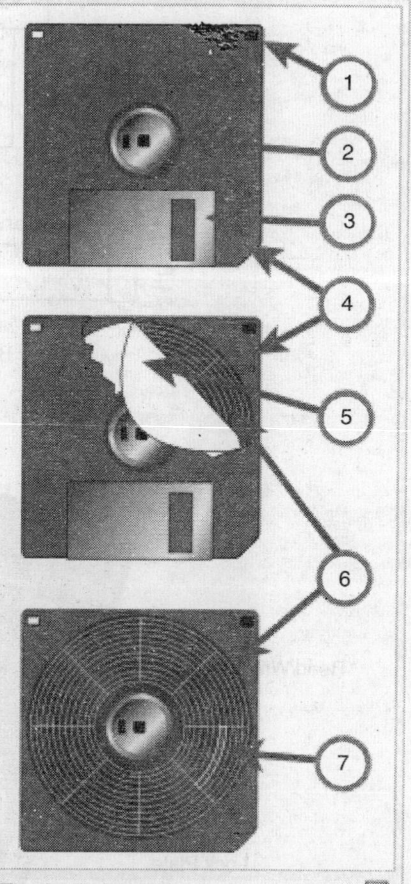

The basic internal components of a 3½-inch floppy disK:
1. Write-protect tab
2. Hub
3. Shutter
4. Plastic housing
5. Paper ring
6. Magnetic disk
7. Disk sector.

Floppy Disk Drives

A disk drive designed to read and write data to a floppy disk for transfer to and from a computer. It can be classified into two sections Mechanical Section and Electronic Section. A Floppy Drive consist of the following:

The following two figures show the block diagram of Floppy Disk Drive and real outlay of Floppy Disk Drive.

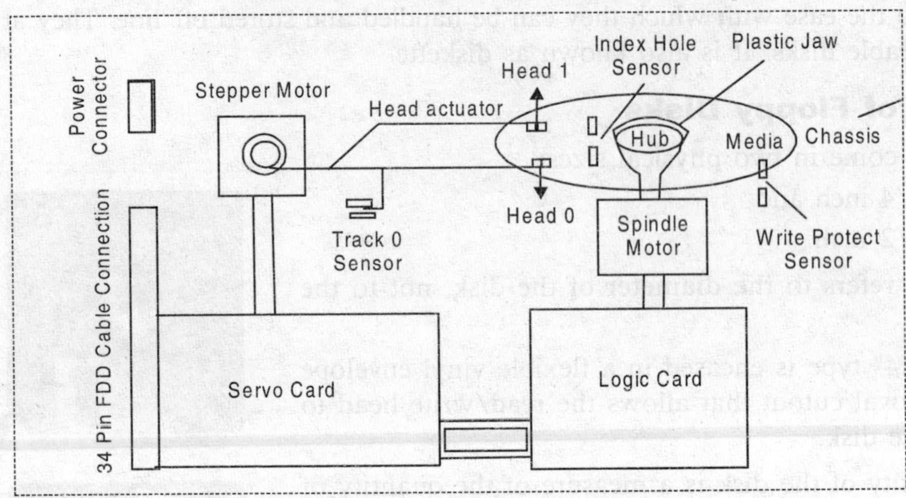

Block Diagram of Floppy Disk Drive

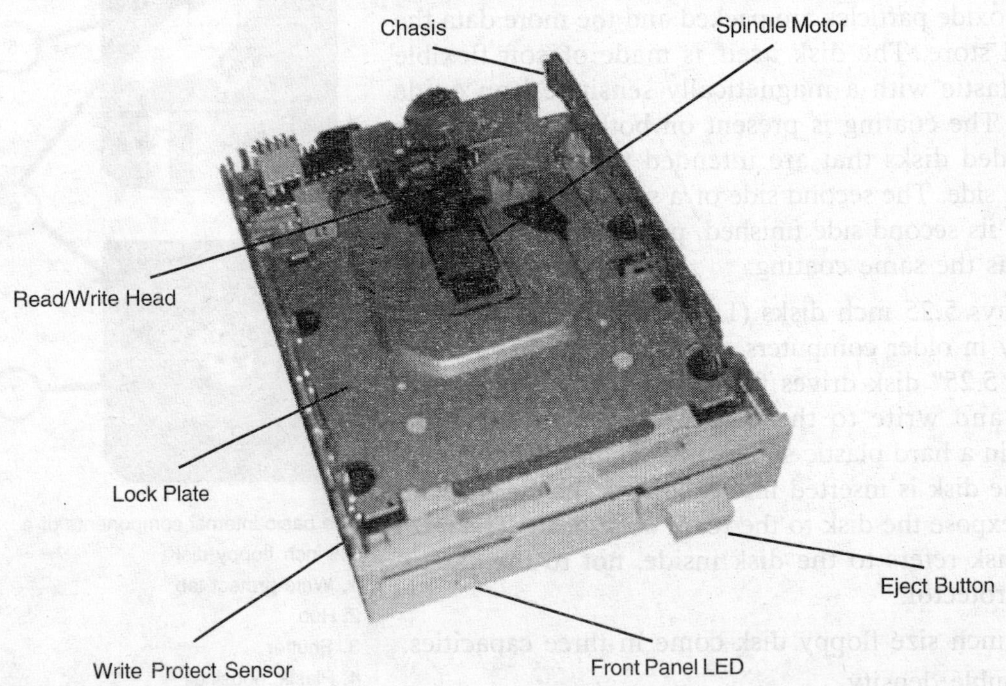

Outlay of Floppy Disk Drive

Mechanical Section

1. Two Motors: (*i*) Stepper Motor
   (*ii*) Spindle Motor
2. Read/Write Heads (Head zero and head one)

3. Chassis
4. HUB
5. Plastic Jaw
6. Head Actuator

Electronic Section:

7. Two cards (*i*) Servo Card
   (*ii*) Logic Card
8. Four Sensor: (*i*) Track Zero Sensor
   (*ii*) Index Hole Sensor
   (*iii*) Write Protect Sensor
   (*iv*) Lock Sensor
9. 34 pin floppy drive connector
10. 4 pin power supply connector

Various parts of the Floppy Disk drive, as shown in the figure are:

Spindle Motor: This motor is used to rotate the floppy disk at 360 revolutions per minute (RPM) so that the sectors can come under the read/write head.

Stepper Motor This motor is used to move the read/write head over the tracks of the disk, it takes step pulses to move to the next track or previous track.

Read/Write Head: The Read/Write head are used to write and read information on the media *i.e.,* floppy, It works on ,the principle of electromagnetism.

Chassis: This is the base for the other parts, which are assembled on it.

Hub: The hub is used to hold the floppy at spindle hole and rotate it at 360 rpm.

Head Actuator: In a disk drive, the mechanism that moves the read/write head radially across the surface of the disk drive.

Plastic Jaw: This is used to hold the floppy at the spindle hole when it is inside the disk, so that it can rotate.

Lock Plate: The lock plate is used to lock the floppy inside the disk.

Electronic Section of FDD: The Electronics section of FDD consists of Two Cards Logic card and Servo card. The Logic card is used to control the stepper motor and the Read/Write Heads and the Servo card is used to control the spindle motor's rpm.

Floppy Disk Drive Cable

FDD cable consists of 34 pin connector, as shown in next figure, which is connected between Floppy Drive Controller (FDC) and floppy drive.

One end of the FDD cable is twisted which is connected with "A" drive, the other end is connected with "B" drive and FDC controller

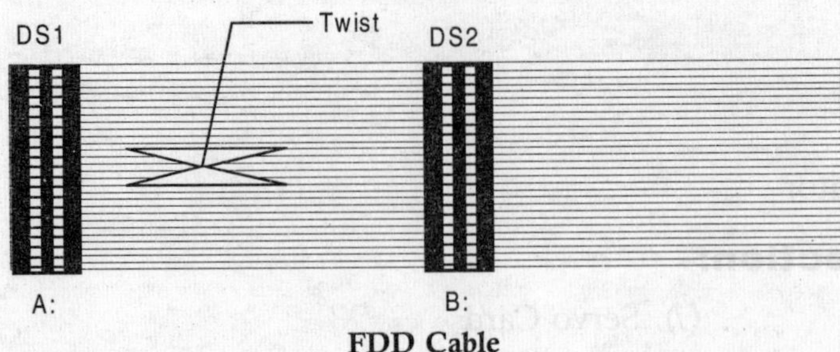

FDD Cable

How to Take Care of Your Floppy Disks

Although diskettes come in protective jackets, users must take at lest ordinary care of them to protect the data contents:

1. Keep floppy disks away from anything that has magnetic charge or that generates magnetic field, including telephone, stereo speakers.
2. Don't slide the cover back on 3.5 inch disks and don't touch the recording medium of any disk.
3. Never force a disk into a disk drive and never remove a disk from a drive when the drive light is on. The light tells you that the drive is working, and removing the disk is likely to damage the data on it.

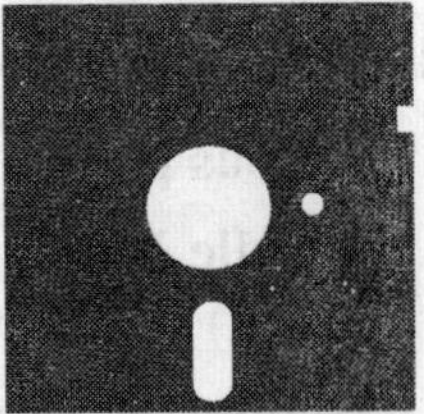

4. Do not expose disks to excessive heat or humidity.

Measuring Drive Performance

When evaluating the performance of common storage devices, you need to be aware of two common measures:

1. The average access time and
2. The data-transfer rate.

Average Access Time

The average access time of a device is the amount of time it takes the device to position its read/write heads over any spot on the recording medium. Access time is the combination of two factors:

1. the speed at which the disk spins (in RPM) and
2. time the read/write head takes to move the heads from one track to another.

Access time is measured in msec. (1/1000 second), so the maximum access time for floppy disks = 60/30 * 1000/1 = 200 m secs.

Average Data- Transfer Rate

It implies at which rate drive can transfer data, *i.e.*, how long it takes to read or write data. For data-transfer rates, the unit of time is almost always the second, but units of data may be measured in bytes, KB or MB. Disk controllers coordinate the flow of data to and from the computer and disk drive. They are often connected to the system as an expansion card and can control the flow of data to several drives.

Drive Interface Standards

Another important factor in determining how quickly a drive can read and write data is the type of controller that the drive uses. A disk controller is connected directly to the computer's bus on some computers, the disk controller is an integral part of the computer's main motherboard. On others, the controller is an expansion board that connects to the bus by plugging into one of the computer's expansion slots.

Integrated Drive Electronics (IDE)

The IDE interface places most of the controller's circuitry on the drive itself to provide a simpler interface with the computer. IDE is capable of providing data-transfer rates of about 1 MB per second under ideal conditions.

Enhanced Small Device Interface (ESDI)

It encodes the data on the drive instead of on the controller card. This results in a higher degree of reliability - which in turn allows for higher speeds. ESDI is capable of transferring data at rate of 3 MB per second.

Small Computer System Interface (SCSI)

It takes an approach to interfacing peripheral devices. Because the original concept of SCSI was to provide peripherals access to the computer's bus, one way to think of SCSI is as an extension of the computer's bus. One benefit of SCSI is that bringing the computer's bus directly into the drive improves efficiency greatly. Because a SCSI interface is essentially an extension of a computer's bus, it can accommodate multiple devices — as many as the bus can handle. Most current implementations of SCSI limit the number of devices to seven.

Internal Structure of a Floppy Disk

The outermost track of any disc is called track zero. Track zero is very important for any disk. It is responsible for booting of a computer, for storing the details of directories and files stored inside the disk.

Track zero has four parts:

1. Master Boot Record (MBR): It stores all the information of the operating system through which the floppy disk is formatted.
2. Dos Boot Record (DBR): It is used to store all the system files, which are required for booting of the computer There are three system files, which are required to boot a computer and they are
   i. IO.SYS
   ii. MSDOS.SYS
   iii. COMMAND.COM
3. Directory Structure (DS): It stores the information of all the directories and files stored inside the disk, such as, Directory name, File name, Size of the files and the date and time of the creation or modification of file etc.

4. File Allocation Table (FAT): It is very-very important part of track zero. It stores all the information about the file and directory stored inside the disk such as track number, sector number and side number It is just like an index of a text book.

Installation of Floppy Disk Drives (FDD)

1. Power off and unplug the computer.
2. Detach all devices, *e.g.*, printer, keyboard, monitor.
3. Remove the computer cover. Refer to your computer system manual.
4. If you are replacing an existing drive, note how the drive is connected. For installation of a second drive or a new drive, go to Step 11.
5. Unplug the four pin power cable and the 34 pin flat interface cable.
6. Remove the screws mounting the old drive and carefully remove the unit.
7. Mount the Imation floppy drive using the screws supplied with the kit.
8. Attach the existing flat interface cable making certain that the red wire, Pin 1, is closest to the motor, near the center rear of the drive, as shown in Figure A.
9. Plug the four wire power connector to the drive to complete the installation.
10. Replace the computer cover and reconnect any peripherals.

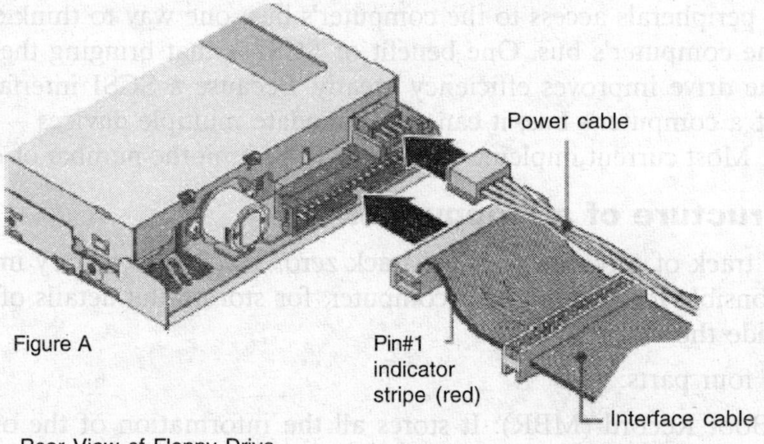

Fig. Floppy Drive

11. For a second drive, complete Steps 1 to 3 above.
12. Remove a floppy disk filler panel at the front of the computer unit.
13. Determine that the interface cable to your existing floppy drive has a second connector near the attached drive. If not, substitute the three-connector interface cable shipped with the Imation kit.
14. Using the screws enclosed in the kit, mount the Imation floppy drive in the space in the computer. If your computer does not have an extra floppy bay, you will need to acquire a 5-inch bay adapter panel from your computer supplier.

15. Connect the cable to the floppy drives with the red stripe closest to the motor assembly as shown in Figure A above.
16. The floppy drive attached to the end connector will appear as Drive A in My Computer or Windows Explorer. The drive attached to the second connector from the end will appear as Drive B.
17. Connect the a four wire power plug to the back of each floppy drive.
18. Reassemble the computer and power on.
19. Follow Steps 1 – 3 from the above instructions.
20. Determine if the mother board of the PC has a 34 pin floppy disk connector and that a 4 pin power connector is available. If the PC does not have an unused small power connector, you may need to obtain a standard power connector to mini adapter from your computer store.
21. Locate the floppy bay at the front of the machine and remove the cover.
22. Mount the floppy drive using the screws from the kit.
23. Attach the end of the 34 pin interface cable without the twist to the floppy disk connector on the mother board of your computer being sure to align the red stripe of the cable with Pin 1. (See your computer documentation or contact the computer manufacturer to locate the proper mother board connector.)
24. Connect the other end of the cable to the floppy drive with the red stripe closest to the motor assembly.
25. Reassemble the computer.
26. During power up, it may be necessary to reconfigure the BIOS of your PC to recognize the new floppy drive. Review the documentation that came with your PC or contact the manufacturer for this procedure.

Troubleshooting Floppy Disk Drives

1. The floppy drive is installed, but the LED on the front of the unit is continually on. The connection of the interface from the PC mother board to the drive may be incorrect. Power off and unplug the computer and recheck. Be certain that the red stripe of the interface cable connects to Pin 1 on the mother board of the PC and also to Pin 1 on the floppy drive. Pin 1 on the drive is closest to the drive motor, at the rear center of the unit.
2. The drive is cabled but is not recognized by the Windows operating system.
   - Go to Control Panel.
   - Click on System.
   - Click on Device Manager.
   - Click the plus sign in front of Floppy Disk Controllers.
   - If there is a yellow exclamation point on the disk controller, highlight the unit and click Remove.
   - Power off the computer and unplug.

- With the system off, check the cable connections to the floppy drive.
- Reboot the system and Windows should automatically recognize your drive.

3. After setting up the system BIOS, a message "DISK BOOT FAILURE. INSERT A SYSTEM DISK AND HIT ENTER" appears. After trying several boot disks, the same message keeps appearing. The BIOS is not set up correctly. Obtain the proper settings by contacting your computer manufacturer or the Internet site for the manufacturer of the BIOS of your machine.

CD-ROM

This is not doubt the latest and the best medium for storing data. Though they look very similar to music CDs, so to differentiate from them, the computer ones are called CD-ROMs. They are round in shape and are about 5" in diameter. Till recently they used to be Read Only but now writeable CDs are also available with the relevant drives to write on them. With capacity to write data of about 600 floppies, it has become very popular over the recent times.

In the form of videodisks or compact disks (CDs), optical disks represent a new trend in small, high-capacity storage of images and sound. A single optical disks stores nearly 1 GB of data on one side. To put this storage capacity into perspective, an optical disk can hold 800 television quality images or 60 minutes of high fidelity music.

The explosive growth in storage needs has driven the computer industry to provide cheaper, more versatile storage devices with greater capacity. New storage technologies using optical disks exceed the storage capacities currently available with magnetic disks of the same size. Optical storage techniques used by computers are basically the same as those used to record music on compact disks.

Optical disks differ from magnetic disk storage by the way data is stored and read from the storage media. A laser beam is used to write and read data on these reflective disks, so they are also known as laser disks. In this technology a laser hits a layer of metallic material spread over the surface of a disk. When data is being entered heat from the laser produces tiny spots on the disk surface. To read the data, the laser scans the disk, and a lens picks up different light reflections from the various spots.

Optical disks are becoming a very inviting option for users. They are less sensitive to environmental fluctuations, and they provide more direct-access storage at a cost than is much less per megabyte of storage than the magnetic disk alternative.

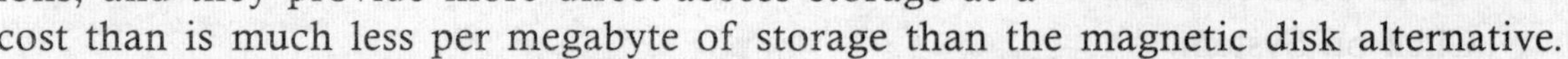

Optical disk technology is still emerging and has yet to stabilize; however at present there are three different types of optical disks in common use:

read-only

recordable, and

erasable

Structure of CD-ROM drive

The CD-ROM has two sections namely Mechanical Section and the Electronics Section.

The center of the drive is a cast aluminum or rigid frame assembly. As with other drives, the frame is the single primary structure for mounting the drive's mechanical and electronic components The front panel consists of lid, volume control, and eject button attached to the frame, and offering a fixed reference slot for CD insertion and removal.

The main PC board, handles the drive control and interfacing, and the headphone PC board, which provides an audio jack for headphones. The main CD subassembly called a drive engine, which uses to hold eject, spin, and read the disk. This interchangeability is part of the genius of CD-ROM drives—a single sub-assembly performs 80 percent of the work. Sony, Philips, and Toshiba are the major manufacturers of CD-ROM engines, but other companies, such as IBM and Ikka, are also producing engines.

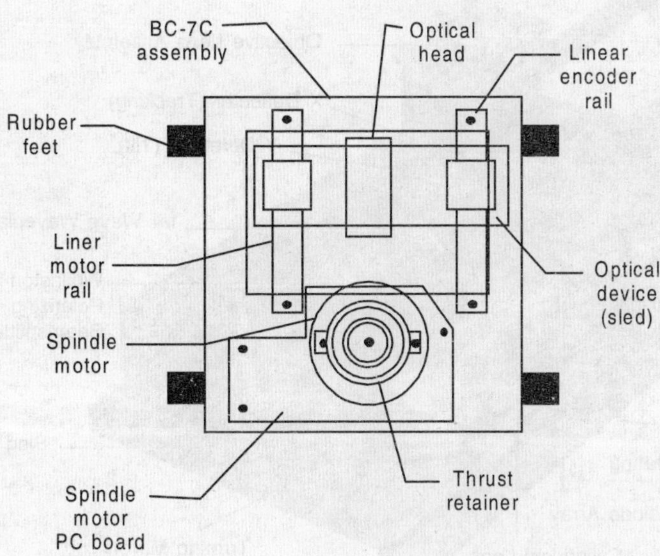

Assembly of CD-ROM drive

The engine features a series of mechanisms that accept, clamp, and eject the disk. The foundation of this engine is the BC-7C assembly. It acts as a sub-frame, the sub-frame is shock-mounted with four rubber feet to cushion the engine from minor bumps and ordinary handling as shown in the figure 5.27 below. The slider assembly, loading chassis assembly, and the cover shield provide the mechanical action needed to accept the disk and clamp it into place over the drive spindle, as well as to free the disk and eject it on demand. A motor/gear assembly drives the load unload mechanics. The work of spinning and reading a disk is handled under the engine.

A spindle motor is mounted on the sub-frame and connected to a spindle motor PC board. The most important part of the CD engine is the optical device that contains the 780-nm (nanometer) 0.6-mW gallium aluminum arsenide (GaAIAs) laser diode and detector, along with the optical focus and tracking components. The optical device slides along two guide rails and shines through an exposed hole in the sub-frame. This combination of device mounting and guide rails is called a full form check.

A CD drive ideally requires a linear motor to act much like the voice coil motor used to position hard-drive R/W heads. By altering the signal driving a sled motor and constantly measuring and adjusting the sled's position, a sled can be made to track very smoothly along a disk—free from the sudden, jerky motion of stepping motors.

Some CD drives still use stepping motors to position the sled. The drive's main PC board is responsible for managing these operations.

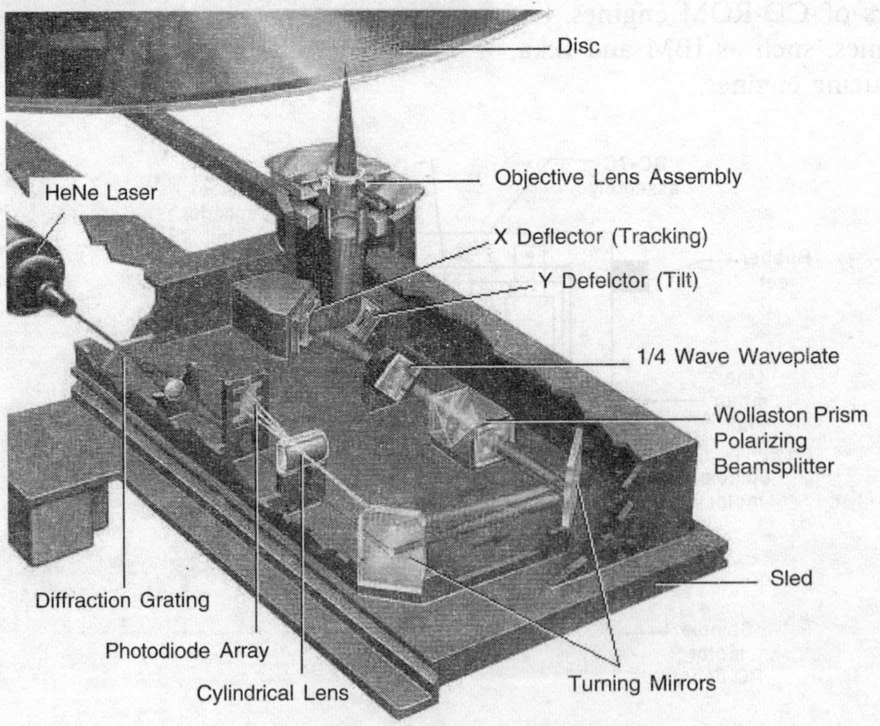

Mechanical Section of CD-ROM Drive

CD-ROM Electronics

The electronics package can be divided into two major areas and they are the controller section and the drive section as shown in the block diagram below. The controller section is dedicated to the peripheral interface—its connection to the adapter board. Much of the reason for a CD-ROM's electronic sophistication can be traced to the controller section. The controller circuitry is dedicated to handling a SCSI interface. This allows the unit's "intelligence" to be located right in the drive itself. Most of the CDROM drives use an EIDE/IDE interface (the same interface used for hard drives).

The drive section manages the CD-ROM's physical operations (i.e., load/unload, spin the disk, move the sled, etc.), as well as data decoding Eight-to-Fourteen Modulation (EFM) and error correction. Drive circuitry converts an analog output from the laser diode into an EFM signal, which is, in turn, decoded into binary data and Cross-Interleaved.

Reed-Solomon Code (CIRC) Information

A drive-controller IC and servo-processor IC are responsible for directing laser focus, tracking, sled motor control (and feedback), spindle motor control (and feedback), and loading/unloading motor control.

Drive Interface

AT Attachment Packet Interface (ATARI) or IDE Interface. The ATARI connection combines more than adequate performance (CDs hardly strain even the slowest of IDE connections) with low cost and easy wiring. Using the ATARI, the system gets exactly the same degree of control over the CDs as with the more complex SCSI link.

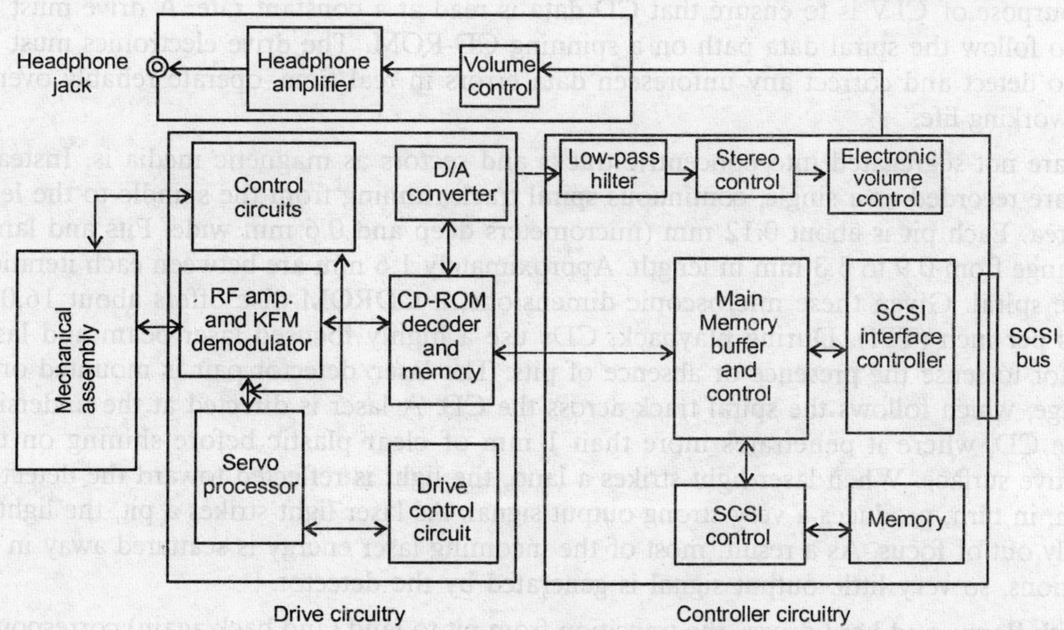

Block diagram of CD-ROM Drive

If one already has two IDE hard disks in the PC, a secondary host adapter will give you the connection one needs. Most cables and connectors are keyed to prevent inadvertent mis-insertion. In any case, the red or blue stripe on the edge of the ribbon cable indicates the side of th'e connector holding the lower numbered pins.

Understanding the Software

Hardware alone is not enough to implement a CD-ROM or CD-R drive. BIOS and MS-DOS provide the software support to handle the drive, Manufacturers provide a hardware-specific device driver used to communicate with the CD-ROM and interface. An MS-DOS extension (MSCDEX) provides file handling and logical drive letter support.

Device Drivers

A device driver allows programs to access the CD-ROM or CD-R drive properly at the register (hardware) level. Because most CD-ROM/CD-R drives are designed differently, they require different device drivers. Device driver uses a SYS extension, and is initiated by adding its command line to the PC's CONFIG.SYS file, such as:

DEVICE=SSCDROM.SYS/D:MSCD000/N:1/P:300

Principles and Working of CD-ROM Drive

CD-ROM/CD-R drives are impressive pieces of engineering. The drive accept standard-sized disks and spin the disk at a Constant Linear Velocity (CLV)—that is, the disk speed varies inversely with the tracking radius. As tracking approaches the disk edge, disk speeds slows, and vice versa. Keep in mind that CLV is different than the Constant Angular Velocity (CAV) method used by floppy and hard drives, which moves the media at a constant speed. The purpose of CLV is to ensure that CD data is read at a constant rate. A drive must be able to follow the spiral data path on a spinning CD-ROM. The drive electronics must be able to detect and correct any unforeseen data errors in real time, operate reliably over a long working life.

CDs are not segregated into concentric tracks and sectors as magnetic media is. Instead, CDs are recorded as a single, continuous spiral track running from the spindle to the lead out area. Each pit is about 0.12 mm (micrometers deep and 0.6 mm wide. Pits and lands can range from 0.9 to 3.3 mm in length. Approximately 1.6 mm are between each iteration of the spiral. Given these microscopic dimensions, a CDROM disc offers about 16,000 tracks per inch (TPI). During playback, CDs use a highly focused laser beam and laser detector to sense the presence or absence of pits. The laser/detector pair is mounted on a carriage, which follows the spiral track across the CD. A laser is directed at the underside of the CD, where it penetrates more than 1 mm of clear plastic before shining on the reflective surface. When laser light strikes a land, the light is reflected toward the detector, which, in turn, produces a very strong output signal. As laser light strikes a pit, the light is slightly out of focus. As a result, most of the incoming laser energy is scattered away in all directions, so very little output signal is generated by the detector.

As with floppy and hard drives, the transition from pit to land (and back again) corresponds to binary levels, not the presence or absence of a pit or land. The analog light signal returned by the detector must be converted to logic levels and decoded. A process known as Eight-to-Fourteen Modulation (EFM) is very common with CD-ROMs.

EFM and Data Storage

A complex decoding process is necessary to convert the arcane sequence of pits and lands into meaningful binary information. The technique of EFM is used with CD-ROMs. For hard-disk drives, such techniques as 2.7 RLL encoding can be used to place a large number of bits into a limited number of flux transitions. The same is true for CDs using EFM.

User data, error-correction information, address information, and synchronization patterns are all contained in a bit stream that is represented by pits and lands. Magnetic media encodes bits as flux transitions—not the discrete orientation of any magnetic area. The same concept holds true with CD-ROMs, where binary 1s and 0s do not correspond to pits or lands. A binary 1 is represented wherever a transition (pit to land or land to pit) occurs. The length of a pit or land represents the number of binary 0s.

The EFM encoding technique equates each byte (8 bits) with a 14-bit sequence (called a symbol), where each binary. 1 must be separated by at least two binary 0s.

A CD-ROM frame is composed of 24 synchronization bits, 14 control bits, 24 of the 14-bit data symbols you saw previously, and eight complete 14-bit Error-Correction (EC) symbols. Each symbol is separated by additional three merge bits, bringing the total number of bits in the frame to 588. Thus, 24 bytes of data is represented by 588 bits on a CD-ROM, expressed as a number of pits and lands. There are 98 frames in a data block, so each block carries (98 x 24) = 2048 bytes (2352 with error correction, synchronization, and address bytes).

The basic CD-ROM can deliver 153.6 KB of data (75 blocks) per second to its host controller.

Advantages

1. Instead of using 15 to 20 diskettes an entire suite of programs and data could reside on a single CD-ROM.
2. CD-ROM are not vulnerable to magnetic fields which can destroy the data on a diskette.
3. Optical media are extremely durable and reliable under normal use. Because the surface of the disk (sealed in its plastic coating) is never touched by anything but light and because the medium itself is virtually unaffected by moisture on temperature conditions.
4. One reason optical technology is so reliable is that the read head is several millimeters away from the disk surface.

However there are two main reasons that prevent CD drives from totally displacing hard devices:

One reason is that CD drives are still slow. A drive that meets the multimedia PC2 standard for performance only has to move 900 KB of data per second. A good hard drive, by comparison, transfers 10 MB of data per second. Whereas on time scale the internal hard drive can find the data your application asks for in 10 msec, and on the other side CD-ROM drive takes upto 300 msec for the same task. The other reason is that you can not write to portions of a writable CD-ROM that already have data written to them. You can add to data that was written to the disk in an earlier session but you can't delete or change what is already there.

Data Transfer Speed in Various CD Drives			
Transfer Speed	Megabytes/s	Megabits/s	Mebibits/s
1x	0.15	1.2	1.1444
2x	0.3	2.4	2.2888
4x	0.6	4.8	4.5776
8x	1.2	9.6	9.1553
10x	1.5	12.0	11.4441
12x	1.8	14.4	13.7329
20x	3.0	24.0	22.8882
32x	4.8	38.4	36.6211
36x	5.4	43.2	41.1987
40x	6.0	48.0	45.7764
48x	7.2	57.6	54.9316
50x	7.5	60.0	57.2205
52x	7.8	62.4	59.5093

CD-ROM Capacity

A standard 120 mm CD-ROM holds 650 or 700 MiB of data. To put this storage capacity into context, the average novel contains 60,000 words. Assume that average word length is 10 letters and that each letter occupies one byte. A novel therefore might occupy 600,000 bytes (600 kB, without layout information). One CD can therefore contain over 1,000 novels. If each novel occupies at least one centimetre of bookshelf space, then one CD can contain the equivalent of over ten metres of bookshelf. However, textual data can be compressed by more than a factor of ten, using compression algorithms, so a CD-ROM can accommodate at least 100 metres of bookshelf space.

In comparison a single layer DVD contains 4.4 GB of data, nearly 7 times the amount of a CD-ROM.

Capacities of Compact Disc types						
Type	Sectors	Data max size		Audio max size		Time
	(MB)		(MiB)	(MB)	(MiB)	(min)
8 cm	94,500	193.536	~ 184.6	222.264	~ 212.0	21
283,500	580.608	~ 553.7	666.792	~ 635.9	63	
650 MB	333,000	681.984	~ 650.3	783.216	~ 746.9	74
700 MB	360,000	737.280	~ 703.1	846.720	~ 807.4	80
800 MB	405,000	829.440	~ 791.0	952.560	~ 908.4	90
900 MB	445,500	912.384	~ 870.1	1,047.816	~ 999.3	99

Note: Megabyte (MB) and minute (min) values are exact.

CD capacities are always given in binary units, although decimal SI prefixes are usually used: a "700 MB" CD has a nominal capacity of about 700 MiB. DVD capacities, on the other hand, are given in decimal units: a "4.7 GB" DVD has a nominal capacity of about 4.38 GiB.

Installing of CD Drive

The following procedure outlines the installation of a CDROM drive.

1. Disconnect the power to the computer.
2. Configure the appropriate master/slave settings or SCSI ID for the drive.
3. Insert the drive into an available drive bay.
4. Screw in the 4 screws — 2 on each side of the bay.
5. If the drive is an IDE, connect the IDE cable to the drive. There should be a stripe along 1 edge of the cable. This stripe denotes pin 1. Pin 1 on the drive is usually closest to the power connector on the drive, however, you should consult the manufacturers documentation. Then connect the signal cable to the motherboard ID1 or ID2 interface making sure to note the pin 1 orientation there as well. If the drive is a SCSI drive, a SCSI cable would be connected from the drive to a SCSI controller card.
6. Connect one of the power supply's power connectors to the drive.

Troubleshooting CD-ROM Drives

The troubleshooting steps for CD-ROM and DVD drives are nearly identical to those of an HDD system. The connections and data paths are very similar. Basically, three levels of troubleshooting apply to CD-ROM problems. These are the configuration level, the operating system level, and the hardware level.In most systems, the CD-ROM and DVD drives share a controller or host adapter with the hard disk drive. Therefore, verify their Master/Slave jumper settings to ensure they are set correctly. Normally, the CD-ROM or DVD drive should be set up as the master on the secondary IDE channel. In this manner, each drive has its own communications channel and does not need to share. If three or four IDE devices are installed in the system, you must determine which devices can share the channels most effectively. In many systems, the CD-ROM and DVD drives share a controller or host adapter with the hard disk drive. Therefore, if the hard drive is working and the CD-ROM drive is not, the likelihood that the problem is in the CD-ROM or DVD drive unit is very high.

Recordable Disk:Write Once, Read Many (WORM)

As with the CD, once data have been etched into the surface of a WORM disk they can not be changed. WORM is an ideal medium for making a permanent record of data, i.e., it can be a feasible alternative to magnetic tape for archival storage.

For example, many banks use WORM disks to store a record of each day's transactions. The transactions are written to an optical disk and become a permanent record that can be read but never altered.

Another popular application of WORM disks is in information systems, that require the merging of text and images that do not change for a period of time. A good example is an "electronic catalog".

A customer can pursue a retailer's electronic catalog on a VDT, or perhaps a PC, and see the item while he reads about it and, with a few keystrokes the customer can order the item as well.

Erasable Disks: Magneto-Optical Disks

A hybrid disk, called magneto-optical (MO), combines the best features of magnetic and optical disk technologies. A magneto-optical disk has the high-volume capacity of an optical disk but can be written over as a magnetic disk. The disk surface is coated with plastic and embedded with magnetically sensitive metallic crystals.

To write data, laser beam melts a tiny spot on the plastic surface and a magnet aligns the crystal before the plastic cools. The crystal are placed in such a way that some reflect lights and others do not. Later on, when the data is read by a laser beam, only the crystals that reflect light are picked up.

Disadvantages

1. Magneto-optical disks are too expensive and do not offer anywhere near the kind of reliability that users have come to expect of magnetic media.
2. The access time in magneto-optical disks are relatively slow, about the same as a low-end, Winchester disk.
3. As optical disk technology matures to offer reliable, cost-effective, read/write operation, it eventually may dominate secondary storage in the future as magnetic disks and tape to today.

DVD

DVD stands for digital video disc or digital versatile disc, is the next generation of optical disc storage technology. It is bigger, faster CD that can hold cinema-like view, better-than-CD audio, and compatriot CD data. Using a DVD you can have home entertainment, computers, and business information with a single digital format. The DVD will eventually replace audio/video CD, videotape, laserdisc, CD-ROM, and video game cartridges.

There are various variations of DVD; DVD-ROM or DVD-R are physical formats and DVD-Video or DVD-Audio are application formats. DVD-ROM is the base format that holds data. Physical format of DVD-ROM includes recordable variations DVD-R, DVD-RAM, DVD-RW, and DVD-RW. The application formats include DVD-Video, DVD-Video Recording, DVD-Audio, DVD-Audio Recording, DVD Stream Recording, and SACD.

Storage Capacity of DVDs

DVDs are of the same diameter and thickness as CDs, and they are made using some of the same materials and manufacturing methods. Like a CD the data on a DVD is encoded in the form of small pits and bumps in the track of the disc. DVD is composed of several layers of plastic, totalling about 1.2 millimeters thick. Each layer is created by injection molding polycarbonate plastic. This process forms a disc that has microscopic bumps arranged as a single, continuous and extremely long spiral track of data.

Once the clear pieces of polycarbonate are formed, a thin reflective layer is sputtered onto the disc, covering the bumps. Aluminium is used behind the inner layers, but a semi-reflective gold layer is used for the outer layers, allowing the laser to focus through the outer and onto the inner layers. After all the layers are made, each one is coated with lacquer, squeezed together and cured under infrared light.

For single-sides discs, the label is silk-screened onto the nonreadable side. Double-sided discs are printed only on the nonredable area near the hold in the middle. If you could lift the data track off a single layer of a DVD, and stretch it out into a straight line, it would be almost 7.5 miles long. A double-sided, double-layer DVD would have 30 miles of data.

Multi-Layer Storage

To increase the storage capacity, a DVD can have up to four layers, two on each side. The laser that reads the disc can actually focus on the second layer through the first layer. Here is a list of the capacities of different forms of DVDs:

DVD disc capacity				
	Single layer capacity		Dual/Double layer capacity	
Physical size	GB	GiB	GB	GiB
12 cm, single sided	4.7	4.38	8.5	7.92
12 cm, double sided	9.4	8.75	17.1	15.93
8 cm, single sided	1.4	1.30	2.6	2.42
8 cm, double sided	2.8	2.61	5.2	4.84

Note: GB here means gigabyte, equal to 10^9 (or 1,000,000,000) bytes. Many programs will display gibibyte (GiB), equal to 2^{30} (or 1,073,741,824) bytes.

Example: A disc with 8.5 GB capacity is equivalent to: (8.5 × 1,000,000,000) / 1,073,741,824 H" 7.92 GiB.

Size Note: There is a difference in size between + and - DL DVD formats. For example, the 12 cm single sided disk has capacities:

Disk Type	Sectors	bytes	GB	GiB
DVD-R SL	2,298,496	4,707,319,808	4.7	4.384
DVD+R SL	2,295,104	4,700,372,992	4.7	4.378
DVD-R DL	4,171,712	8,543,666,176	8.5	7.957
DVD+R DL	4,173,824	8,547,991,552	8.5	7.961

Capacity Nomenclature

The four basic types of DVD are referred to by their capacity in gigabytes, rounded up to the nearest integer.

DVD type	Name
Single sided, single layer	DVD-5
Single sided, dual layer	DVD-9

Double sided, single layer DVD-10

Double sided, dual layer DVD-18

Another format in limited use is a double sided DVD with one side comprising a single layer of data while the opposite side comprises two layers of data (effectively a DVD-5 on one side bonded to a DVD-9 on the other). This format holds approximately 12.3 GB of data and is known as DVD-14.[6]

Tape Drive

Like your tape recorder's cassette, it has magnetic coated plastic material. It is very useful to store large volumes of data. While larger tape spools with magnetic tape units are used with mainframe computers, the small cassette tapes, similar to music cassettes are used with Personal Computers.

Physical Characteristics of a Magnetic Tape

The tape is made of plastic material with iron oxide (ferrite) coating on one side of the tape, which is magnetically sensitive, and it is this surface that is used for the recording of data. The magnetized spots or bits are extremely small and not visible to the human eye.

One main advantage of tape is that large volumes of data can be condensed into a relatively small area. Typically magnetic tape is 1/2 inch wide and comes in reels which are 2400 to 3600 feet long and have a diameter of about 10 1/2 inch.

Representation of Data on a Magnetic Tape

Tracks run across the length of the tape with a tape having typically 7 to 9 tracks across its width. For IBM and IBM-compatible mainframe that use the 9-bit EBCDIC code, a tape would have 9 longitudinal tracks on channels or recording surfaces each capable of storing magnetized bits.

The data is recorded in a string of successive positions called columns or frames with one data character per column. Each column is subdivided into a number of rows called channels or tracks.

The magnetic state of each track within each frame is said to be binary in that the presence of a particular magnetic state or bit is:

1. taken to represents a 1
2. absence of bit represents a 0

At any point along the length of the tape, the combination of bits on the tracks represent a character

For example, A to Z, a to z, 0 to 9
special characters like ;,;$@ etc.

Each track with a column contains 1 bit and the bit combinations in each column represent data characters according to the particular coding system such as ASCII (7 bit) EBCDIC (8 bit).

Three coding systems frequently used are the 7 track code, 9 track code and binary code.

1. In case of the 7 track code, 6 tracks are used for data bits and one track contains the parity bit used for increasing hardware operating accuracy.
2. In the case of 9 track code, 8 tracks are used for data bits and 9th is the parity bit.
3. In the binary coding system data is recorded in terms of the binary system rather in terms of alphabetic characters and decimal numeric values.

For example, if a particular machine utilizes 24-bit binary words and 7-track tape is being used, 4 columns of the tape can be used to encode each binary word.

Tape Density

The actual number of characters that can be represented in an inch of tape is called the tape density.

or

The number of columns or frames per inch of magnetic tape is a measure of the density of the tape.

Density is expressed in terms of bytes per inch (bpi). Here the term byte refers to the set of bits that can be entered in a single column of the tape.

Typical tape densities are in the range of 800 to 1600 dpi, although higher as well as lower densities are possible. Since there are enough tracks across the width of the tape to represent characters, so this density also gives the number of character per inch of tape.

If characters are packed onto a tape at a density of 800 dpi then a 2400 ft tape would hold

= 800x2400x12

= 23,04,00,00 character

A density of 1600 bpi would double this figure.

Magnetic Tape Units

The magnetic tape drive is a specialized input/output device used for reading and writing magnetic tapes. The file reel contains the tape to be read or be written on, and machine reel contains the tape that has already been processed.

The tape advances past the read/write head the rated speed of reading or writing is a function of two factors:

1. the recording density of the tape and
2. the linear speed of the tape drive

For example, if the recording density is 1600 bps and the speed is 200 inches per second rated read/write speed = 1600x200 = 320000 bps

Tape Records, Blocks and Interblock Gaps

Data is recorded on magnetic tape in the form of blocks. Where each block consists of a grouping of data written (or read) in one continuous operation. For example, a grouping of data written on magnetic tape in one continuous operation and which may include one or more records is called a block. Between physical disk or tape records, the computer automatically reserves some blank space called on interblock gap (IBG). It permits proper timing for accessing records and activating read/write heads.

Blocks are separated by a gap, which is a blank space about 1/2 inch in length. Gaps are required in order to differentiate different blocks of data. The greater the number of inter-record gaps, the smaller the storage capacity of the tape.

For example,

let each record = 800 bytes

density = 1600 bytes/inch

In case where two consecutive records have 1/2 inch gap, i.e., inter-record gap = 1/2 inch then in one inch length of tape contains 800 bytes and 1/2 inch is a gap between two records. Therefore, only half of the length of tape is used for storing data. To circumvent this problem, records are often grouped in blocks. If records are blocked, i.e., grouped together, one write command can transfer a number of consecutive records to the tape without requiring inter-record gaps between them. Gaps appropriately called interblock gaps are placed between successive blocks. In using magnetic tape the record size is not restricted and can be as long as it is suitable for the application involved.

Records can be of two-types:

1. Fixed length record - records are of same size.
2. Variable length record - records length differ.

For example, variable-length record is a record containing the transactions for the month for an individual flow of cheques. The record for a customer who wrote 40 cheques during the month is substantially shorter than the record of another customer who wrote 200 cheques.

Just as record-size can be variable so can be the number of records per block. So we can have fixed-length or variable-length records and fixed-length or variable-length blocks. Even though the block size is variable, but its size cannot be unlimited. The programmer has to define the maximum limit on block size in each tape operation.

To distinguish variable length records written in a block, we have a control field at the beginning of each record, which contains the length of the record. The utilization of a tape's storage capacity increases as the number of records in a block is made larger

Blocking factor = number of records in a block.

For example, let number of records = 10

record capacity = 800 bytes

density = 1600 bpi

inter-record gap = 1/2 inch.

Parity and Error Control

In order to interpret correctly the data that are stored on a tape, the encoding scheme (EBCDIC, ASCII etc) that was used when data were written must be known. Additionally the technique used to record error-control bits has to be known in order for that information to be used.

One common technique for error control on magnetic tapes is parity. Odd parity : there must be an odd number of 1-bits represented for each character. If the bits making up a character's binary representation already have an odd number of 1-bits, then the parity bit (in 9th track) is a 0-bit.

If there is an even number of 1-bits, the parity bit for that character is 1-bit making the total number of 1-bits for that character's representation odd. Parity bits are written when data on the tape are written, then they are checked when the tape is read to verify that an error has not occurred.

Blocking

Data are read from or written to a tape in groups of characters called blocks or physical records. A block is the smallest amount of data that can be transferred between secondary memory and primary memory in one access. A block may contain one or more records. In order to read or write data properly the tape medium must be moving at a constant speed when it passes by the head mechanism.

Because requests to read or write blocks do not arrive at a tape drive at a constant rate, there must be a gap (interblock gap) between each pair of blocks, forming a space to be passed over as the tape slows from read/write speed and as the tape accelerates to read/write speed. Because the tape is not moving at a constant speed while the read/write head is positioned at a gap, a gap cannot contain user data.

Drawbacks of Tape

1. Records must be processed in the order in which they reside on the tape. Therefore, accessing a record requires the scanning of all records that precede it. This form of access is called Sequential Access.
2. Operations such as rewinding a tape or block-spacing a certain number of records or blocks increase the performance and flexibility of a magnetic-tape device.

Tape File Organization Format

In addition to data, other items of information required in a tape file are:

Beginning-of-tape (BOT)

It is a reflective strip with adhesive backing. The reflective marker identifies the starting point for tape use and is automatically sensed by the read/write head in both forward and rewind operations.

Header Label

This is a block of data containing identifying information about the tape file. We can use adhesive label but to be on safer side we use a magnetic label, which serves as a means of machine verification of the content of a reel of tape.

It contains:

Field Identification : in terms of file name or a file number

Retention Period : date prior to which the tape cannot be over written.

Creation Date : the date on which the file was established.

Reel sequence and number

Trailer Label

Trailer label is last record on the tape. It contains the same information as the header label, but in addition it contains a block count, which is a count of the number of data blocks written on the reel. This block count is used for control purposes.

End-of-tape (EOT)

It is again a reflective strip and serves to stop the tape drive in order to prevent the tape from dethreading. When EOT marker is sensed, the tape drive will not advance forward even if a programming command so directs the computer. It is particular for stopping for further writing.

Zip Drives

A high-capacity floppy disk drive developed by Iomega Corporation. Zip disks are slightly larger than conventional floppy disks, and about twice as thick. They can hold 100 or 250 MB of data. Because they're relatively inexpensive and durable, they have become a popular media for backing up hard disks and for transporting large files.

A Zip drive is a small, portable disk drive used primarily for backing up and archiving personal computer files. The trademarked Zip drive was developed and is sold by Iomega Corporation. Zip drives and disks come in two sizes. The 100 megabyte size actually holds 100,431,872 bytes of data or the equivalent of 70 floppy diskettes. There is also a 250 megabyte drive and disk. The Iomega Zip drive comes with a software utility that lets you copy the entire contents of your hard drive to one or more Zip disks.

The Zip drive can be purchased in either a parallel or a Small Computer System Interface (SCSI) version. In the parallel version, a printer can be chained off the Zip drive so that both can be plugged into your computer's parallel port.

SCSI Drive

SCSI originally stood for Small Computer System Interface, It's a fast bus that can connect

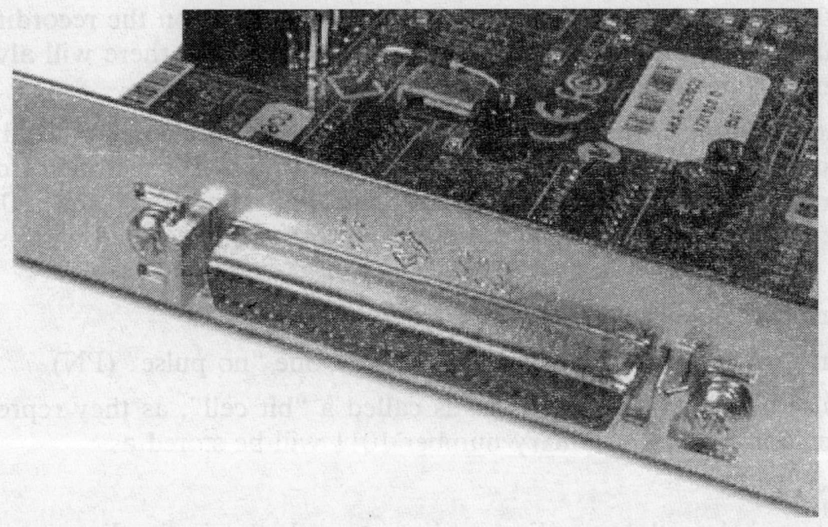

Fig. SCSI

lots of devices to a computer at the same time, including hard drives, scanners, CD-ROM/RW drives, printers and tape drives. Other technologies, like serial-ATA (SATA), have largely replaced it in new systems, but SCSI is still in use.

SCSI has several benefits. It's fairly fast, up to 320 megabytes per second (MBps). It's been around for more than 20 years and it's been thoroughly tested, so it has a reputation for being reliable. Like Serial ATA and FireWire, it lets you put multiple items on one bus. SCSI also works with most computer systems. SCSI is often used to control a redundant array of independent discs (RAID). A RAID is a series of hard drives treated as one big drive. These drives can read and write data at the same time, known as striping. The RAID controller determines which drive gets which chunk of data. While that drive writes the data, the controller sends data to or reads it from another drive. A SCSI controller coordinates between all of the other devices on the SCSI bus and the computer. Also called a host adapter, the controller can be a card that you plug into an available slot or it can be built into the motherboard. The SCSI BIOS is also on the controller. This is a small ROM or Flash memory chip that contains the software needed to access and control the devices on the bus.

Each SCSI device must have a unique identifier (ID) in order for it to work properly. For example, if the bus can support sixteen devices, their IDs, specified through a hardware or software setting, range from zero to 15. The SCSI controller itself must use one of the IDs, typically the highest one, leaving room for 15 other devices on the bus.

FM

FM or Frequency Modulation was the original data-encoding scheme used for storing the data on the magnetic recording surface. This method of data encoding is also known as the "single density recording", as this method was used to write to the single density floppy diskettes. This method was popular in the 1970s and is no longer used today.

In this method, a clock signal is put with every data signal on the recording surface. This clock signal is used for synchronizing the read operation, as there will always be a clock signal, whether the data signal is there or not.

Let us see one example, supposed you want to store the binary digit 1011 on a magnetic recording media using the FM recording technique. In this FM method of data recording a 1 bit is stored as two pulses (one clock pulse and one data pulse), and a 0 bit is stored as a one pulse and one gap or no pulse (1 clock pulse and one "no pulse" to show that is a 0 bit).

1. A binary digit 1 is stored as two pulses (PP)
2. A binary digit 0 is stored as one pulse and one "no pulse" (PN)

A clock pulse and data pulse together is called a "bit cell", as they represent one bit of information. For example, a binary number 1011 will be stored as:

PP PN PP PP

A pulse is recorded on the recording medium as a change in the direction of the magnetic field from the last magnetic field and a "no pulse" is recorded as no change in the direction of the magnetic field from the last magnetic field, i.e., if the last magnetic field was NS then a pulse or bit 1 is recorded as SN, and a no pulse or a 0 is recorded as NS.

For example 1011 or PP PN PP PP will be stored as:

NSSN NSNS SNNS SNNS

When using the FM encoding technique, the synchronization signal will always be available for the disk read operations.

FM method of data recording is also known as (0,1) Run Length Limited (RLL) recording. The reason behind this name is, in a series or in a running length the minimum number of 0s is zero, i.e., you can have two pulses next to each other without any 0 or "no pulse" in between and the maximum number of 0s is one, i.e., you will never have more than one position without a 0 or "no pulse" signal.

MFM

More data can be stored on the same surface or the data storage density can be increased, if the number of pulses required to store the data can be minimized. When minimizing the pulses, one should be careful that the number of no pulses together should not be very long, otherwise the disk controller may go out of synchronization with the data.

The MFM (Modified Frequency Modulation) method of data storage, by reducing the number of pulses, is able to store more data without any data and synchronization loss.

In MFM recording the 0s and 1s are encoded as given below:

- 1 is always stored as a no pulse, and a pulse (NP)
- 0, when preceded by another 0, is stored as a pulse, and no pulse (PN)
- 0, when preceded by a 1, is stored as two no pulses (NN)

If you store 1001 on the disk surface using the MFM storage method, it would be stored as

NO NN PN NP

As you can see, this requires only three pulses in MFM method, let us store the same data using the FM method of data recording.

PP PN PN PP

Total six pulses are required to store the same data using the FM method.

In this MFM method of data recording the minimum number of 0s together is one and the maximum number of 0s is three, this is a (1,3) RLL, Run Length Limited data recording, i.e., in MFM recording there will always be at least one "no pulse" signal, i.e., two pulses will never come together, and the maximum number of positions without any pulse will never be more than three.

Revision

1. Storage devices are used to store data and programs.
2. A hard disk is a stack of metal platters that spin on one spindle, like a stack of rigid floppy disks.
3. Access time is the interval between the instant a computer makes a request for transfer of data from a disk-storage device to RAM and the instant this operation is completed.
4. Data can be recorded on disk tracks with or without the use of keys. A key is a label that is used to identify a particular record.
5. There are two kinds of floppies, 3½" and 5¼" in sizes.
6. The 3.5 inch size floppy disk come in three capacities: double density, high density and very high density.
7. A floppy-disk drive is a device that reads and writes data to and from floppy disks.
8. Every new floppy disk must be formatted.
9. Optical disk technology is still emerging and has yet to stabilize; however at present there are three different types of optical disks in common use: read-only, recordable, and erasable.
10. CD-ROM (Compact disk-read only memory) are created at a mastering facility.
11. A magneto-optical disk has the high-volume capacity of an optical disk but can be written over as a magnetic disk.
12. DVD stands for digital video disc or digital versatile disc, is the next generation of optical disc storage technology.
13. Magnetic tape units are used with mainframe computers.
14. Zip disks are slightly larger than conventional floppy disks.
15. SCSI drive is a fast bus that can be connected to lot of drives to a computer at the same time.
16. FM or Frequency Modulation was the original data-encoding scheme used for storing the data on the magnetic recording surface.
17. The MFM (Modified Frequency Modulation) method of data storage, by reducing the number of pulses, is able to store more data without any data and synchronization loss.

Multiple Choice Questions

1. Hard disk is a _______ device.
   (a) Storage (b) Display
   (c) Removable
2. There are two types of floppies 5¼ and ____:
   (a) 3½ (b) 3¼
   (c) 5½
3. Every new floppy disk has to be _______.
   (a) stored (b) formatted
   (c) labelled
4. DVD stands for:
   (a) Direct Video Disc (b) Data Video Disc
   (c) Digital Video Disc
5. CD-ROM stand for:
   (a) Current Disk Read Only Memory
   (b) Compact Disk Read Only Memory
   (c) Close Disk Read Only Memory
6. FM stand for:
   (a) Frequent Module (b) Frequency Module
   (c) Frequency Modulation
7. Magnetic tapes are used in:
   (a) Personal Computers (b) Mainframe Computers
   (c) Laptops
8. CD ROM storage is .... MB.
   (a) 650 (b) 702
   (c) 750
9. .... is used to write protect a floppy.
   (a) Write Protect Notch (b) Write Paper Notch
   (c) With Protect Notch
10. Floppy drive connector is of .... Pins.
   (a) 34 (b) 50
   (c) 72
11. Spinning speed of each platter of IDE Hard disk is
   (a) 10,000 rpm. (b) 5,000 rpm.
   (c) 7,200 rpm. (d) 6,000 rpm.
12. A Zip drive is used to:
   (a) Storage backup (b) Compress data
   (c) Hide data (d) None of these.

13. Storage capacity of 5-1/4 inch floppy is ....
    (a) 512 KB (b) 1 MB
    (c) 1.44 MB
14. Numbers of heads/platter are ....
    (a) 1 (b) 2
    (c) 3
15. Which one is optical storage media:
    (a) HDD (b) Floppy disk
    (c) Pen drive (d) DVD.
16. Formatting is the process of arranging:
    (a) Tracks (b) Sectors
    (c) Both (a) and (b) (d) None of these.

True/False Questions

1. Access time is the interval between the instant a computer makes a request for transfer of data from a disk-storage device to RAM and the instant this operation is completed.
2. There are two kinds of floppies, 3¼" and 5½" in sizes.
3. The 3.5 inch size floppy disk come in three capacities: double density, high density and very high density.
4. New floppy disk need not be formatted.
5. Optical disk technology is still emerging and has yet to stabilize; however at present there are three different types of optical disks in common use: read-only, recordable, and erasable.
6. A magneto-optical disk has the high-volume capacity of an optical disk but can be written over as a magnetic disk.
7. Magnetic tape units are used with laptop computers.
8. Zip disks are slightly larger than conventional floppy disks.
9. SCSI drive is a fast bus that can be connected to lot of drives to a computer at the same time.
10. Data storage capacity of DVD is very high.
11. Each Platter in the HDD has magnetic coating on it.
12. The HDD has various working modes for its logic card.

Short Answer Type Questions

1. How the storage capacity is calulated of magnetic media?
2. Why SCSI hard disk is costly than IDE hard disk?
3. Draw back panel of CD ROM drive?
4. What is access time of hard disk?
5. What is SCSI hard disk?

Descriptive Questions

1. Describe the working of Hard Disk.
2. What do you understand by Access Time?

3. How the data is written on the floppy disks?
4. Why are CD-ROM preferred over the floppy disks?
5. What are Optical Disks?
6. Describe the working of DVD.
7. Describe the working of Magnetic Tape.
8. What do you understand by FM and MFM?
9. What is floppy disk? Explain contraction and its working?
10. Give the block diagram of CD-ROM?
11. How the hard drive works? Explain its internal working.
12. Explain the working principle of FDD.
13. Explain the types of HDD availlable in the market along with the difference.
14. What are the types of storage devices?

Answers to Objective Type Questions

Multiple Choice Questions

1. a	2. a	3. b	4. c
5. b	6. b	7. b	8. a
9. a	10. a	11. c	12. a
13. b	14. b	15. d	16. c

True False Questions

1. T	2. F	3. T	4. F
5. T	6. T	7. F	8. T
9. T	10. T	11. T	12. T

4 Computer Serial Devices

Introduction to Serial Devices of Personal Computers

In computer you can have devices fitted at both serial, parallel and USB ports. These days personal computers come with 4 serial, 2 parallel and 1 USB ports. This is the common configuration, but, you can have different from this too. There are attachments available which can make your 1 USB into 4 USB ones. In this chapter, we will read about the devices which are connected to the serial ports.

Mouse

Don't be afraid, it is not a real one. It is so called since it resembling a "Rat". In fact, it is a pointing device. These days it is almost essential for personal computers. Click at any place on the monitor with mouse to point out the location where you want to input the information. All Windows-based programs use mouse, making working with computers easier as you are not required to type commands.

It is a pointing device that lets you move a cursor or pointer on the screen just by moving the mouse around on a flat surface. A mouse also allows you to create graphic elements on the screen, such as lines, curves and freehand shapes and makes using menus and message boxes easier.

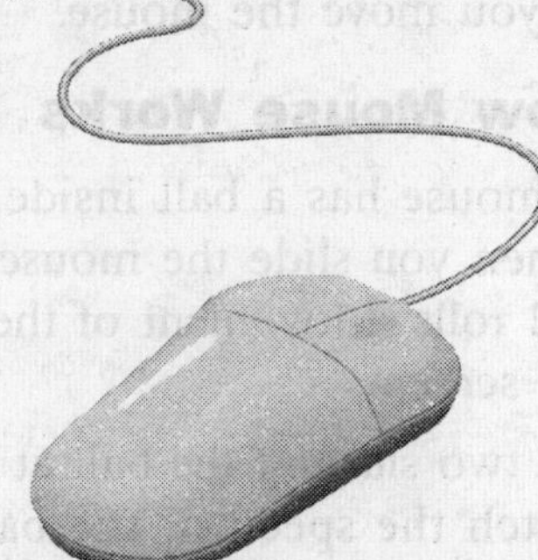

Types of Mouse

There are three basic types of Mouse

1. Mechanical Mouse
2. Optomechanical Mouse
3. Optical Mouse

Mechanical Mouse

A mechanical mouse has a rubber or metal ball on its underside that can roll in all directions. Mechanical sensors within the mouse detect the direction of the rolling ball and make a movement of the screen pointer accordingly.

Optomechanical Mouse

Optomechanical mouse is also similar to a mechanical mouse except that it uses optical sensors to detect the movement of the ball on the Mouse Pad.

Optical Mouse

Optical mouse uses a laser beam to detect the movement of mouse on specially designed Mouse Pad. We must move the mouse along a special mat with a grid so that optical mechanism has a frame of reference. This type of mouse has no mechanical moving parts.

Optical mouse respond more quickly and precisely than any other mouse. These are very expensive.

A mouse can be used for many applications ranging from games to designing products with graphics. It provides an alternative for people who are uncomfortable with a keyboard or it can be used in combination with a keyboard to enhance input operations.

The mouse is also used to draw sketches, diagram, etc., on the CRT screen. It is also moved on graphic tablet for drawing work and the same is also used to edit text. For editing text on the screen the cursor is quickly moved to the desired point of the screen by moving the mouse.

How to use the mouse

There are three simple techniques — clicking, double-clicking and dragging

Clicking

To click on something with the mouse means to move the pointer or cursor to the item on the screen and to press the release the mouse button once.

Double-Clicking

Press and release the mouse button twice in rapid succession.

Dragging

After positioning the mouse pointer over the item, then depress the button and hold it down as you move the mouse.

How Mouse Works

A mouse has a ball inside of it that extends just below the housing of the mouse itself. When you slide the mouse around on a flat surface such as a desktop or mouse pad the ball rolls. Movement of the mouse result in a corresponding movement of the pointer on the screen.

On two sides of the ball at 90 angle each other are two small rollers or wheels that spin to match the speed of the ball. Sensors detect how much each roller spins and send this information to the computer in the form of changes to the current pointer position.

Like the keyboard, a mouse does not actually send a message directly to the program that

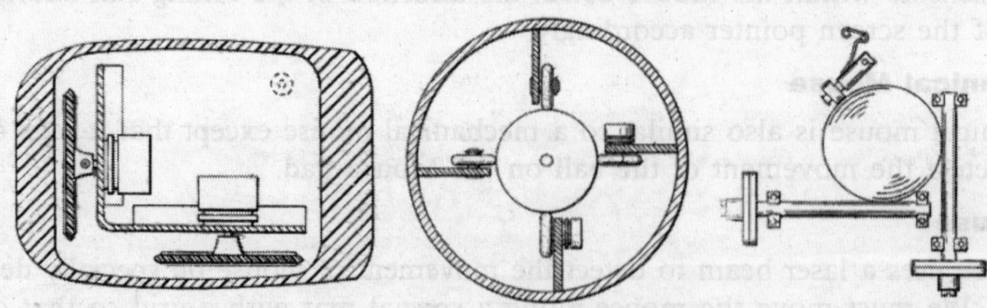

Mouse Diagram

the computer is running. Rather it sends an interrupt request to the CPU. The program that is running checks regularly to see whether a mouse event has occurred or not.

Buttons on the Mouse

A mouse can have one, two or three buttons with a two or three-button mouse the primary or main button is the one on the left because most people are right-handed. We can reconfigure mouse device to make another button primary.

Connectivity and Communication Protocols

To transmit their input, typical cabled mice use a thin electrical cord terminating in a standard connector, such as RS-232C, PS/2, ADB or USB. Cordless mice instead transmit data via infrared radiation or radio (including Bluetooth).

The electrical interface and the format of the data transmitted by commonly available mice has in the past varied between different manufacturers.

Serial interface and protocol

Standard PC mice once used the RS-232C serial standard (released in 1969), via a DB-9 connector. The Mouse Systems Corporation version used a five-byte protocol and supported three buttons. The Microsoft version used an incompatible three-byte protocol and only allowed for two buttons. Due to the incompatibility, some manufacturers sold serial mice with a mode switch: "PC" for MSC mode, "MS" for Microsoft mode.

PS/2 interface and protocol

With the arrival of the IBM PS/2 personal-computer series in 1987, IBM introduced the eponymous PS/2 interface for mice and keyboards, which other manufacturers rapidly adopted. The most visible change was the use of a round 6-pin mini-DIN, in lieu of the former 5-pin connector. In default mode (called stream mode) a PS/2 mouse communicates motion, and the state of each button, by means of 3-byte packets.

Extensions: IntelliMouse and others

A Microsoft IntelliMouse relies on an extension of the PS/2 protocol: the ImPS/2 or IMPS/2 protocol (the abbreviation combines the concepts of "IntelliMouse" and "PS/2"). It initially operates in standard PS/2 format, for backwards compatibility. After the host sends a special command sequence, it switches to an extended format in which a fourth byte carries information about wheel movements. The IntelliMouse Explorer works analogously, with the difference that its 4-byte packets also allow for two additional buttons (for a total of five).

The Typhoon mouse uses 6-byte packets which can appear as a sequence of two standard 3-byte packets, such that ordinary PS/2 driver can handle them. Mouse-vendors also use other extended formats, often without providing public documentation.

For 3D or 6DOF input, vendors have made many extensions both to the hardware and to software. In the late 90's Logitech created ultrasound based tracking which gave 3D input to a few millimeters accuracy, which worked well as an input device but failed as a money making product.

Other input devices, such as PhaseSpace's 3D optical tracking, have served to create VR and AR input devices[citation needed], and experiments in this arena continue at Cambridge, Cardiff, UCSC and other universities as well as in government labs.[citation needed] This type of input device tracks multiple LED sources to provide sub-millimeter tracking for input to control tools and robots in a real or virtual space as well as in computer training.

Advantages

1. It is simple device and very easy to use.
2. It is not that very expensive.
3. It moves the cursor faster than the arrow keys of keyboard do.

Drawbacks of a Mouse

1. The movement of the cursor is not very sensitive to movement of mouse.
2. If the contact between wheels and mouse pad is lost, the cursor does not move.
3. It is not useful in word-processing or in computer programming applications.
4. It requires space on tabletop or other hard surface to roll.
5. It requires serial port for connection with computer system.

A recent development in the wireless mouse or remote mouse, which works on transmission of infrared or radio waves.

Troubleshooting Mouse

If you experience problems with your mouse, the problem could be because of the mouse, mouse driver software, the application software you are using, cables or the main system itself. So, before you throw away your mouse, try the following troubleshooting techniques:

- Make sure the mouse cable is correctly connected to its port.
- Turn your PC's system unit power off and back on and see if the error disappears.
- If you have a second mouse available, turn off your PC's power and connect the new mouse. Power the PC back on to see if the error disappears.
- Try the mouse on some other system where a mouse of the same type is working without any trouble.
- Some software do not support mouse. Try mouse with a program that is known to support the mouse.
- Make sure the mouse device driver being used is correct one and is setup correctly.
- If the mouse is a serial mouse, try using a second serial port. You might need to update the mouse device driver to use the second serial port.
- If you are using a bus mouse, make sure that the mouse adapter card is properly seated in its expansion slot.

Installing Mouse

A mouse connects to one of the serial ports, such as COM1 or COM2 on your computer. This is one of the most simple and commonly used mouse.

To replace or to install a serial mouse, perform these steps.

- First of all check if you have a spare serial port for the mouse. If you do not have a spare serial port, then you need to first install a serial interface board or a multi I/O board into your computer.

If you have a spare serial port or if you are replacing an already available serial mouse then perform the following steps:

- Power off the PC's main system unit.
- Remove the existing mouse by removing the mouse from the serial port.
- Select the new serial port into which you want to install a new mouse, connect the new mouse into the port. Sometime you may require 9 to 25 pin or 25 to 9 pin converter to connect the mouse to the available serial port.
- Power on your system, update your mouse driver and other software as necessary. Test the mouse.

Keyboard

The most common input medium in computer is Keyboard. Without it many consider the computer as incomplete. Let us see how the data is accepted by computer when fed in by the keyboard.

How Computer Accepts Input from the Keyboard

When we press a key on a keyboard key say the letter S, then a tiny computer chip inside either the computer or the keyboard called the keyboard controller, takes a note that a key has been pressed and places a code into part of its memory buffer, indicating which key was pressed. This code is called the key's Scan Code (identifying number). Now without specifying what has happened the keyboard controller signals (*i.e.*, sends interrupt) the computer processing components that something has happened at the keyboard. The keyboard controller sends an interrupt request to the CPU (using the interrupt number 9 assigned to the keyboard interrupt) when it receives a complete keystroke.

Interrupts cause the CPU to put aside what it is doing and jump to an interrupt handling program. In this case the interrupt handles an integral part of the ROM-BIO software. When the computer's processing components receive an interrupt request, the program that is controlling the computer at that moment evaluates the request to determine the appropriate response. In the case of a key press, the program reads the memory location in the keyboard buffer that contains the scan code of the key that was pressed and places the keyboard letter in the computer's main memory.

The keyboard buffer can actually store a number of keystrokes at once. This is necessary because some time elapses between the pressing of a key and the computer's reading of that key from the keyboard buffer. Also programmers must put instructions into their programs to read keystrokes and program might be doing something else when the key is pressed.

With the keystrokes stored in a buffer the program can react to them when convenient. Because reading the keyboard to get the scan code of a key action is a function of software, we can reassign scan codes to represent different letters or symbols.

Keyboard Keys

There are more keys on computer keyboard than on typewriter. Most commonly used keyboards has **101 keys** and more. With XT, 84 key keyboard was used but it has now become obsolete. The 101 key keyboard has the important keys:

Alphabetic Keys

These are alphabet keys from [A] to [Z]. As in typewriter, you can use [SHIFT] to make them capital, i.e., ABCDE, etc. So if you press a b c d e .... etc. With [SHIFT] key already pressed, you will get A B C D E .... etc. Similar results can be obtained by putting CAPS LOCK key ON.

a = [A]

[SHIFT]+[A]=A

For typing [A], you press [SHIFT] key and then while keeping [SHIFT] key pressed, press the "a". Otherwise for typing a, you don't need to press the [SHIFT] key, just press the a key.

Numeric Keys

The numeric keys (with the characters 0 to 9) are located on the computer's keyboard at two places. You can see them in the top row above the alpha keys (as in typewriter). A second set of these keys is provided on the right-hand side of the keyboard. The numeric keys in the top row can be used straightaway to type in numeric characters. By simultaneously holding down the Shift key (as in the typewriter), you can also type in special upper characters like ! % $ *, etc. However, to type numeric characters by using the keys on the right side, you will need to press the Num Lock key ON.

Function Keys

These keys are marked [F1] to [F10] in the 84 key format and to [F12] in the 101 format. These keys are used for specific purposes as defined in the computer (a computer program is a set of instructions given to a computer to perform a specific task) which you may be using.

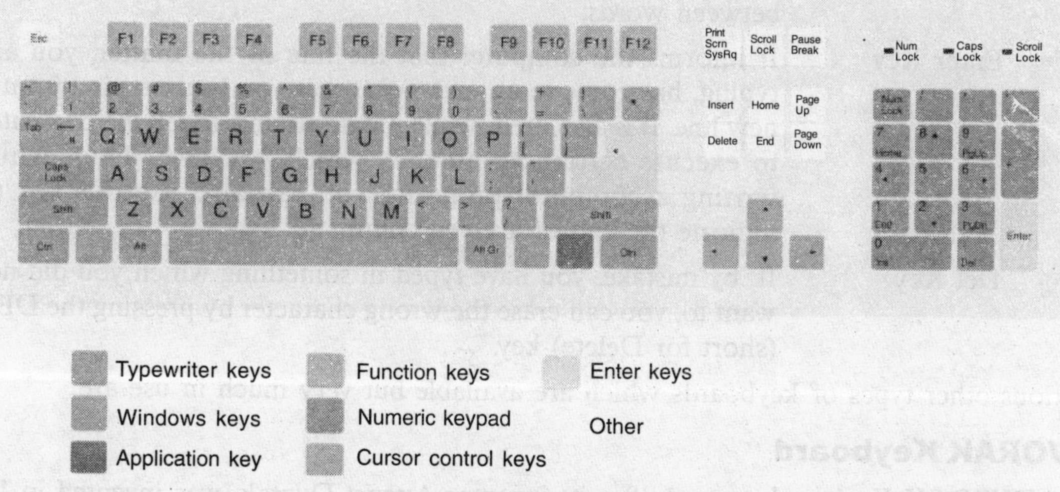

Keyboard Layout

For example, in BASIC programming (BASIC is a computer language used for writing programs) F3 will load the program, F1 will list the program after loading and F2 will run the program.

Arrow Keys

On 101 keys keyboard these are placed at two places. The first is called the cursor pad which works independently. The other is the numeric-cum-cursor pad. It is similar to the one on the 84 key keyboard. When the Num Lock key is not in the ON position, pressing the key of the numeric keypad moves the cursor in the direction shown on each key. Otherwise, this portion is used to enter numbers.

Special Keys including Spacebar

There are several other keys which serve some definite purposes. Some of these keys are available on the typewriter too. The special keys are:

SHIFT	Shift Key	It is used for typing capital letters and special characters. In combination with both Control and Alternate keys, it is sometimes used to execute a particular command too.
CTRL	Control Key	On its own, this key does not have any purpose. However, combined with different keys, it performs some useful operations. For example, in WordStar software, Control if pressed alongwith B, will make the character Bold.
←	Backspace	It allows the cursor to go back by one character. Some types of computer programs allow the backspace to delete the last character. A cursor is usually a blinking line (_), on the screen, which shows where the character you type on your keyboard will appear.

Spacebar	As in the typewriter, the Spacebar is used to leave space between words.
ENTER Enter Key	It informs the computer that the line of the matter, you are typing, has come to an end. After that you begin typing from a new line. It is also used, while programming, to tell the computer to execute certain commands which you give. Thus, while writing a computer program, you can also use this key to indicate the end of a given command.
DEL Del Key	If, by mistake, you have typed in something which you did not want to, you can erase the wrong character by pressing the DEL (short for Delete) key.

Various other types of keyboards which are available but very much in use are:

DVORAK Keyboard

The DVORAK Keyboard, named after its inventor August Dvorak, was invented in 1932. Through ergonomic studies of typists, he noticed that the QWERTY layout forces that majority of the work to be done by the weakest finger — the fourth and fifth fingers of the left hand. The stronger, quicker right hand and middle fingers are used only for the least frequently typed characters. The Dvorak keyboard layout, places the most frequently used characters in the center, i.e., on the home row (the vowels plus, d, h, t, n and s).

The next most frequently used characters are placed up one row because it is easier to reach up than down. Because this layout distributes the typing work load among the fingers according to their strengths, awkward strokes are reduced by 90%. Operators who are involved with word processing have found 75% improvement in their production after switching over to Dvorak keyboard.

PC users who want to try the Dvorak layout do not need to replace their QWERTY keyboard. The switch can be made electronically.

AZERTY Keyboard

The AZERTY layout of keyboards are used in some European typewriters. The term describes the sequences of the first six letters in the first row of alphabetic keys.

Troubleshooting Keyboard

Most of the problem faced in keyboard operation can be divided into two categories:

- complete non-operation of the keyboard and.
- broken or stuck keys

First problem could be either because of a broken connection between the keyboard and the system or because of some problem in the keyboard or the main system itself. If you find that your keyboard is not working then to see if the problem is with the keyboard or the main system you can try a different working keyboard on your system.

If the new keyboard is also not working then the problem most probably is with the main system. If the new keyboard is working properly then the problem is with your old keyboard. You can also try your old keyboard on some other machine to make sure that the fault is really with the keyboard.

When the keyboard of a system is not working then some of the points that must be checked are:

- Some old keyboards have a small switch at their bottom side to select the operating mode of the keyboard. Using this switch one can select either XT (8088/8086) or AT (80286) operating mode.
- Many old computers have a keyboard lock on the front panel. This lock disables the keyboard. Forgetting to unlock this lock, or not properly unlocking this could be one reason of the keyboard not working.
- Another problem could be the connector from lock to the motherboard coming loose at the lock or the motherboard side.
- The keyboard socket on the motherboard—into which the keyboard is plugged—is often one of the reason of keyboard failure. This socket sometimes become loose and may not connect properly with the keyboard. A loose socket may give intermittent problems in the keyboard operation.
- Check the connection between the socket and the motherboard. Check for any loose solder on motherboard.
- Check the keyboard cable. Open the keyboard, remove the cable and using a Multi-meter test each wire for continuity and cross-connection. If some fault is found then replace the cable.

Installing Keyboard

1. Position the keyboard cable over the connector, and pull the keyboard slightly to the right so the cable is not bent. Hold the cable as close as possible to the connector and press straight down. Press the cable firmly into the connector.
2. Flip the keyboard over and insert the small tabs at the bottom of the keyboard into the openings in the PowerBook case.
3. Pull down on the keyboard release tabs (located to the left of the F1 and F9 keys) and then press down on the top portion of the keyboard.
4. Let go of the keyboard release tabs to secure the keyboard in place.
5. Replace the PowerBook battery or plug in the power adapter.
6. Restart the computer.

Removing the Installed Keyboard

1. Place your computer on a clean, flat surface.
2. Shut down your computer, remove the battery from the expansion bay, and disconnect the power adapter, modem, and any other cables connected to the computer.
3. Make sure that the keyboard locking screw is not in the locked position. Your new PowerBook comes with the keyboard unlocked, so unless you or someone else locked the keyboard, you can skip this step.

4. Release the keyboard by pulling down on the keyboard release tabs (located to the left of the F1 and F9 keys) until the top portion of the keyboard pops up.
5. Lift the top portion of the PowerBook keyboard up slightly near the top row of keys and pull it back far enough to release the small tabs that hold the bottom of the keyboard in place.
6. Flip the keyboard over and lay it on the palm rests.
7. Touch a metal surface inside the computer to discharge any static electricity.
8. Grasp the keyboard cable as close as possible to the connector and pull up to disconnect the keyboard from the logic board. Rock the cable carefully if additional leverage is needed.

Understanding Ports and Their Functions

A port is defined as the part of a computer through which serial or parallel communication of data will take place. Ports are the portion of the computer system from where the signals are sent and received. The ports of a PC can be Input Port, Output Port and Input/Output Port. Input port are those which receives data, Output port which transmit data and Input/ Output port receives as well as sends the data. It is bi-directional in nature. Some of the ports, which are most commonly used, are:

- Serial Port
- Parallel Port
- USB Port
- IRDA Port
- WOL
- AIRBUS
- IDE Port
- SB-LINK Port
- Super I/O Port
- PC Game Port and MIDI Port

Serial Port

In serial port 'serial communication' takes place. A personal computer has two external Serial ports, which are commonly known as COM-1 and COM-2. The Serial port supports the serial devices such as Mouse, Modem, Serial Printer, and other external devices, which have serial interface. It is so called because the data transferred from this port is serially, there is only one data line to transmit data and one data line to receive data. The serial port has 9 pin or 25 pin Male D type connectors as shown next.

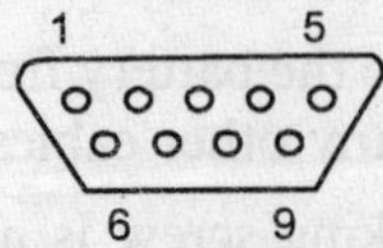

Pin D-SUB Male Serial Port

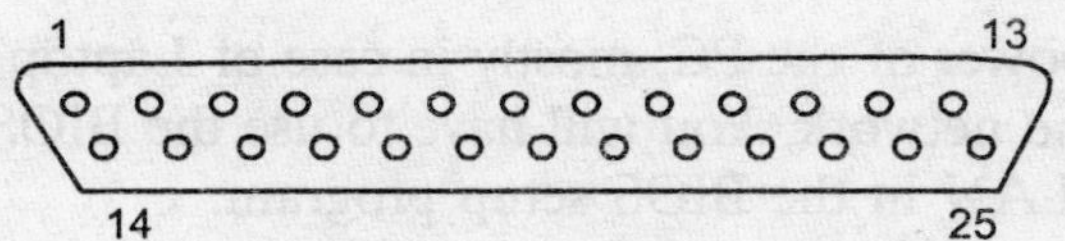

25 Pin D-SUB Male Serial Port

Parallel Port

In parallel port 'parallel communication' takes place. A personal computer has one external Parallel port, which is commonly known as LPT-1, it has three modes (SPP/EPP/ECP Mode). The Parallel port supports the parallel devices such as Printer, Scanner, and other external devices, which have parallel interface. It is so called because the data transferred from this port is parallely, there are eight data line D0–D7 to transmit and receive data. The parallel port has 25 pin Female D type connector as shown in fig below. Parallel port consists of Address 378, 379 and 37A all in Hex.

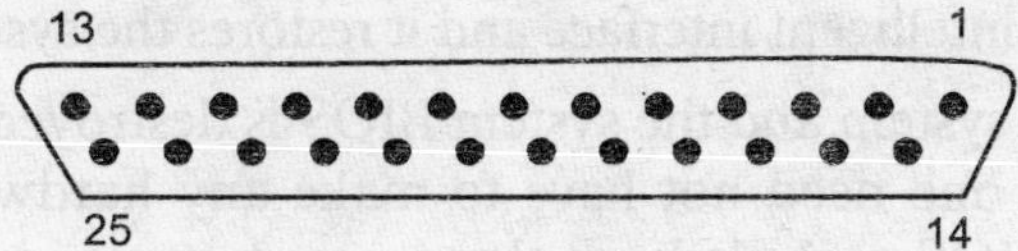

25 Pin D-SUB Female Parallel

USB Port

The USB Universal Serial Port is the latest concept, It was first introduced in 1996, the USB is more than a successor to the RS-232C serial port. It provides the basic mechanism for connecting most, if not all, peripherals to the PC. Everything from the keyboard to cash register drawer can be connected simply and quickly with a USB plug.

It is a fast serial type port but different than the Serial port. A personal computer has two external USB ports. The USB can support upto 256 Devices which can be connected with the support of USB Hub (a USB Hub is a device which is used to share various USB devices). The USB supports the devices such as Video Cam, Camcoder, USB Printer, USB Scanner, USB Mouse, and other devices which has USB interface. It consists of four pins. If one is installing USB device one has to go to the BIOS Setup and Enable the option under Advance BIOS Setup.

Infra Red Device Access (IRDA) Port

The Infra Red Device Access Port (IRDA) supports the IRDA devices which are remote controlled such as IRDA Keyboard, IRDA Mouse, IRDA Printers, etc.

Wake on Lan (WOL)

The Wake On Lan (WOL) is also a very new concept, which is very much useful for a computer connected in a network. A cable from the LAN card is connected with this port in order to generate ring-in-signal and wake up automatically to receive the message for you, whenever some message is generated for the client or a client is requested by some other user the WOL wakes the clients PC knocking for the demand. This is very good for those who prefer to save power of the PC, mostly in case of Laptop computer or Notebook computer connected on the network. You will have to use the BIOS setup utility to enable the "Power On by Ring/LAN in the BIOS setup program.

Airbus

The AIRBUS is a revolutionary new interface designed on the motherboard. There is a KEYBIOS device, which is designed to connect to this port which gives lots of incredible features to the PC system.

One of the most significant and immediate feature for AIR bus is, it rescues the system BIOS from virus attack. There is a virus called CIH virus and it made users start to aware that the virus could also make serious damage to the motherboard. Such virus kills the system BIOS and make the PC system failed to work. Unfortunately, similar virus can become popular and the protection to the motherboard may be surely necessary and extremely important

In this case the AIR bus can be one of the best solution to rescue the PC system from virus attack because it is an intelligent interface and it restores the system BIOS automatically.

In case virus infects the PC system and the system BIOS is destroyed the recovery procedure is done automatically and one need not have to make any hardware or software setting. Simply plug in the KEYBIOS and click on the power button and then leave everything done by the KEYBIOS.

IDE Ports

There are two channels of Ultra DMA Bus Master IDE ports, which support up to four IDE devices like IDE Hard Disk, ATARI CD-ROM and ZIP devices. It has 40 pin male connector.

SB-Link Ports

In some of the Motherboards one SB-LINK feature connector to support PCI sound cards are used.

Super I/O Ports

The following are the Ports in this category.

1. PS/2 Mouse connector and AT type Keyboard connector.
2. One Floppy Disk Control port for connecting FDD.
3. One digital Game and MIDI port
4. One TV Output optional port to provide video signal output for TV.

PC Game Port and Midi Port

Some soundcards have some MIDI signals included in their Game Port. Ground and VCC has been used for this.

This port consists of 15 PIN D-SUB FEMALE connector at the computer as shown next.

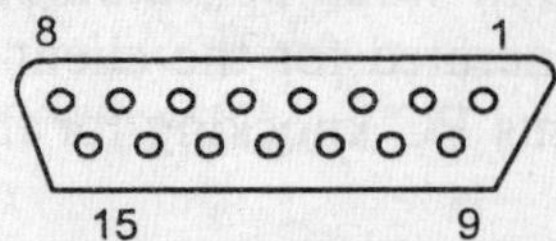

Modem

The modem is a device which allows you to connect your computer to any other computer, anywhere else in the world using a telephone line. This allows you to communicate with the connected person, transfer data, copy software/programs from the connected computer, sent and received mail using e-mail, etc.

Currently, the modem can also be used to sent and receive fax, for this you use modem as fax device. Also you can use modem to connect to the Internet. There are two main types of modems: Internal and External Modems.

Let us see how modem works?

When the computer is switched on and is ready to transmit data, it sends a Data Terminal Ready (DTR) signal to the modem. When the modem is ready to receive data or instruction from the computer, it sends a Data Set Ready (DSR) signal to the computer. Both these signals must be present before the next step can happen. Next, the computer sends a command to the modem to go "Off Hook", i.e., to open communication with the phone line. Next, the computer issues a command to modem to dial a phone number.

Installing the Modem

There are two ways by which the modem can be installed. One of them is Automatically and the other is Manually.

Automatically

After connecting the modem when you switch on the computer system, Windows 95/98 should automatically detect the modem and ask for the modem driver software. If the auto detection does not work then:

1. Click on the Start/Setting/Controls Panel.
2. In the control panel window double click on Add New Hardware icon.
3. In the next Add New Hardware Wizard screen, to automatically detect new hardware click on Next>option.
4. In the next screen select Yes for Do you want Windows to search for your new hardware? question and click on Next option.
5. Click on Modem to select it.
6. Click on the Next>option, it will start the auto detection process, which may take some time.
7. Finally next screen will appear with an option to click on Details..... button to see the list of detected hardware.
8. Click on Finish option to install the drivers for the detected hardware.

If your modem was not detected during this process then you need to manually install the modem driver software.

Manually

For this, follow the above instructions for step 1 & 2 and in the 3rd, in Add New Hardware Wizard screen, do the following:

1. Click on No, I want to select the hardware for a list, to the Do you want Windows to search for your new hardware? question.
2. Click on Next>option.
3. In the next screen a list of hardware appear, from the list click on Modem.
4. Click on Next>option.
5. Next Windows will try to automatically detect the modem.

To manually install the modem driver,

1. Click on Don't detect my modem; I will select it from a list.
2. Click on Next>option. A list of modem manufacturers and their modem models are shown on the next screen. There is also an option called Have Disk ....., if you have received a modem driver disk or CD with your modem then.
3. Click on the Have Disk . . . . option.
4. Place the driver disk/CD into proper drive and in the next Install From Disk screen select the proper drive. You can also click on Browse . . . . option to search for the driver disk/CD.
5. Once the driver is found on disk, click on OK, this will install the modem driver into the computer system. The driver could be on some sub-directory of the driver disk/CD, check the manual that came with the modem.
6. Restart the computer to make the modem active.

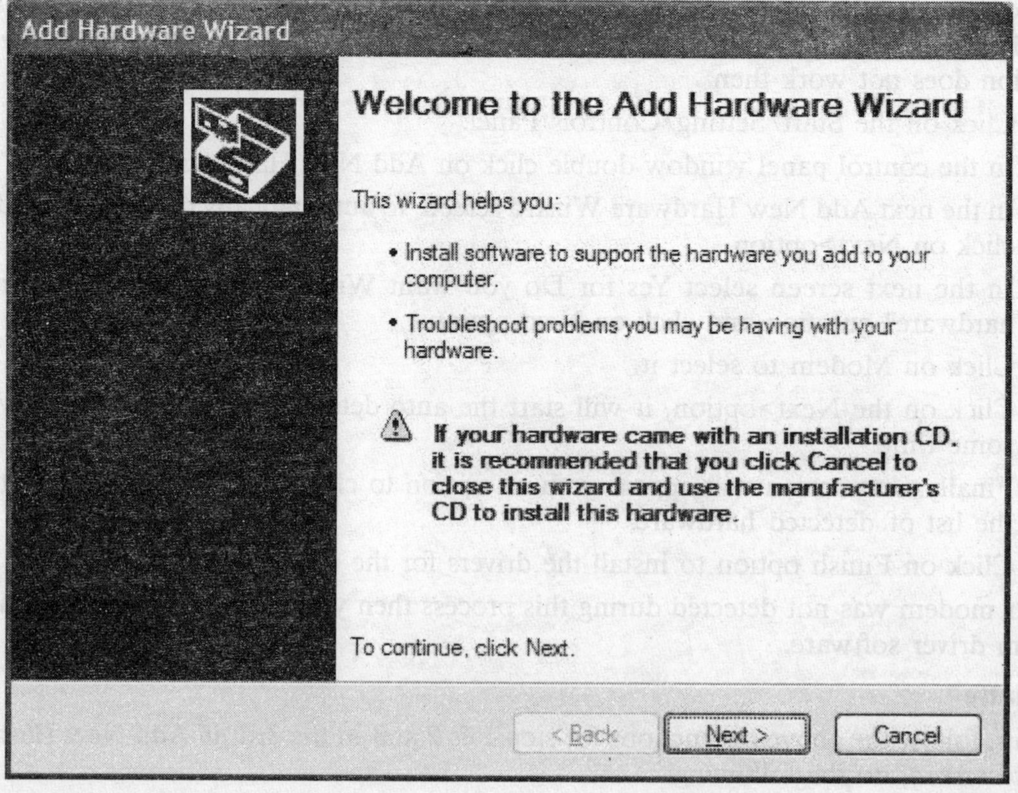

Sometimes the driver disk/CD that comes with the modem contains a SETUP.EXE or INSTALL.EXE program. Running this program will automatically install the modem driver to the Windows.'

Revision

1. Mouse is a pointing device.
2. There are three basic types of Mouse: Mechanical Mouse, Optomechanical Mouse and Optical Mouse.
3. Mouse can be used by clicking, double-clicking and dragging.
4. Keyboard is the main input device of the computer.
5. The main keys on the keyboard are: Alphabetic keys, Numeric keys, Function keys, and Arrow keys.
6. Computers have a few built in interfaces called ports.
7. A 25-pin or 9-pin D-shell subminiature male connector is used on the system as connector for the serial interface.
8. The modem is a device which allows you to connect your computer to any other computer, anywhere else in the world using a telephone line.

Multiple Choice Questions

1. Mouse is a _______ device.
   (a) Input (b) Pointing
   (c) Output
2. The mouse which is now commonly used is:
   (a) Optical (b) Optomechanical
   (c) Mechanical
3. Mouse can be used by clicking, double-clicking and:
   (a) biting (b) eating
   (c) dragging
4. The main keys of the Keyboard are Alphabetic, Arrows, Numeric and:
   (a) Function (b) Future
   (c) Faulty
5. A male connector for the serial interface can have 9 or __ pin:
   (a) 30 (b) 20
   (c) 25
6. A modem performs
   (a) Modulation (b) Demodulation
   (c) Analog to digital and digital to analog conversion
   (d) All of these.
7. The fastest communication port is:
   (a) Parallel port (b) Serial port
   (c) USB port (d) All.
8. Serial connector is of .... pins.
   (a) 9 pin (b) 16 pin
   (c) 20 pin

True/False Questions

1. Mouse is an input device.
2. There are three basic types of Mouse: Mechanical Mouse, Optomechanical Mouse and Optical Mouse.
3. Mouse can be used by clicking, double-clicking and dragging.
4. Keyboard is the main ouput device of the computer.
5. The main keys on the keyboard are: Alphabetic keys, Numeric keys, Function keys, and Arrow keys.
6. Computers have a few built in interfaces called ports.
7. A 25-pin or 9-pin D-shell subminiature male connector is used on the system as connector for the serial interface.
8. The modem is a device which allows you to connect your computer to any other computer, anywhere else in the world using a telephone line.
9. Modem is used to create a dialup connection.

Short Answer Type Questions

1. What is multimedia keyboard?
2. Describe the various types of mouse.
3. Describe the various type of keys on the keyboard.
4. How would you install a keyboard?

Descriptive Questions

1. Explain the working of Mouse.
3. How mouse works? Explain.
4. Describe the process of troubleshooting the mouse.
5. Describe the various types of ports.
6. What is modem? Explain its working.
7. Explain the working of modem at Transmitting end as well as receiving end.
8. Explain the working of keyboard?

Answers to Objective Type Questions

Multiple Choice Questions

1. b	2. b	3. c	4. a
5. b	6. d	7. c	8. c

True False Questions

1. F	2. T	3. T	4. F
5. T	6. T	7. T	8. T
9. T			

5 Computer Parallel Devices

Introduction to Parallel Devices of Personal Computers

In the last chapter, we read about the devices which were connected to the serial port. Now, in this chapter, we will read about the devices which are connected to Parallel ports.

First among them are Printers.

Printers

They are hardcopy output devices and can be divided into two distinct categories:

1. Impact Printers
2. Non-impact Printers

Various Features of Printers

Modes

Some printers operate in a number of different modes that trade off print quality for speed. These modes vary with the technology used by the printer.

Three of the most common modes for impact dot matrix printers are draft, near letter quality, and letter quality. Draft mode delivers the highest speed and the lowest quality. To achieve the highest possible speed, in draft mode the printers move their print heads faster than they can fire to print at each dot position on the paper. Typically, in draft mode these printers can blacken only every other dot. The thinly laid dots give text and graphics a characteristic gray look in draft mode. Near letter quality mode slows the print head so that text characters can be rendered without the machine gun, separated dots look of draft mode. Because the dot density is higher, characters appear fully black and are easier to read. Letter quality mode slows printing further, often using two or more passes to give as much detail as possible to each individual character. The printer concentrates on detail work, adding serifs and variable line weights to characters to make them look more like commercially printed text.

Color

Printers start with the primaries when it comes to color. They start with inks corresponding to the three primary colors—red, yellow, and blue. If you want anything beyond those, the printer must find some way of mixing them together. This mixing can be physical or optical.

The physical mixing of colors requires that two or more colors of ink actually mix together while they are wet. Printer inks are, however, designed to dry rapidly so the colors to be mixed must be applied simultaneously or in quick succession. Few printers rely on the physical mixing of inks to increase the number of colors they produce.

Optical mixing takes place in either of two ways. One color of ink can be applied over another (that has already dried), or the colors can be applied adjacent to one another.

Applied multiple layers of color require that the inks be to some degree transparent, as a truly opaque ink would obscure the first color to be applied. Most modern printer inks are transparent, which allows them to be used on transparencies for overhead projection as well as paper. The exact hue of a transparent ink is, of course, dependent on the color of the medium it is applied to.

Optical mixing also takes place when dots of two or more colors are intermixed. If the dots are so close together than the eye cannot individually resolve each one, their colors blend together on the retina, blending the individual hues together. Most PC color printers take advantage of this kind of optical mixing by dithering

Print Engines

The actual mechanism that forms an image on paper is called the print engine. Each uses a somewhat different physical principle to put ink on paper. Although each technology has its strengths, weaknesses, and idiosyncrasies, you might not be able to tell the difference between the pages they print. Careful attention to detail has pushed quality up to a level where the paper rather than the printer is the chief limit on resolution, and color comes close to photographic, falling short only on the depth that only a thick gelatin coating makes possible. In making those images, however, the various print engine technologies work differently at different speeds, at different noise levels, and with different requirements. These differences can make one style of print engine a better choice for your particular application than others.

Impact Printers

A printer in which printing is the result of mechanically striking the printing medium. An impact printer makes contact with the paper to produce an image. The impact may be produced by a print hammer character, like that of a typewriter key striking a ribbon against the paper or by a print hammer hitting paper and ribbon against a character.

An impact printer must be used if printing a multiple copy report so that the duplicate copies will receive the imprint.

Impact printers are of following types:

Solid Font

A complete character, such as on a typewriter key, strikes a carbon ribbon or other inked surface against paper to produce an image of the character. The solid-font characters are mounted on one of several types of printing heads such as a ball, wheel or cup.

Advantage

- The advantage of a solid-font over non-solid is that they give the best quality formed character images.

Disadvantage

- Solid-font print heads are usually slower than other types.

Dot Matrix

It is made of separate pinlike (needles) hammers that strike the ribbon against the paper in computer-determined patterns of dots. This type of printer is usually faster than solid-font type, but the image quality is not as good. All of printers print the characters in ASCII character set. This is a set of 128 printable and special control characters. Print speeds are critically important in computer environments because of the volume of output involved. On the basis of speed printers can further be classified as:

Serial or Character Printers

It is the slowest printer. The two major types of character-at-a-time impact printer are:

1. Dot-matrix printers and
2. Daisywheel printer

Dot-Matrix Printer

In it the individual characters are formed by a matrix of wires or styluses. Dot-matrix printers are also called serial printers. The images are formed by a print head that is composed of a series of little print hammers that look like the heads of pins. The print head usually has nine pins or 24 pines. The bottom 2 pins are used to form the descenders of lower case letters viz., p, q, g and y. Many expensive dot-matrix printers do not provide descenders, but print quality is improved when they are used.

The modern minimal printer uses an impact dot matrix print engine. The heart of the machine is a mechanical print head that shuttles back and forth across the width of the paper. A number of thin print wires act as the hammers that squeeze ink from a fabric or Mylar ribbon to paper.

Working Principle of Dot Matrix Printer

In most impact dot matrix printers, a seemingly complex but efficient mechanism controls each of the print wires. The print wire normally is held away from the ribbon and paper, and against the force of a spring, by a strong permanent magnet. The magnet is wrapped with a coil of wire that forms an electromagnet, wound so that its polarity is the opposite of that of the permanent magnet.

To fire the print wire against the ribbon and paper, this electromagnet is energized (under computer control, of course), and its field neutralizes that of the permanent magnet. Without the force of the permanent magnet holding the print wire back, the spring forcefully jabs the print wire out against the ribbon, squeezing ink onto the paper. After the print wire makes its dot, the electromagnet is de-energized and the permanent magnet pulls the print wire back to its idle position, ready to fire again. The Mechanical Section or DMP is shown next.

The two-magnets-and-spring approach is designed with one primary purpose—to hold the print wire away from the paper (and out of harm's way) when no power is supplied to the printer and the print head. The complexity is justified .by the protection it affords the delicate print wires.

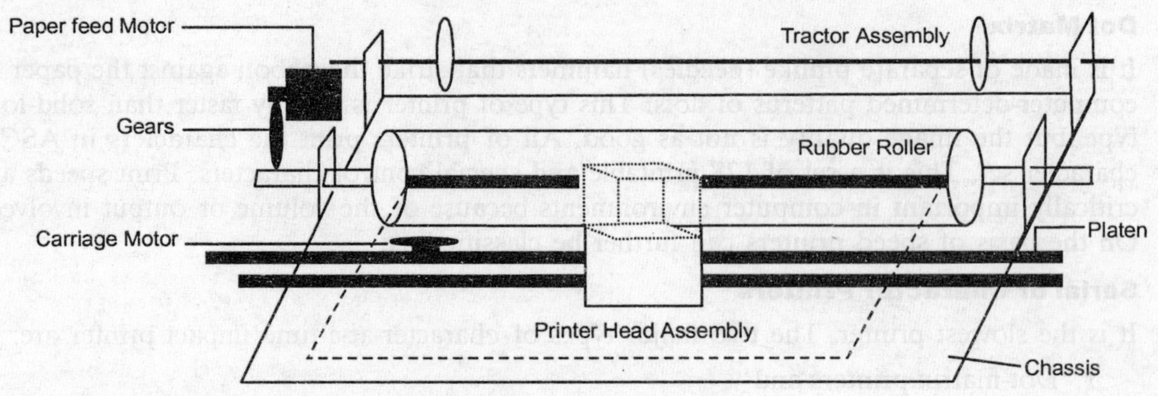

Mechanical Section of DMP

The print head of a dot matrix printer is made from a number of these print wire mechanisms. Most first generation personal computer printers and many current machines use nine wires arrayed in a vertical column. To produce high quality, the second generation of these machines increased the number of print wires to 18 or 24. These often are arranged in parallel rows with the print wires vertically staggered, although some machines use different arrangements. Because the larger number of print wires fit into the same space (and print at the same character height), they can pack more detail into what they print. Because they are often finer than the print wires of lesser endowed machines, the multitude of print wires also promises higher resolution.

No matter the number of print wires, the print head moves horizontally as a unit across the paper to print a line of characters or graphics. Each wire fires as necessary to form the individual characters or the appropriate dots for the graphic image. The impact of each wire is precisely timed so that it falls on exactly the right position in the matrix. The wires fire on the fly—the print head never pauses until it reaches the other side of the paper.

When computer sends series of hex data in hex format this code type of data represents the character to be printed with the help of printer this data may be punctuation mark tabs, enter and various other types of keyboard words that are sent to the printer by the computer. These codes are first of all stored into buffer Ram or memory because usually printer is a slower device as compare to computer so printer sends this data slowly when the printer Ram is full of the data then printer sends the acknowledgement signals to the computer so that computer can stop sending more data to the printer. The codes stored into the buffer Ram of printer are hexal decimal numbers in the form of binary and these codes represent alphabets like A, B, C in both types of formats capital and small also codes indicate various character and special symbols after storing data the printer microprocessor will send this data to the print head so that a definite print out can be taken. Electrical signals from the microprocessor are amplified and travel to particular circuits to the head which contain 9 pins or 24 pins called printing pins that are erroring in stat lines one and of each pins is connected to an electromagnetic the current from the microp cessor activates the magnetic and creates a magnetic field around the so line.

Oid (electromagnet) which repels a magnetic on the end of the pin causing the pin to strike the surface of the ribbon.

The moving pin strikes a ribbon which is coated with ink the impact of pin is used to create a dot on the surface on paper. Due to impact action DMP is also called impact type of printer. The force of impact transfer ink from ribbon to paper surface.

To speed operation, some impact dot matrix machines print bi-directionally, rattling out one row from left to right, then the next row right to left. This mode of operation saves the time that would ordinarily be wasted when the carriage returns to the left side of the page to start the next line. Of course, the printer must have sufficient memory to store a full line of text so that it can be read backwards.

Adding color to an impact dot matrix printer is relatively straightforward. The color the impact printer actually prints is governed by the ink in or on its ribbon. Although some manufacturers build color impact printer using multiple ribbons, the most successful (and least expensive) designed used special multi-colored ribbons lined with three or four bands corresponding to the primary colors. To change colors, the printer shifts the ribbon vertically so a differently hued band lies in front of the print wires. Most of the time the printer will render a row in one color, shift ribbon colors, then go across the same row in a different color. Of course, the color ribbon costs more and does not last as long as its monochrome equivalent.

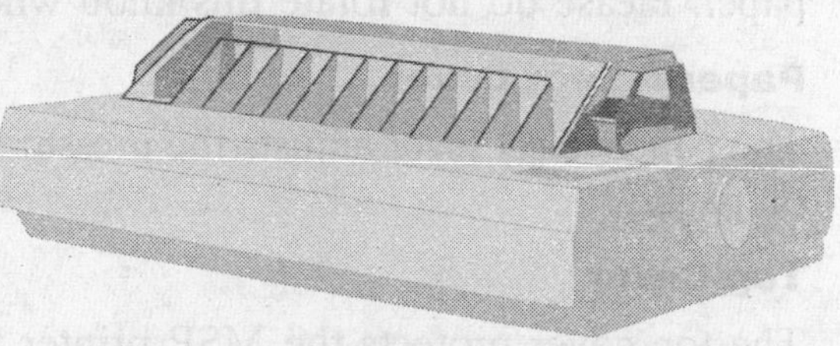

Outlook of Dot Matrix Printer

As with their typewriter progenitors, all impact dot matrix printers have a number of desirable qualities. Owing to their heritage of more than a century of engineering refinement, they represent a mature technology. Their designs and functions are relatively straightforward and familiar.

Impact technology takes the lead when you share one of the most common business needs, making multi-part forms. Impact printers can hammer an impression not just through a ribbon, but through several sheets of paper as well. Slide a carbon between the sheets or, better yet, treat the paper for non-carbon duplicates, and you get multiple, guaranteed identical copies with a single pass through the mechanism. For a number of business applications—for example the generation of charge receipts—exact carbon copies are a necessity, and impact printing is an absolute requirement. The output from DMP is in the form of dots.

Principle of DMP

The head of DMP works on the basic of electromagnetic induction.

The DOT MATRIX PRINTER (DMP) is an example of Impact printer because while printing the printer head comes in contact with the printing paper. Printer is a simple device consists of mechanical section and Electronic section. It has two sections in electronics.

1. Power Supply Unit (PSU)
2. Logic Card.

Dot Matrix Printer consists of the following:

Power Switch

The power switch is used to turn power to the printer on and off. It is on the left side near the back.

Tractors

The tractors are the sprockets that feed continuous fan-folded paper into the printer and keep the paper properly aligned.

Platen

The platen is the hard steel rod on which the cartridge assembly move.

Paper Feed Knob

The paper feed knob turns the platen. By turning this knob, you can manually feed the paper. Please do not rotate this knob when the printer is powered on.

Paper Select Lever

The paper select lever adjusts the pressure on the platen according to the type and thickness of paper.

Top Cover

The top cover protects the MSP printer from dirt and dust as well as reducing the sound level while printing. The top cover helps hold the paper against the platen when the tractor is installed in the "push" position. The top cover has special beveled edge for tearing off the paper.

Single-Sheet Guide/Paper Separator

The single-sheet guide is used for loading single sheets of paper. It also acts as a paper separator (in the down position) when using continuous paper.

Paper Thickness Lever

The paper thickness lever adjusts the print head to accommodate different paper thickness and types of forms. You can also increase the life of your ribbon by adjusting this lever.

Paper Park Lever

The paper park lever adjusts the printer's tractor mechanism for switching between continuous paper and single sheets, without having to manually remove the continuous paper.

Pressure Release Lever

The pressure release lever is used when you have the tractor mechanism installed in the push position or when you are feeding single sheets. It improves the paper feeding and hence quality of graphics printing.

Control Panel

The control panel is located on the right front of the MSP. It consists of four tactile switches and six lights to indicate the printer status.

On Line Light

The online light is built into the online switch. When this light glows, the printer is online and is ready to work.

Font Lights

The font lights indicate which typeface one is currently using. Selections include: Draft, High sped draft, NLQ Roman, NLQ Sans serif and NLQ Script. By pressing the FONT switch when the printer is OFGFLINE, you can scroll through the options and the lights will indicate, which one is to be selected.

Pitch Lights

These lights indicated the character pitch you are using. By pressing the switch wile the printer is OFFLINE, you can scroll through the options such as Pica Elite and condensed.

ONLINE Switch

Pressing the switch toggles the printer between ONLINE and OFFLINE states.

OFFLINE Mode

Micro line feed (reverse): While holding the ONLINE switch press LF/FF switch. Each time one presses, the printer reverses the paper in micro steps (1/72 Inch).

In MENU mode

Save: Press ONLINE switch to save the current filed selection in the non-volatile memory of the printer. While powering on.

Configuration reset: Hold the ONLINE switch and power on the printer to reset the content's of the non-volatile memory to the factory default settings.

Self-Test Of DMP Printer

1. With the paper loaded on the printer and the power switch- OFF, plug the power cord into an electrical outlet
2. While holding down the LF/FF switch, turn ON the power switch.
3. If you want to interrupt the self-test, press the ONLINE switch.
4. To resume, press ONLINE switch again.
5. If you want to stop the self-test, turn the power switch OFF. The printer will continue printing until you turn the printer OFF.

Connecting Printer with Computer

Computer and Printer communicate by means of a cable, which is usually sold separately. Each computer uses a slightly different cable so you'll need one made specifically for your computer. The cable one needs is called a Centronics parallel printer cable or a parallel printer interface cable as shown in next two figures. It's possible to purchase a cable with the connector attached perpendicular to the cable; this allows you to place the printer close to a wall.

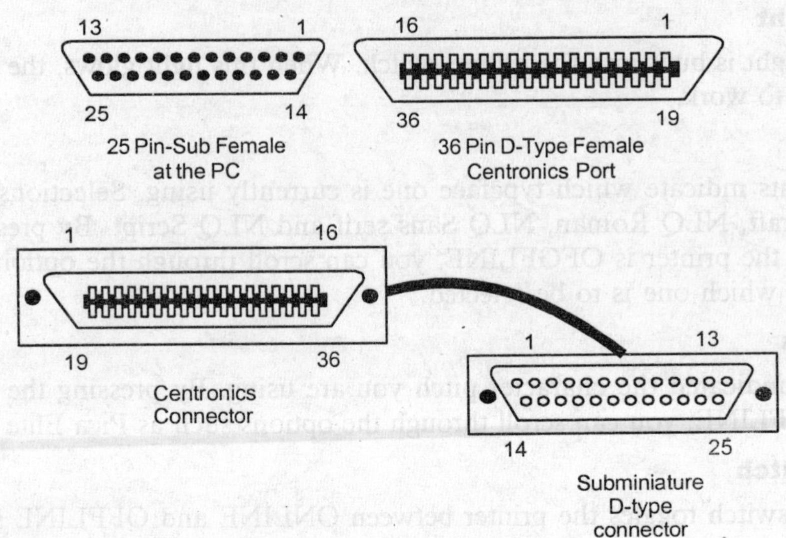

Parallel and Centronics Port

Drawbacks

1. Their speed limitation is slow as compared to line printers.
2. Their print resolutions are inferior to the daisywheel printers.
3. These printers may not be able to print graphic objects adequately but can handle applications such as accounting, personnel and payroll very well.

Daisywheel Printers

A serial impact printer in which the printing element is a plastic hub that has a large number of flexible radial spokes, each spoke having one or more different raised printing characters, the wheel is rotated as it is moved horizontally step by step under computer control, and stops when a desired character is in a desired print position so a hammer can drive that character against an inked ribbon.

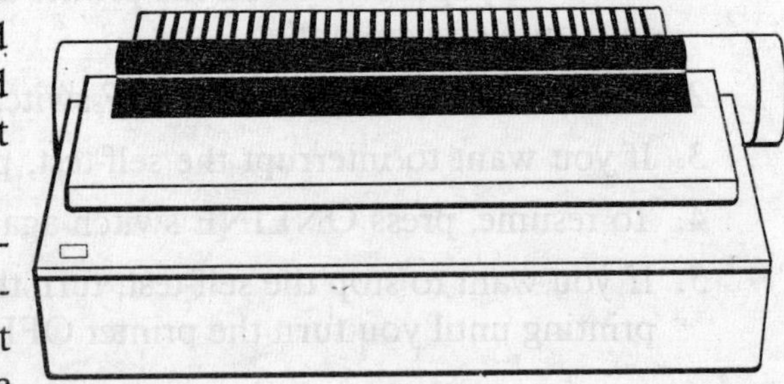

Daisy Wheel Printers are slower than dot-matrix printers, but they produce a high-resolution output. This high-resolution output is often called letter quality printing because it is suitable for business letters and memos. You can print in as may type fonts or foreign languages on a daisywheel printer as there are print wheels to fit your particular model of machine.

It is also called as a smart printer because of its bi-directional printing and built-in microprocessor control features.

Disadvantages

1. They are noisy

2. They are still too slow for many large volume output situations.
3. To change the typeface style, machine has to be stopped and then the print wheel is changed.
4. They cannot produce graphic output.

Line Printers

It prints an entire line in a single operation without necessarily printing one character at a time. These are generally electro-mechanical devices which print complete lines of print, up to 160 characters in width, at speeds about 300 to 2000 lines per minute. Line printers are used primarily in the mini/mainframe processing environment. Examples of line-at-a-time impact printers are:

1. Chain Printers
2. Band Printers and
3. Drum Printers

Chain Printers

It is a high-speed printer in which the type are carried by the links of a revolving chain. As the characters on the print chain revolve in a horizontal loop, a desired character eventually aligns in a given column. At this instant, the hammer strikes the paper forcing the page into the inked ribbon and the ribbon against the character thus creating the desired symbol on the print page. The chain is cycled continuously until a complete print line has been formed. The print page is then advanced one line and the process is repeated.

Band Printers

On a band printer, several similar sets of fully formed characters are embossed on a horizontal band that is continuously moving in front of the print hammers. In band printer, the paper is momentarily stopped and, as the desired character passes over a given column, the hammer activates, pressing the ribbon against the paper to form the image. It is a line printer that uses band of type characters as its printing mechanism.

Drum printers or (barrel Printers)

A printer in which all the characters for printing are placed round the surface of a cylinder (the barrel) the entire character set being placed round the cylinder at each print position. Print hammers opposite each print position can be activated by the computer striking the paper and bringing it in contact with a continuous ink ribbon between the paper and the surface of the barrel. The barrel rotates at high speed, the appropriate character being selected as it reaches a position immediately opposite the print hammers. A complete line of output is printed for each revolution of the drum since all the characters in each set pass their print stations during revolution.

Non-Impact Printers

Printers that do not strike characters against ribbon or paper when they print, are non-impact printers. Example of non-impact printers include

1. Ink-jet printers
2. Laser printers

These printers makes much less noise than impact printers.

If you are using a non-impact printer, do not try to print on multiple-part carbon forms: because no impact is being made on the paper you will end up with no copies.

A drum printer uses 80 or more character sets embossed on a cylindrical drum. A separate hammer for each character set forces the print page into an inked ribbon and the character when the character aligns at the print position.

Advantages of Non-impact Printers

1. They are faster and quieter
2. They have got the ability to change typefaces automatically and their ability to produce high-quality graphics.

Ink-jet Printers

It uses a technique of projecting droplets of ink at paper to form the required image. Ink-jet printer create an image directly on paper by spraying ink through as many as 64 tiny nozzles. It provides a print resolution of around 360 dots per inch.

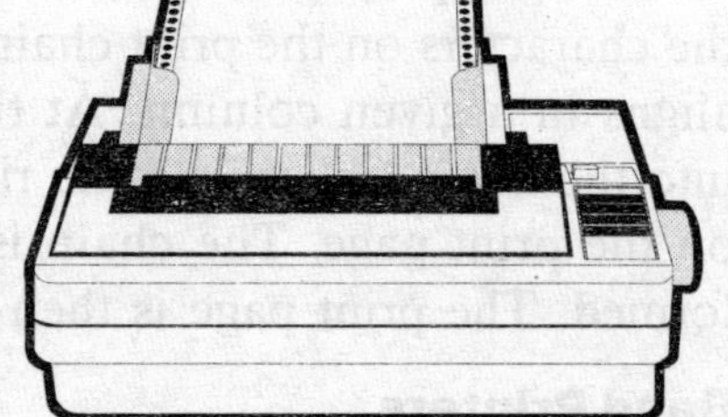

The InkJet printers consist of a special nozzle type head. Ink passes through ionic chamber (special) Ink charges in this chamber. The charged ink is passed through the given to electrical field and variation is done in electronic field the charges shape come in the drop.

The ink is passed through the special ink chamber so as to provide it with the charge the changed ink drop when ejected through the nozzle has to pass through various deflection field produced by deflecting coils which are controlled by logic circuit. The charge in drop after passing through this field attains the necessary shape on the paper.

Today's most popular personal printers use inkjet print engines. The odd name "inkjet" actually describes the printing technology. The outlook of inkjet printer is shown here. It sprays droplets of ink onto paper-it works well enough to deliver image sharpness on a par with most other output technologies.

In essence, the inkjet printer is a line printer, little more than a dot matrix printer with the hammer impact removed. Instead of a hammer pounding ink onto paper, the inkjet flings it into place from tiny nozzles, each one corresponding to a print wire of the impact dot matrix printer. The motive force can be an electromagnet or, as is more likely today, a piezoelectric crystal (a thin crystal that bends when electricity is applied across it). A sharp, digital pulse of electricity causes the crystal to twitch and force ink through the nozzle into its flight to paper. The types of inkjet engines are commonplace: thermal, piezoelectric, and phase-change.

At heart, the basic technology of all three kinds of inkjets is the same. The machines rely on the combination of the small orifice in the nozzle and the surface tension of liquid ink to prevent a constant dibble from the jets. Instead of oozing out, the ink puckers around the hole in the inkjet the same way that droplets of water bead up on a waxy surface. The tiny ink droplets scrunch together rather than spreading out or flowing from the nozzle because the attraction of the molecules in the ink (or water) is stronger than the force of gravity. The inkjet engine needs to apply some force to break the surface tension and force the ink out, and that's where the differences in inkjet technologies arise.

InkJet printers are mostly used medium type of printers between Laser and DMP. These are very small type of printers, which provide higher resolution as compare to DMP cost of inkjet printers is the cost of DMP so we can say that these are the cheaply used printers with respect to DMP but the per page cost of InkJet printer must higher then the DMP. These printers are void ally used because lost of these printers is best speed is also best and quality is also some much better DMP and Laser. The print out taken with the help of InkJet printer is all most same with that taken with a Laser another quality of inkjet is that these printers print very silently but high amount of noise is associated with DMP so we can say that InkJet printer is the best for there similarly to Laser printers the InkJet printer really works better then a DMP also InkJet have print head that can travel approach the width of page that can print the almost line with one pass. This mechanical movement puts inkjet printer in the same category as the DMP. As the inkjet printer print character by character so the speed of inkjet printer is specified in character per second. Usually it is 100 to 200 characters per second the main different between resolutions of a printer is defined as number of dots per inch. The main different between inkjet printer and DMP is the inkjet printer head an inkjet printer spits all through ink on the surface of paper to produce a print out but its technology is much better as compare to DMP.

An inkjet is attached to the head which moves across the width of paper which is the colored data is given to the print head contains four ink cartages one for Red, Blue, Yellow, Black and each cartages of printer head is made up of ink filled chambers each attached to a nozzle smaller than hair. An electrical current flows to thin resistances at the bottom of all the color that printer will use to form a small section of a word or picture. A resistance used here is called film type resistance when current passes through the resistance a high amount of heat is produced it will occur. The temperature produced here is more than 900^{0}f only for a second. The ink jets boiled due to this and forms a bubble of vapor. As the vapor expands it pushes ink through the nozzle. The vapor of printer in the form of a drop jet at the tip of nozzle. The drop jet over comes the pressure of the bubble forces the drop Jet over to the paper. The volume of the ink is above one million of a drop of water from an eyedropper. A typical character is formed by twenty drops across and 30 high.

How printer colors are Created

All colors are made up of different combinations of light we see all the wavelength that make white light through a prism a white light is broken into various color by the prism. The various colors are called spectrum. The spectrum is a mixture of colors. Different mixture of primary color can create any color from the spectrum by either enabling colors or subtracting. Color mixing is of two types additive color mixing subtractive color mixing. Additive color mixing is used to create colors and television. Computer monitors and in movies. Three colors Red, Green, Blue are used to produce all other colors.

Subtractive color Mixing

Reflection properties are used. All color printer use small dots of four inks to make various shades are made by learning dots of unprinted while some printers uses this type of process. Most common color computer can operate up to 3001. But now a day's printer of 700 DPI and 1440 DPI are also used.

Advantages

1. Many of ink-jet printers can also be programmed to print unusual symbols, *e.g.*, Japanese or Chinese characters.
2. It provide an excellent middle ground between dot-matrix and laser printers.
3. Multiple-nozzle print heads enables them to print in several colours.

Disadvantages

1. They can only create one character at a time and therefore cannot match the print speed of line printers.
2. They are expensive

Laser Printers

The one revolution that has changed the faces of both offices and forests around the world was the photocopier. Trees plummet by the millions to provide fodder for the duplicate, triplicate, megaplicate. Today's non-impact, bi-image laser printer owes its life to this technology. The outlook of Laser Printer shown here.

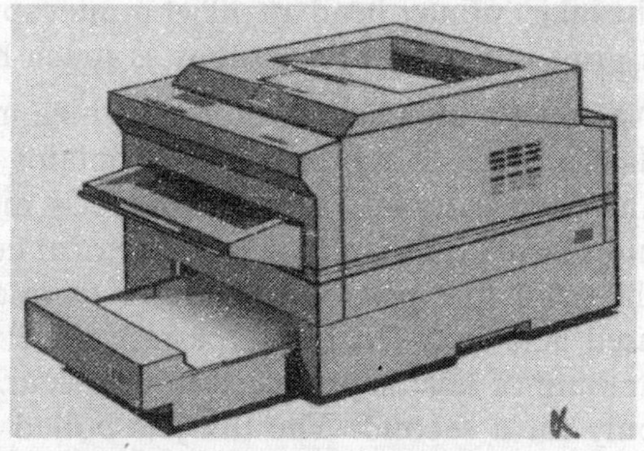

At heart, the laser printer principle is simple. Some materials react to light in strange ways. Selenium and some complex organic compounds modify their electrical conductivity in response to exposure to light. Both copiers and laser printers capitalize on this photoelectric effect by focusing an optical image on a photo-conductive drum that has been given a static electrical charge. The charge drains away from the conductive areas that have been struck by light but persists in the dark areas. A special pigment called a toner is then spread across the drum, and the toner sticks to the charged areas. A roller squeezes paper against the drum to transfer the pigment to the paper. The pigment gets bonded to the paper by heating or "fusing" it.

The laser printer actually evolved from the photocopier. Rather than the familiar electrostatic Xerox machine, however, the true ancestor of the laser printer was a similar competing process called electro-photography, which used a bright light to capture an image and make it visible with a fine carbon-based toner. The process was developed during the 1960s by Keizo Yamaji at Canon. The first commercial application of the technology, called New Process to distinguish it from the old process (xerography), was a Canon photocopier released in 1968.

The first true laser printer was a demonstration unit, made by Canon in 1975, that was based on a modified photocopier. The first commercial PC laser printer came in 1984 v/ hen Hewlett-Packard introduced its first LaserJet, which was based on the Canon CX engine. At heart, it and all later lasers use the same process, a kind of heat set, light inspired offset printing.

The magic in a laser printer is forming the image by making a laser beam scan back and forth across the imaging drum. The trick, well known to stage magicians, is to use mirrors. A small rotating mirror reflects the laser across the drum, tracing each scan line across it. The drum rotates to advance to the next scan line, synchronized to the flying beam of laser light. To make the light and dark pattern of the image, the laser beam is modulated on and off. It's rapidly switched on for light areas, off for dark areas, one minuscule dot at a time to form a bit image.

The major variations on laser printing differ only in the light beam and how it is modulated. LCD-shutter printers, for example, put an electronic shutter (or an array of them) between a constant light source (which need not be a laser) and the imaging drum to modulate the beam. LED printers modulates ordinary Light-Emitting Diodes as their optical source. In any case, these machines rely on the same electro-photographic process as the laser printer to carry out the actual printing process.

The basic laser printer mechanism requires more than just a beam and a drum. In fact, it involves several drums or rollers, as many as six in a single-color printer and more in color machines. Each has a specific role in the printing process. The Mechanical Section of Laser Printer is shown here.

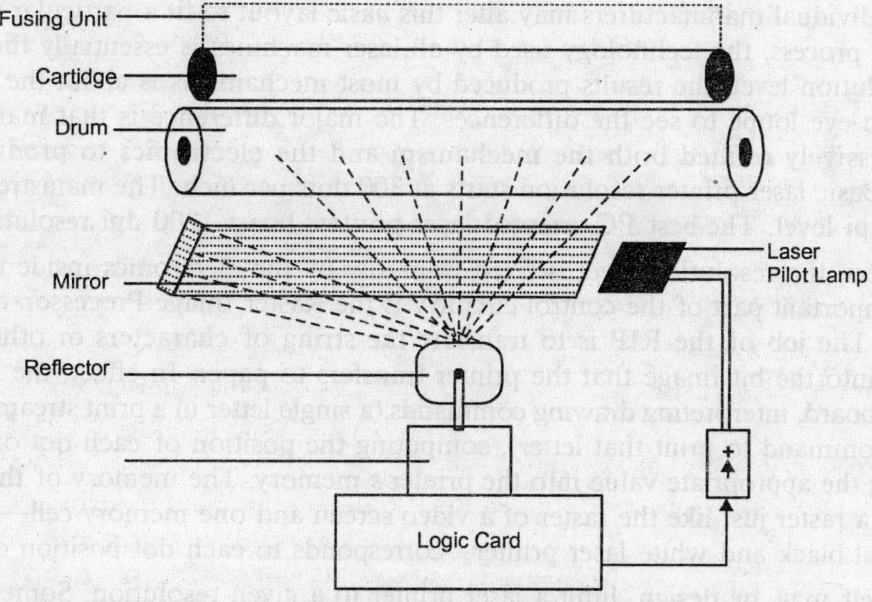

Mechanism of Laser Printer

The imaging drum, often termed the OPC for optical photoconductor, must first be charged before it will accept an image. A special roller called the charging roller applies the electrostatic charge uniformly across the OPC.

After the full width of an area of the OPC gets its charge, it rotates in front of the modulated light beam. As the beam scans across the OPC drum and the drum turns; the system creates an electrostatic replica of the page to be printed.

To form a visible image, a developing roller then dusts the OPC drum with particles of toner. The light-struck areas with an electrostatic charge attract and hold the toner against the drum. The unexposed parts of the drum do not.

The printer rolls the paper between the OPC drum and a transfer roller, which has a strong electrostatic charge that attracts the toner off the drum. Because the paper is between the transfer roller and the OPC drum, the toner collects on the paper in accord with the pattern that was formed by the modulated laser. At this point only a slight electrostatic charge holds the toner to the paper.

To make the image permanent, the printer squeezes the paper between a fuser and backup roller. As the paper passes through, the printer heats the fuser to a high temperature—on the order of 350 degrees Fahrenheit (200 degrees Celsius). The heat of the fuser and the pressure from the backup roller melt the toner and stick it permanently on the paper. The completed page rolls out of the printer.

Meanwhile, the OPC drum continues to spin, wiping the already-printed area against a cleaning blade that scrapes any leftover toner from it. As the drum rotates around to the charging roller again, the process repeats. Early lasers used OPC drums large enough to hold an entire single-page image. Modern machines use smaller rollers that form the image as a continuous process.

Although individual manufacturers may alter this basic layout to fit a particular package or to refine the process, the technology used by all laser machines is essentially the same. At a given resolution level, the results produced by most mechanisms is about the same, too. You need an eye loupe to see the differences. The major difference is that manufacturers have progressively refined both the mechanism and the electronics to produce higher resolutions Basic laser printer resolution starts at 300 dots per inch. The mainstream is now at the 600 dpi level. The-best PC-oriented laser printers boast 1200 dpi resolution.

In most lasers, the resolution level is fixed primarily by the electronics inside the printer. The most important part of the control circuitry is the Raster Image Processor, also known as the RIP. The job of the RIP is to translate the string of characters or other printing commands into the bit image that the printer transfers to paper. In effect, the RIP works like a video board, interpreting drawing commands (a single letter in a print stream is actually a drawing command to print that letter), computing the position of each dot on the page, and pushing the appropriate value into the printer's memory. The memory of the printer is arranged in a raster just like the raster of a video screen and one memory cell—a single bit in the typical black and white laser printer—corresponds to each dot position on paper.

The RIP itself may, by design, limit a laser printer to a given resolution. Some early laser printers made this constraint into an advantage, allowing resolution upgrades through after-market products that replaced the printer's internal RIP and controlled the printer and its laser through a video input. The video input earns its name because its signal is applied directly to the light source in the laser in raster scanned form (like a television image), bypassing most of the printer's electronics. The add-in processor can modulate the laser at higher rates to create higher resolutions.

Moving from 300 dpi to 600 dpi and 1200 dpi means more than changing the RIP and adding memory, however. The higher resolutions also demand improved toner formulations because, at high resolutions, the size of toner particles limits sharpness much as the size of print wires limits impact dot matrix resolution. With higher resolution laser printers, it becomes increasingly important to get the right toner, particularly if you have toner cartridges refilled. The wrong toner limits resolution just as a fuzzy ribbon limits the quality of impact printer output.

Adding color to a laser printer is more than dumping a few more colors of toner. The laser must separately image each of its three or four primary colors and transfer the toner corresponding to each to the paper. The imaging process for each color requires forming an entire image by passing it past the OPC drum. Forming a complete image consequently requires three or four passes of the drum.

Exactly what constitutes a pass varies among manufacturers. Most color laser printers use three or four distinct passes of each sheet of paper. The paper rolls around the drum and makes four complete turns. Each color gets images separately on the drum, then separately transferred to the sheet. The printer wipes the drum clean between passes.

So-called "one-pass" printing, pioneered by Hewlett-Packard, still requires the drum to make four complete passes as each color gets separately scanned on the drum, and toner is dusted on the drum separately for each color. The paper, however, only passes once through the machine to accept the full color image at once and to have all four colors fused together onto the paper. The first three colors merely transfer to the drum. After the last color—black—gets coated on the drum, the printer runs the paper through and transfers the toner to it. The paper thus makes a single pass through the printer, hence the "one-pass" name. This single-pass laser technology yields no real speed advantage. The photoconductor drum still spins around the same number of times as a four-pass printer. The speed at which the drum turns and the number of turns it makes determines engine speed, so the one-pass process doesn't make a significant performance increase.

The advantage to one-pass color laser printing comes in the registration of the separate color images. With conventional color laser systems, the alignment of the paper must be critically maintained for all four passes in order for all the colors to properly line up. With the one-pass system, paper alignment is not a problem. Only the drum needs to maintain its alignment, which is easy to do because it is part of the mechanism rather than an interloper from the outside world.

No matter the number of passes, adding color in laser printing subtracts speed. In general, color laser speed falls to one-quarter the monochrome speed of a similar engine because of the requirement of four passes. (With three-pass printing, speed falls to one-third the monochrome rate). For example, a printer rated at 12 pages per minute in monochrome will deliver about 3 ppm in color. Even allowing for this slowdown, however, color lasers are usually faster than other color page printers. They are also often quieter. Compared to thermal wax transfer printers, a popular high quality color technology, they are also economical because a laser uses toner only for the actual printed image. Thermal wax machines need a full page of ink for each page printed no matter the density of the image.

Working of Laser Printer

1. Eraser Lamp clears residual charge from drum
2. Main corona puts-6KV charge on drum surface
3. Laser beam selectively hits parts of the EP drum, making that part conductive. The conductive part loses voltage, dropping from –600V to –100V.

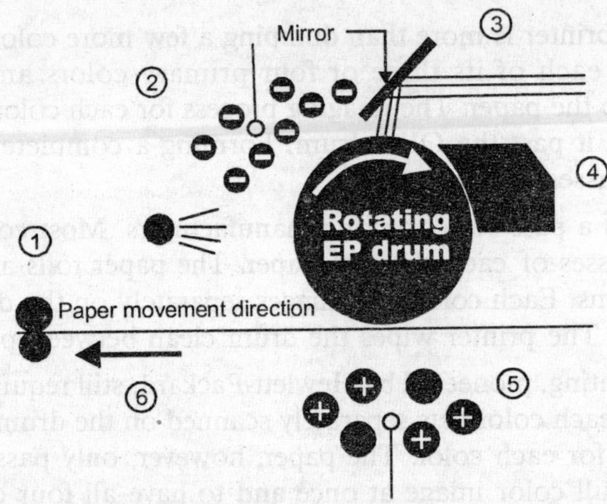

Working of Laser Printer

4. Developer Roller Squeezes Toner (represented by the #4 area) into a uniform layer on the EP drum. The parts that are charged to -6KV, however, repel the toner. Toner only remains where the laser has touched, as it is the most positively charged part of the drum.
5. The paper is pulled under the drum, which now contains the desired image written in toner. A second corona, drawing the toner from the drum to the paper.
6. The image now only sits on the paper as fine, dust-like toner. The toner must be fixed to the page. The fuser roller actually melts the toner into the page with heat at a temperature of 180 degrees C.

Cartridges

Laser printers use up a bit of their mechanism with every page they print. The organic photoconductor drum on which images are made gradually wears out. (A new drum material, silicon, is supposed to last for the life of the printer, but few printer models currently use silicon drums.) In addition, the charging corona or other parts may also need to be periodically replaced. And, of course, you need toner.

Laser printer manufacturers have taken various approaches to replacing these consumables. Hewlett-Packard's LaserJets, for example, are designed with one-piece cartridges that contain both the drum and toner. The whole assembly is replaced as a single unit when the toner runs out. Other laser printers are designed so that the toner, drum, and sometimes the fuser, can be replaced individually.

The makers of the latter style of printer contend that the drum lasts for many times more copies than a single shot of toner, so dumping the drum before its time is wasteful. On the other hand, the all-in-one cartridge folks contend that they design their drums to last only as long as the toner.

Surprisingly, from a cost standpoint the choice of technology does not appear to make a difference. (From an ecological standpoint, however, the individual replacement scheme still makes more sense.)

A similar situation reigns among inkjet printers. Some designs incorporate the print head nozzles into the ink cartridge. Others make the nozzles a separately replaceable item. Although the latter should have a cost advantage and a convenience disadvantage, as a practical matter the differences are not significant.

A more important issue to consider with inkjets is single versus separate cartridges for ink colors. Many printers, typically the less expensive models, use a single cartridge for all three primary ink colors. If you use all three colors equally, this is a convenient arrangement. Most of the time, however, one color will run out before another and force you to scrap a cartridge still holding a supply of two colors of rather expensive ink. If you are frugal or simply appalled at the price of inkjet ink, you'll want a separate cartridge for each ink color.

Refilling

One way to tiptoe around the high cost of laser printer consumables is to get toner or ink cartridges refilled. Most manufacturers do not recommend this—because they have no control over the quality of the toner, they can't guarantee that someone else's replacement works right in their machines. Besides, they miss the profits in selling the toner or ink.

Quality really can be an issue, however. The Resolution Enhancement technology of the HP's LaserJet III series, for example, requires toner with a particle size smaller than that of toner used by other printers. You cannot tell the difference in toner just by looking at it—but you can when blotchy gray pages pour out of the printer. When you get cartridges refilled, you must be sure to get the proper toner quality

Printer Control

To make what you see on paper resemble what you preview on your monitor screen, your printer requires guidance from your computer and your software to tell it exactly how to make a printout look. The computer must send the printer a series of instructions, either to control the most intimate operation of the dumb printer or to coax special features from the brainy machine.

The instructions from the computer must be embedded in the character stream because that is the only data connection between the printer and its host. These embedded instructions can take on any of several forms.

Character Mode

In printing text from your PC, a printer receives a stream of ASCII code characters. The printer matches those characters to one of the fonts in its memory, which may be ROM or RAM. It then uses the pattern from memory to control the placement of bits on paper. All commands to the printer guide the formation and arrangement of these characters.

Because the entire process is oriented toward making characters, the commands to the printer are gauged in terms of characters and lines of text. Most commands deal with fonts and character positioning. For example, the printer may have several fonts in memory and use specific commands to select each one. Other commands tell the printer to emphasize characters or to slant them into italics. Placement commands tell the printer where to put the characters including how to space them.

The printer's interface uses the same signals to carry character data as well as commands. The printer needs some way to distinguish one from the other so that it doesn't print its commands on paper garbled with the text you actually want to see as hard copy. To prevent this confusion, most printers use a combination of two ideas for their commands: special control characters that code commands that also tell the printer not to print the character symbol; and escape sequences, a series of characters preceded by a special command telling the printer not to print the command characters.

Advantages of Laser Printers

1. Very high speed
2. Low noise level
3. Very high image quality
4. Excellent graphics capabilities
5. A variety of type sizes and styles
6. Uses standard, inexpensive copy paper which is loaded into a paper tray.

Thermal Printers

The thermal printers (a non-impact) is an alternative to the other serial printers. Heat elements produce dot-matrix images on heat-sensitive paper. Some fax machines use technique similar to thermal printers to produce documents on heat-sensitive paper. Output on thermal paper fades quickly when exposed to light, but the hardware is often inexpensive.

Advantages

- The advantages include compact size, limited noise, and low purchase price.

Disadvantages

- The major disadvantage is the cost of the heat-sensitive paper.

A thermal printer uses heated dot-matrix wires to print output on specially treated paper.

Electrostatic Printers

Electrostatic printers are devices in which the parts of paper which are to be printed are electrostatically charged, and attract a fine dust which is then fused to the paper by the application of heat. An electrostatic printer may be used in some instances as a plotter. Some properties associated with printers.

Spooling and Printer Buffers

The term spooling is derived from the expression Simultaneous Peripheral Operation On Line. Spooling is a temporary storage of input and output on high-speed input-output devices, which helps in reducing processing delays when transferring data between peripheral equipment and the processors of a computer. The speed of the printers is incredibly slow as compared with the processing speed of the computers to which they are connected. Which makes CPU to sit idle during printing process. To overcome this, two approaches are used.

Spooler Program

It allows the processor to alternate between processing a user's ongoing activity and controlling the printing process. Of course disk space or a dedicated block of primary storage must be available to store the text to be printed by the spooler.

Printer Buffer Hardware

It is an additional storage device that can accept text to be printed as fast as the computer can send it. The buffer then slowly releases the test data to match the printer's speed while the computer is free to do other things.

Printer Installation

Windows Millennium/98/95 Installation Instructions

1. Click the Windows Start button.
2. Choose Settings, and then click Printers.
3. Double-click the Add Printer icon.
4. Click Next.

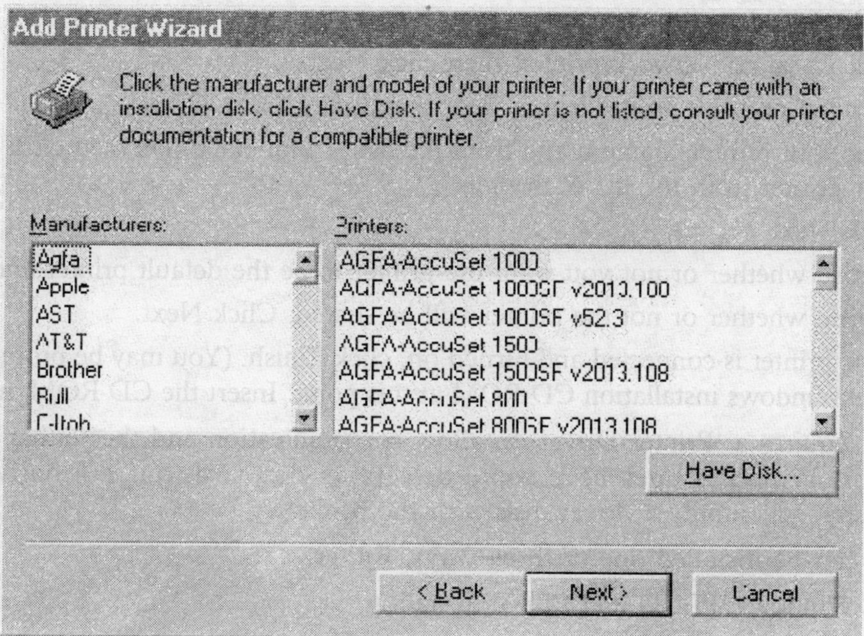

5. A screen may appear asking you "How is the printer attached to your computer?" Click local, then click Next.
6. Click your printers name brand from the list of Manufacturers then click the model of your printer from the list of printers.
7. Click Next.
8. Click the port the printer is attached to and click Next.
9. Choose whether or not you want the printer to be the default printer and click Next.
10. If the printer is connected and turned on, click Finish. (You may be prompted to insert your Windows installation CD-ROM at this point. Insert the CD-ROM and click OK.)

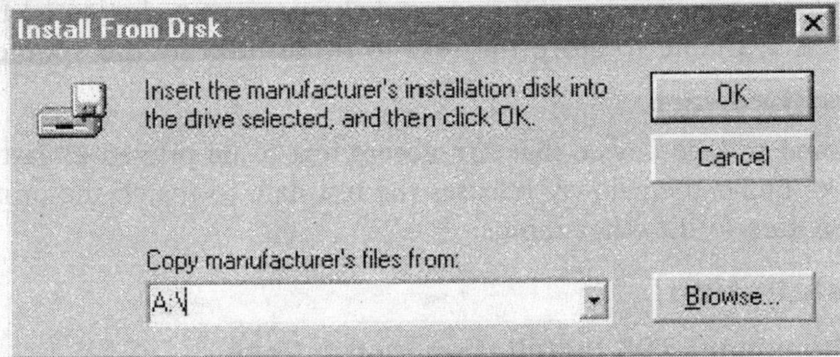

Windows 2000 Installation Instructions

1. Click the Windows Start button.
2. Choose Settings, then click Printers.
3. Double-click the Add Printer icon.
4. Click Next.
5. Click Local or Network printer, then click Next.
6. Click the port the printer is attached to and click Next.
7. Click your printers name brand from the list of Manufacturers then click the model of your printer from the list of printers.
8. Click Next.
9. Choose whether or not you want the printer to be the default printer and click Next.
10. Choose whether or not the printer will be shared. Click Next.
11. If the printer is connected and turned on, click Finish. (You may be prompted to insert your Windows installation CD-ROM at this point. Insert the CD-ROM and click OK.)

Windows requires a 'Printer Driver' to allow communication and the setting up of printer parameters. Windows does have some drivers as standard, but normally the Printer manufacturer will supply a driver disk with the printer.

A printer can be installed one of three ways. Either

- Let Windows 'PLUG and PLAY' install it;

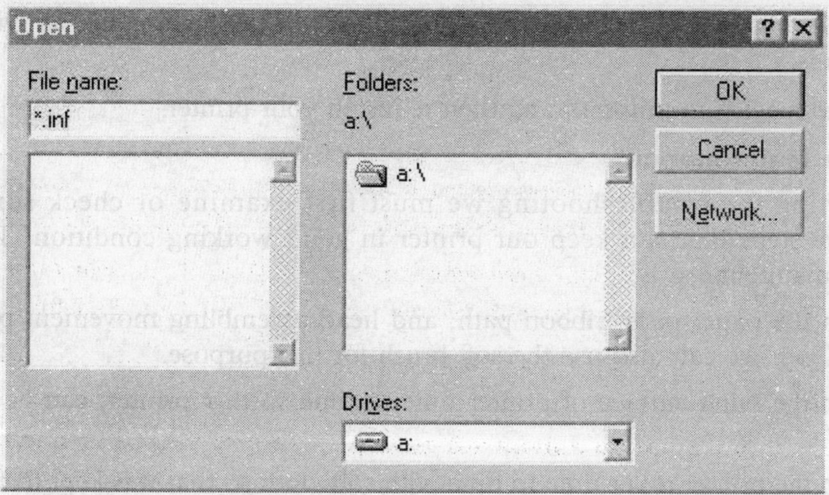

- Run the '*setup*' on the printer driver disk;
- By double clicking on the 'ADD PRINTER' icon in the PRINTERS window. *i.e*, START>SETTINGS>PRINTERS

Once this is done the 'ADD PRINTER WIZARD' will appear click 'NEXT'
Select the drive that has the manufacturer's disk inserted and using the 'FOLDERS' window browse to the relevant folder. In the 'FILE NAME' window will be the correct driver file (Windows selects the file!) Click 'OK' twice and follow the onscreen prompts. Windows will then print a test page to verify that all is OK.

Troubleshooting Printer

Here are a few simple techniques that will solve many printer problems.

1. Reboot your computer. This generally solves most printing problems.
2. If it's not printing, or you're getting a message about the Fax printer, change your default printer: Start — Settings — Printers/Faxes. Right-click the printer you want, and then select (left-click) Set as Default.
3. Check and make sure all connections going to and coming from the printer are firmly in place.
4. Check that the printer is on-line:
   (*i*) Start — Settings — Printers, right-click the printer.
   (*ii*) If there isn't a checkmark by "Set as Default", left-click that option to select it.
5. Print a test page. If that prints and the application you are using doesn't, you probably will need to contact the application's vendor for support.
6. Turn off your printer for 10 seconds and turn it back on. Make a note of any error messages or flashing lights when the printer is turned back on.
7. If your printer is connected directly to another computer, try rebooting that computer.

If your printer is connected to a JetDirect box, try unplugging the Jet Direct box for 10 seconds.

8. You may wish to uninstall and then re-install your printer.

Preventive Maintenance

Before starting the troubleshooting we must first examine or check some preventive maintenance steps that can keep our printer in good working condition. The main steps preventive maintenance is.

1. Clean the paper path, ribbon path, and head assembling movement path with a dry soft Cloth we can also use the soft brush for this purpose.
2. Clean the outer surface of printer time to time so that printer; can be kept free from dust.
3. Clean the printer roller time to time with soft cloth so that it is kept free from dust and rust.
4. If you clean time to time and oil the printer then we can avoid expenses repair
5. Check for loose belt because in some DMP the print head is connected to the motor with the help of belt if be it is loose then replace it.
6. Lubricating (oiling) of head assembling mechanism will keep the printer away from heaving unnecessary fault.
7. Do not extra oiling the various part of printer because extra oiling can cause serious fault in a printer due to dusted so for log life of printer its head must be kept cool as can it is possible. If your printer has fraction feed and tractor feed then do not use both these at the same time. If you use both them the paper feeding will not be paper and the paper may get struck in side the printer.

Scanner

Whereas a keyboard, mouse or trackball requires manual input of data, scanners allow input of printed data. A scanner reads text, photographs and graphics from paper which are then converted into bit patterns for processing, storage or output. Scanner is a device that examines a spatial pattern one part after another and generate analog or digital signals corresponding to the pattern. Scanners are often used in mark sensing, pattern recognition or character recognition.

Practically scanner uses light for examining the spatial patterns. In a scanner, as the image is scanned, it is converted into light and dark picture elements, or pixels, similar to newspaper photo. This technique makes the images usable by word processing, desktop publishing, and graphic packages.

There are two main types of scanners, Hand-held scanner and Flat-bed scanner

Hand-held Scanner

These devices read data on price tags, shipping labels, inventory part number, book ISBNs, and the like. Hand-held scanner, sometimes called wand scanners, use either contact or laser technology. It has a set of light emitting diodes. It is placed over the material to be scanned and slowly dragged from the top to the bottom. The light emitted by the diodes are not reflected by black lines and are reflected by whole areas. The material is converted and stored in a bitmap. Typical applications are to store images and reproduce them in publications.

Flat-bed Scanner

It consists of a box with glass plate on top, which is used for placing the document to be scanned. The light beam is situated below the glass plate and is moved from left to right horizontally. After scanning one line the beam moves up little and scans the next line. The scanner can also store colour images.

Other types of scanners are:

Drum Scanners

These scanners use photo multiplier (PM) tubes and are expensive, sensitive devices that can capture information at a higher resolution and higher pixel-depth than flatbed scanners, which are based on charge coupled devices (CCDs). A PM tube is a light-sensing device with a much higher sensitivity and lower noise-to-signal-ration than a CCD. A drum scanner can capture shadow information that is not visible to the human eye. It can transform that information into the visible region and improve the image. This is particularly useful in scanning transparencies. However, drum scanners are too slow and expensive to use for OCR or document management applications.

Sheetfed Scanners

These scanners take up less desk space and are easier to install. But most of these can only scan loose sheets. Sheetfed scanners have been made more compact in size by turning the scanner design inside out. Instead of the head moving over the paper, tiny rubber wheels pull the paper over the scan head. The wheels, however, do not track perfectly, so pages at times get skewed, resulting in a crooked scan. Sheetfed scanners focus more on managing paper flow than on getting an optimal scan.

Installing Scanner

To install a scanner follow the steps below:

(*i*) Parallel Port Scanner

1. Shutdown system.
2. Hook parallel connector to printer port of your computer. If you have a SCSI scanner, or USB simply hook into one of those ports.
3. Unlock scanner head. This is usually done underneath scanner of on sides by power switch.

4. Plug in power for scanner boot system up Windows will recognize new device and hardware manager will appear.

(ii) SCSI Scanner

1. If you have a SCSI scanner first cover installing the SCSI Adapter Card.
2. Make sure and refer to your adapters documentation for jumper settings. You will want to set the jumpers if any before we install the adapter.
3. Turn Off PC and unplug from outlet.
4. Remove case cover
5. Unscrew a slot on case for adapter card
6. Connect any necessary internal cables. (drives)
7. Align card with Bus slot and seat evenly. Be careful of any catching the cards ports on anything.
8. Tighten down card snug
9. Close case
10. Hook up power

(iii) USB Scanner

1. This one is very simple. You will simply plug in with computer running and install a driver for it.
2. Exit all programs running.
3. With only windows running plug in your scanner into the USB port
4. Give windows a few seconds
5. you should be brought to a hardware wizard
6. Now you are ready to load a driver for it.

Scanning The Scanner

A flatbed scanner uses a light source, a lens, a charge coupled device (CCD) array and one or more analog-to-digital converters (ADCs) to collect optical information about the object to be scanned, and transforms it to a computer image file. A CCD is a miniature photometer that measures incident light and converts that measured value to analog voltage.

When an object is placed on a scanner's copy board or glass surface and start scanning, the light source illuminates a thin horizontal strip of the object called a raster line. Thus, when an image is scanned it can scan one line at a time. During the exposure of each raster line, the scanner carriage (optical imaging elements, which is a network of lenses and mirrors) is mechanically moved over a small distance using a motor. The reflected light is captured by the CCD array. Each CCD converts the light to an analog voltage and indicates the gray level for one pixel. The analog voltage is then converted to a digital value by an analog-to-digital converter (ADC), using.8,10 or 12 bits per colour.

The CCDs elements are all in one row, with one element for each pixel in a line. If you have 300 CCD elements for each inch across the scanner, you can have a maximum potential optical resolution of 300 pixels per inch (ppi) also referred to as dots per inch (dpi). In case you have 600 CCD elements for each inch, then the maximum optical resolution will be 600 ppi or 600 dpi.

There are two methods by which the incident white light is sensed by the CCD. The first involves a rapidly rotating light filter that individually filters the red, green and blue components of the reflected light and is sensed bya single CCD device. Here, the colour filter is fabricated into the chip directly. In the second method, a prismatic beam splitter first splits the reflected white light and three individual CCDs sense the red, green and blue light beams. High precision is required in the optics and in the alignment of the sensing mechanisms for this method.

A Scanner for You

How can one identify a first-rate scanner? The answer is not so simple, though it would suffice to say that it is one that combines accuracy and minimal loss with maximum power and ease in compensating for the distortions. One of the most potentially confusing claims for scanners is the number of bits that they offer. You often come across terms like 24, 30, or 36 bit scanners, but what do they actually mean?

Bits are the basic elements of digital data. A single bit is either on or off, usually expressed as 1 or 0 so that there are only two variations. Each pixel of a scanned image has a 'depth' of one to 32 bits. 1-bit images are black and white (for example, line art). A 2-bit pixel contains four variations (00 01 1011) and allows a variation of the colour from, white to light grey to dark grey to black;

An 8-bit pixel can vary anywhere within the full range of 256 grey values. 24-bit images are actually three 8-bit channels, one each for red, green and blue light. A 32-bit image can be an RGB image with a fourth channel (for example an alpha channel in Adobe Photoshop) or, more commonly, a CMYK image with one 8-bit channel for each of cyan, magenta, yellow and black.

A 24-bit scanner divides each of its primary colours-red, green, or blue (RGB) into 8 bits, or 256 (28) shades. (In grey scale mode, a 24-bit scanner captures 256 shades of grey). This 256^3 gives you 16.7 million possible colours. This is the maximum that most high-end graphics boards will display. A 30-bit scanner offers 10 bit or 1,024 shades for each colour, while a 36-bit scanner offers 12 bits or 4,096 shades.

However, even this data is not enough for a perfect picture. Once the seventh and eighth bits are reached, accuracy takes a nosedive. This results in loss or distorted details—especially in the highlight and shadow regions. Further applying tone corrections—adjusting gamma curve results, brightness and contrast-reduces the size of the colour palette, esulting in loss of data. You can still change the colours but you cannot work with what is not there!

The solution lies in adding more bits and making it a 30-bit scanner. A 30-bit scanner offers 10 bits per colour or captures 1,024 shades of red, green, or blue for over a billion colours. The first 8 bits are fairly accurate, so the scanner can just junk the last couple of bits and leave you with superior 24-bit colour.

If the scanner performs tonal corrections of colour at the hardware level, greater advantage can be derived from the larger number of colours. If one expands part of the tonal range of a 24-bit image to bring out, say, the shadow details, one will automatically end up compressing it elsewhere, thus losing midtones and highlight details. A 30-bit scanner can use the instructions imparted to select and deliver the best 24 bits of data for the required needs, giving one the corrected image with much greater detail retention and smoother tonal continuity.

However, 30-bit and 36-bit scanners use the extra bits internally, and generally send only 24 bits to the computer.

Colour Models

Colour models are closely related to bit depth. Greyscale goes up to 8-bit, which renders 256 shades. Colour images are multiples of 8-bit channels. RGB, the normal model for computer graphics, goes up to 24-bit (three 8-bit channels for red, green, and blue). CMYK, the standard for printing colour images, is a 32-bit model.

RGB Colour

Red, green and blue are the primary colours of light. The human eye responds to stimuli from varying RGB wavelengths and renders the appropriate signals to the brain so that we perceive such colours as cherry, mauve and beige. Most of the scanners use an RGB colour model for recording digital image data. RGB colours is called additive because colours throughout the spectrum are created by adding varying intensities of red, green, and blue light to black (no light). These intensities vary from 255 (full intensity) to 0. Each colour channel has 256 variations and their combinations allow creating a total of 16,777,216 colours. A combination of R:255 G:255 B:255 creates white, while R:0 G:0 B:0 is black (no light).

CMYK Colour

Cyan, magenta and yellow are the secondary colours of RGB and are opposites. When RGB light strikes an object, the amount of cyan, magenta and yellow in the object's pigmentation affects how much light is reflected back (it's the reflected light that we see). Cyan absorbs red light, magenta absorbs green light and yellow absorbs blue light. The degree of absorption depends on the amount of pigment or, in printing terms, the amount of CMY ink. This is why CMYK is considered subtractive; the colours displayed by CMYK are the result of subtracting varying amounts of red, green, and blue light.

In the example below, a printed object composed of 39% cyan, 47% magenta, 0% yellow and 1% black (which absorbs all light) would reflect back 60% red light, 52% green light, and 99% blue light.

Resolve the Resolution

A pixel can have many colours (24 bits or as many as 16.7 million colours), while a dot is a special pixel that has two colours (black and white). Scanners capture pixels, hence we say pixels per inch (ppi). Most printers print dots, hence the term dots per inch (dpi). Pixels contain more information than dots. For scans of photographs you do not need to scan at the resolution of the printer because the extra information contained in the pixels is dispersed among the many dots. Even though scanner specifications are mostly mentioned in dpi these are actually in ppi only.

The true optical resolution is the ability of a scanner to resolve fine details in an original. It is actually the optical sampling rate or ppi rating of the scanner. The optical sampling rate is the number of samples captured in the x-axis by the scanner. This is determined by the width of the scanned area and the number of elements in the CCD. This is only one of the crucial components of resolution. There can be several other important factors that determine the final resolution. These include the optics quality (lens, mirrors, filters), mechanical stability of the optical system, motion of the carriage, vibration of the object, CCD, and optical components, focal range and stability of the optical system, impact of temperature and humidity changes on the optical system, frequency response of the electronic system and image processing applied to the images.

Thus, a high optical sampling rating of a scanner does not necessarily guarantee better resolution than one with a lower optical sampling rate. For example, the resolution of a scanner with a high sampling rate of 600 ppi but low-quality optical system may not be as good as a scanner with a 400 ppi sampling rate and a high-quality optical system.

Interpolation

The true optical resolution of the scanner is also referred to as the horizontal resolution while the y-direction sampling rate is also called the mechanical resolution or the vertical resolution, since it indicates the minimum movement of the scanner's mechanics—the number of steps per inch that the scanner takes in the y direction. This figure is typically double the optical resolution. This vertical resolution is interpolated. Interpolation means the scanner or scanning software generates data based on the real, captured data. If you see something saying 'EOO-b, -9,600 ppi optical', this means that it is a 600 ppi scanner, the interpolated number makes no difference—whether, it is 9,600 or 600, or infinity. Also, in most of the cases, some marketing masterminds reverse three specification. You would be on safer grounds assuming that the lower number is the actual optical resolution of the scanner.

Interpolation guesses the values for pixels at a finer level than the scanner samples them, based on the values of nearby pixels. It is easy to interpolate between two measurements on the same scan line because the scanner measures the entire line and has all the information available. It is harder to interpolate in the other direction–to fill in an interpolated line–because the scanner has not scanned the lines after the interpolated line yet. By taking extra steps in the y direction, one eliminate the need to interpolate in the direction.

Scanners that offer higher interpolated resolutions than the scanner's optical and mechanical resolutions so their interpolation for the higher resolutions at the computer. That gives them the luxury of being able to receive later lines in the images before they interpolate between lines.

Unfortunately, both the scanner-based and software-based interpolations can be less sophisticated than the interpolation routines in a sophisticated program such as Adobe

Photoshop, one will often get better results by scanning at the maximum optical resolution for the scanner, and then resampling at a higher interpolated resolution image editor.

If one work involves scanning photos for Web pages or output to an inkjet printer, a 300 ppi scanner will capture enough detail for you. But if printing is carried out with high-resolution output devices or scanning small targets like slides and enlarging them, or reproducing line art, then a 600 ppi scanner is a much better option.

Scanner Software

The scanner comes with a TWAIN driver, which functions as a standalone program for scanning, and enable yours scan images directly into most Windows programs. If an application supports TWAIN driver by entering a sear command. If it supports OLE instead of TWAIN, one can use OLE to call up the driver and insert the scanner image. In addition, all scanners today also come with image editing, OCR and sometimes other applications as we.

Image Quality

In the ultimate analysis, the most important issue for any scanner is image quality. Understanding what affects image quality will not only help you make a more informed buying decision but will also help to take best advantage of whatever scanner are gets.

High on the list is colour balance–the ability to capture neutral colours in neutral form. If you scan a black-and-white photo in colour and the result has a colour tinge one can be sure that the colours will be off on one's colour photos too. A closely related issue is colour accuracy, or the ability to capture colours that closely match the original. Many scanners often impart a pinkish tinge to scans.

For any given scanner at any given setting, both tonal quality and the colour accuracy will vary depending on the screen or printer you are using to look at the result. That is why an easy-to-use calibration feature is critical. It must be borne in mind that images that look good on screen will not necessarily look good when printed, and images that look good while printed may not look good on the screen, one will want to calibrate for both screen and printer; making sure one uses the appropriate calibration file when you scan, typically by telling the TWAIN driver the final destination for the image.

Another important image quality criterion is gamma correction. Gamma correction essentially lets one modify contrast level at different levels of brightness. Changing the gamma setting can make a tremendous difference to an image.

Noise level and the closely related signal-to-noise ratio are important indicators of how much detail one will be able to see in a scan. A signal-to-noise ratio is the ratio of the usable signal, in this case the image to noise in a scan. Noise is a distortion in the image's analog signal. This is an analog problem and is confined to the analog electronics in a scanner. One can change the signal-to-noise level substantially by changing settings in the TWAIN driver. Turning down the brightness settings also reduces the amount of noise in an image.

Colour registration-a measure of how well the three colours line up with each other– is not usually an issue for colour photos but may be an issue if one is scanning line art. If the registration is off, one will see an extra 'halo' of colour at the edges. When one is scanning a Web page, even a full pixel off is generally acceptable in a 600-dpi scan, though it will be noticeable to those who look for it in 300-dpi scan.

Plotters

It is an output unit that directly produces a hardcopy record of data on a removable medium, in the form of a two-dimensional graphic representation. Plotters are designed to produce large drawings or images such as construction plans for buildings or blueprints for mechanical objects.

There are two major types of pen plotters:

1. Flatbed plotters
2. Drum plotters

Flatbed Plotters

It uses a bed or tray to hold paper in a fixed position. A movable pen is usually held by a single arm that can move the pen both horizontally and vertically. The computer instructs the flatbed plotter by directing the pen to x-y position on the page.

Drawback

1. It limits picture sizes to the page dimensions of their tray.
2. Slow output device : can take hours to complete a complex drawing.

Drum Plotter

It has a single arm that can only move across the drum horizontally. The drum itself moves the paper forward or backward to enable the pen to draw in any vertical direction. Any type of diagonal line is drawn by combining a horizontal movement of the pen arm with a vertical page movement via the drum.

Drum plotters are used to produce continuous output, such as plotting earthquake activity, or for long graphic output, such as the structural view of a 'skyscraper'.

Working of Plotter

A plotter uses a robotic arm to draw with coloured pens on a sheet of paper. The instructions that a plotter receives from a computer consists of a colour and beginning and ending coordinates for a line.

With that information, the plotter picks up the appropriate pen, positions it at the beginning coordinates, drops the pen down to the surface of the paper and draws to the ending coordiantes. Plotter draw curves by creating a sequence of very short straight lines. There is one major type of plotter that does not use pens i.e.; Electrostatic plotter

Electrostat plotters use electrostatic charges to create images out of very small dots on specially treated paper. The paper is run through a developer to allow the image to appear Electrostatic plotters are faster than pen plotters and can produce images of very high resolution.

Revision

1. Printers are used to get the ouput on paper.
2. There are two main types of printers: Impact and Non impact printers.
3. An impact printer makes contact with the paper to produce an image.
4. Dot-matrix printers are also called serial printers.
5. Daisy Wheel Printers are slower than dot-matrix printers, but they produce a high-resolution output.
6. Line printer prints an entire line in a single operation without necessarily printing one character at a time.
7. Chain printer is a high-speed printer in which the type are carried by the links of a revolving chain.
8. On a band printer, several similar sets of fully formed characters are embossed on a horizontal band that is continuously moving in front of the print hammers.
9. Printers that do not strike characters against ribbon or paper when they print, are non-impact printers.
10. The physical properties of LASERS (Light Amplification by Stimulate Emission of Radiation) allows for the very precise positioning of narrow beam of light, transferring a high energy source to a very small area.
11. Electrostatic printers are devices in which the parts of paper which are to be printed are electrostatically charged, and attract a fine dust which is then fused to the paper by the application of heat.
12. Scanner is a device that examines a spatial pattern one part after another and generate analog or digital signals corresponding to the pattern.
13. There are two types of scanners, Hand-held scanner and Flat-bed scanner.

Multiple Choice Questions

1. Printer is a ________ device.

   (a) Input (b) Pointing

   (c) Output
2. Dot matrix printers are so called because they print characters in terms of :

   (a) Squares (b) Dots

   (c) Circles
3. Line printers print a ______ at a time.

   (a) character (b) dot

   (c) line
4. Full form of LASER is:

   (a) Light Amplification by Stimulate Emission of Radiation

   (b) Low Amplification by Stimulate Emission of Radiation

   (c) Light Around by Stimulate Emission of Radiation
5. The two scanners known are Hand held and :

   (a) mouse held (b) Flat bed

   (c) print bed

6. LASER printer's drum is charged with:
   (a) –300 V (b) +300 V
   (c) –600 V (d) +600 V
7. Which of the following is not print-head standard:
   (a) 9 pin (b) 18 pin.
   (c) 24 pin. (d) 16 pin.
8. Printer is a
   (a) Communcation equipment (b) Input device.
   (c) Output device. (d) Processing device.

True/False Questions

1. Printers are used to get the ouput on paper.
2. There are two main types of printers: Impact and Non impact printers.
3. Dot-matrix printers are also called parallel printers.
4. Daisy Wheel Printers are faster than dot-matrix printers, and they produce a high-resolution output.
5. Chain printer is a high-speed printer in which the type are carried by the links of a revolving chain.
6. On a band printer, several similar sets of fully formed characters are embossed on a horizontal band that is continuously moving in front of the print hammers.
7. Printers that do not strike characters against ribbon or paper when they print, are impact printers.
8. Electrostatic printers are devices in which the parts of paper which are to be printed are electrostatically charged, and attract a fine dust which is then fused to the paper by the application of heat.
9. There are two types of scanners, Hand-held scanner and Flat-bed scanner.
10. DMP printers cannot print multiple copies of print output at a time.
11. DMP printers have a good photo quality.
12. Explain the construction of various print heads of DMP printer.

Short Answer Type Questions

1. Describe the various type of printers.
2. Which are Electrostatic Printers?
3. Describe the working of Flat-bed scanner.

Descriptive Questions

1. What are the advantages and disadvantages of Dot Matrix Printers?
2. Describe the working of Daisywheel printers.
3. What are Chain, Band and Drum printers?
4. What are the advantages and disadvantages of using Ink-jet printers?
5. Which are the different type of scanners?
6. Explain the working principal of LASER printer?
7. What is scanner? Give working of scanner.

Answers to Objective Type Questions

Multiple Choice Questions

1. c	2. b	3. c	4. a
5. b	6. d	7. b	8. c

True False Questions

1. T	2. T	3. F	4. T
5. T	6. T	7. T	8. T
9. T	10. F	11. T	12. T

6 USB Devices

Introduction to Parallel Devices of Personal Computers

Now, we come to the last type of devices, *i.e.*, USB Devices.

USB (Universal Serial Bus) is a protocol that allows two way communication between peripheral devices and a host computer. It is hot pluggable, allowing the device to be connected and/or removed while the computer is running.

USB Devices

Universal Serial Bus (USB) is a serial bus standard to interface devices. It was originally designed for computers, but its popularity has prompted it to become commonplace on video game consoles, PDAs, portable DVD and media players, cellphones; and even devices such as televisions, home stereo equipment (*e.g.*, digital audio players), car stereos and portable memory devices.

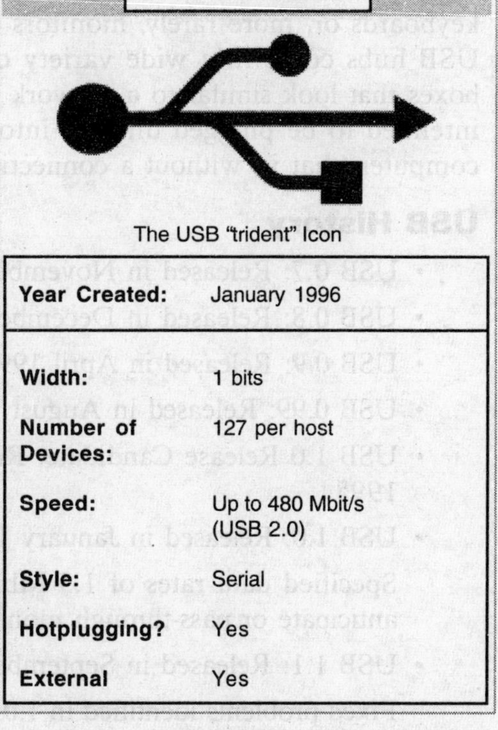

The USB "trident" Icon

Year Created:	January 1996
Width:	1 bits
Number of Devices:	127 per host
Speed:	Up to 480 Mbit/s (USB 2.0)
Style:	Serial
Hotplugging?	Yes
External	Yes

The Hardware

A USB cable has four wires: power, ground, D+ and D–. The signal wires usually operate in differential mode. There are two types of USB devices: high speed and low speed. There are differences in the type, length and connectors that can be used with the two types. Generally the requirements are stricter for high speed devices. A high speed device can transfer data at a maximum of 12 Mbs while low speed is limited to 1.5 Mbs. The PIC 16C745 can only operate at low speed standard. The connector at the computer (A End) is a flattened rectangle while at the device (B end) the connector is square with two cut-off corners. Each USB device is able to draw 100 mA from the cable which allows a device to be bus powered. A device can negotiate up to 500 mA once connected to the USB cable but this power may not be available. If the power is unavailable the device must stay in a low power setting. Obviously devices can be powered externally as well.

The Software

When a device is connected, the computer (or a hub) detects the device by a pullup resister (see circuit). A pullup resister on the D– wire signals a low speed device, while a high speed device has a pullup on the D+ wire. When detected a series of enumeration steps are started. The enumeration process assigns an identifier number to the device (there can be a maximum of 127 devices on a network) and also tells the host computer what sort of capabilities a device has (input, ouput, etc). The device also informs the computer of its name (Vendor, Product, Version and Serial Number). If the device identifies itself as a HID (Human Interface Device) then the device describes how the data should be interpreted.

A USB Series "A" plug

USB Hub

A USB hub is a device that allows many USB devices to be connected to a single USB port on the host computer or another hub.

USB hubs are often built into equipment, normally keyboards or, more rarely, monitors or printers. Separate USB hubs come in a wide variety of form factors from boxes that look similar to a network hub to small designs intended to be plugged directly into the USB port on a computer (that is, without a connecting cable).

A USB Series "A" plug

A USB hub with the plastic cover removed

USB History

- USB 0.7: Released in November 1994.
- USB 0.8: Released in December 1994.
- USB 0.9: Released in April 1995.
- USB 0.99: Released in August 1995.
- USB 1.0 Release Candidate: Released in November 1995.
- USB 1.0: Released in January 1996.

  Specified data rates of 1.5 Mbps (Low-Speed) and 12 Mbps (Full-Speed). Did not anticipate or pass-through monitors. Few such devices actually made it to market.
- USB 1.1: Released in September 1998.

  Fixed problems identified in 1.0, mostly relating to hubs. Earliest revision to be widely adopted.
- USB 2.0: Released in April 2000.

  Added higher maximum speed of 480 Mbps (now called Hi-Speed).
- Mini-B Connector ECN: Released in October 2000.

  Specifications for Mini-B plug and receptable. These should not be confused with Micro-B plug and receptable.

- Errata as of December 2000: Released in December 2000.
- Resistor ECN: Released in May 2002.
- Errata as of May 2002: Released in May 2002.
- Interface Associations ECN: Released in May 2003.

  New standard desriptor was added that allows multiple interfaces to be associated with a single device function.
- Rounded Chamfer ECN: Released in October 2003.
- Unicode ECN: Released in February 2005.
- USB On-The-Go Supplement 1.0: Released in December 2001.
- USB On-The-Go Supplement 1.0a: Released in June 2003.
- USB On-The-Go Supplement 1.2: Released in April 2006.
- USB On-The-Go Supplement 1.3: Released in December 2006. This is the current revision

USB connectors

Connector types

There are several types of USB connectors, and some have been added as the specification has progressed. From the original USB specification:

- Standard-A plug
- Standard-A receptacle
- Standard-B plug
- Standard-B receptacle

Added in the first engineering change noticed to the USB 2.0 specification:

- Mini-B plug
- Mini-B receptacle

Added in the Universal Serial Bus Micro-USB Cables and Connectors Specification:

- Micro-A plug (white)
- Micro-AB receptacle (gray)
- Micro-B plug (black)
- Micro-B receptacle (black)

Adapters, also from the Universal Serial Bus Micro-USB Cables and Connectors Specification (Note that no other adapters are allowed.):

- Standard-A receptacle to Micro-A plug
- Micro-USB is a connector announced by the USB Implementers Forum (USB-IF) on January 4, 2007. It is intended to replace the Mini-USB plugs used in many new smartphones and PDAs. The Micro-USB plug is rated for 10,000 connect-disconnect

cycles. It is about half the height of the mini-USB connector in widespread use today but features a similar width.

USB Device classes

Devices that attach to the bus can be full-custom devices requiring a full-custom device driver to be used, or may belong to a device class. These classes define an expected behavior in terms of device and interface descriptors so that the same device driver may be used for any device that claims to be a member of a certain class. An operating system is supposed to implement all device classes so as to provide generic drivers for any USB device.

Device classes are decided upon by the Device Working Group of the USB Implementers Forum. If the class is to be set for the entire device, the number is assigned to the bDeviceClass field of the device descriptor, and if it is to be set for a single interface on a device, it is assigned to the bInterfaceClass field of the interface descriptor. Both of these are a single byte each, so a maximum of 254 different device classes are possible (values 0x00 and 0xFF are reserved). If bDeviceClass is set to 0x00, the operating system will look at bInterfaceClass of each interface to determine the device class. Each class also optionally supports a SubClass and Protocol subdefinition. These can be used as the main device classes are continuously revised.

The most used device/interface classes (grouped by assigned class ID) are:

0x00 Reserved value - used in the device descriptor to signify that the interface descriptor holds the device class identifier for each interface.

0x01 USB audio device class, sound card-like devices.

0x02 USB communications device class (“CDC”), used for modems, network cards, ISDN connections, Fax.

0x03 USB human interface device class (“HID”), keyboards, mice, etc.

0x06 Still image capture device class, identical to the Picture Transfer Protocol as used across USB

0x07 USB printer device class, printer-like devices.

0x08 USB mass storage device class used for flash drives, portable hard drives, memory card readers, digital cameras, digital audio players etc. This device class presents the device as a block device (almost always used to store a file system).

0x09 USB hubs.

0x0B Smart card readers.

0x0E USB video device class, webcam-like devices, motion image capture devices.

0xE0 Wireless controllers, for example Bluetooth dongles.

0xFF Custom device class - used to establish that a device or interface does not support any standard device class and requires custom drivers.

USB devices

1. Printers
2. Scanners
3. Mice
4. Joysticks
5. Flight yokes
6. Digital cameras
7. Webcams
8. Scientific data acquisition devices
9. Modems
10. Speakers
11. Telephones
12. Video phones
13. Storage devices such as Zip drives
14. Network connections

USB Mouse

The USB mouse uses the Universal serial bus interface to communicate with computer. With Windows and other Operating Systems that support USB interface, USB has become one of the most advanced (and one of the best) connections around for mice, printers and other peripherals. Installation of USB mouse is quite simple. It's hot-swappable, that means, you need not reboot your machine in order to detect for the mice device by the Operating system. So, you can plug it in even when your computer is running. The mouse is immediately recognized and you can use it right away.

Types of USB Mouse

There are basically three different types of USB mice : mechanical, optomechanical and optical.

The mechanical mouse has a small hard rubber ball underneath that moves against two rollers as it's passed across a flat surface. Mechanical sensors detect the movement of the rollers as an 'x' and 'y' axis and the cursor on screen is moved accordingly.

An optomechanical mouse works on the same principal. The rollers have wheels on the end of them with evenly spaced holes. As the wheels spin, a light-sensitive optical device counts the number of holes that pass by and convert those numbers to an 'x' and 'y' axis. An optical mouse is more accurate or precise and has no moving parts. It uses a laser to detect movement and has to be paired with a special pad or mat that has an embedded optical reference grid.

USB Keyboard

USB keyboards are compatible with Windows computers. The Command key works as the Windows key, the Option key as the Alt key, the Help key as the Insert key, and the Clear key as the Num Lock key. The volume keys function as they would on a Macintosh, and the eject key has no function.

The additional function keys placed where the Print Screen/SysRq, Scroll Lock, and Pause/Break keys are on most IBM PC keyboards (F13/F14 through F15/F16) do not work as those keys in Windows without a special driver.

The USB keyboard can also be used on PlayStation 2 game consoles. The USB keyboard is also combined with a USB hub of two ports. This is a handy feature for using a USB flash drive and other devices.

USB keyboard may hold a hub, so other USB units are connected. Each unit may hold two USB connectors, so they all can be daisy chained.

USB Flash Drivers

USB flash drives are NAND-type flash memory data storage devices integrated with a USB (universal serial bus) interface. They are typically small, lightweight, removable and rewritable. As of November 2006, memory capacities for USB Flash Drives currently are sold from 32 megabytes up to 64 gigabytes. Capacity is limited only by current flash memory densities, although cost per megabyte may increase rapidly at higher capacities due to the expensive components. (USB Memory card readers are also available, whereby rather than being built-in, the memory is a removable Flash memory card housed in what is otherwise a regular USB flash drive, as described below.)

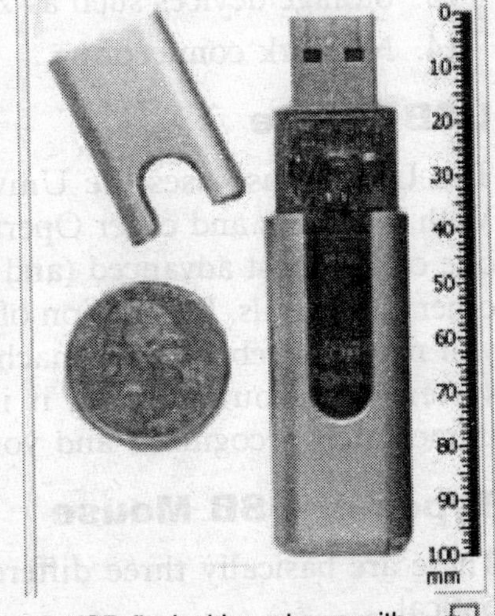

A USB flash drive, shown with a 24 mm U.S. quarter coin for scale.

USB flash drives offer potential advantages over other portable storage devices, particularly the floppy disk. They are more compact, generally faster, hold more data, and are more reliable (due to both their lack of moving parts, and their more durable design) than floppy disks. These types of drives use the USB mass storage standard, supported natively by modern operating systems such as Linux, Mac OS X, Unix, and Windows.

A flash drive consists of a small printed circuit board encased in a plastic or metal casing, making the drive sturdy enough to be carried about in a pocket, as a key fob, or on a lanyard. Only the USB connector protrudes from this protection, and is usually covered by a removable cap. Most flash drives use a standard type-A USB connection allowing them to be connected directly to a port on a personal computer.

To access the data stored in a flash drive, the drive must be connected to a computer, either by plugging it into a USB host controller built into the computer, or into a USB hub. Flash drives are active only when plugged into a USB connection and draw all necessary power from the supply provided by that connection. However, some flash drives, especially high-speed drives utilizing the USB 2.0 standard, may require more power than the limited amount provided by a bus-powered USB hub, such as those built into some computer keyboards or monitors. These drives will not work unless plugged directly into a host controller (i.e., the ports found on the computer itself) or a self-powered hub.

USB 2.0

Its speed reached a performance level sufficient for consumer equipment while retaining compatibility with older devices. An example of how the popularity of USB displaced FireWire in a commercial device is the Apple iPod. It was originally released with a FireWire connector, which was eventually modified to allow for both USB and FireWire connections when the product was released for Windows. 3rd generation iPods used USB and Firewire for data transfer and only allows a FireWire connection to charge the battery from the main adapter. The iPod does charge via both cables when connected to the host computer. With the 4th generation and newer, iPods use USB for data transfer and both USB and Firewire for charging. The Firewire controller chip set has been removed in favour with reduced costs. The iPod Nano and shuffle don't even support Firewire, only supporting USB.

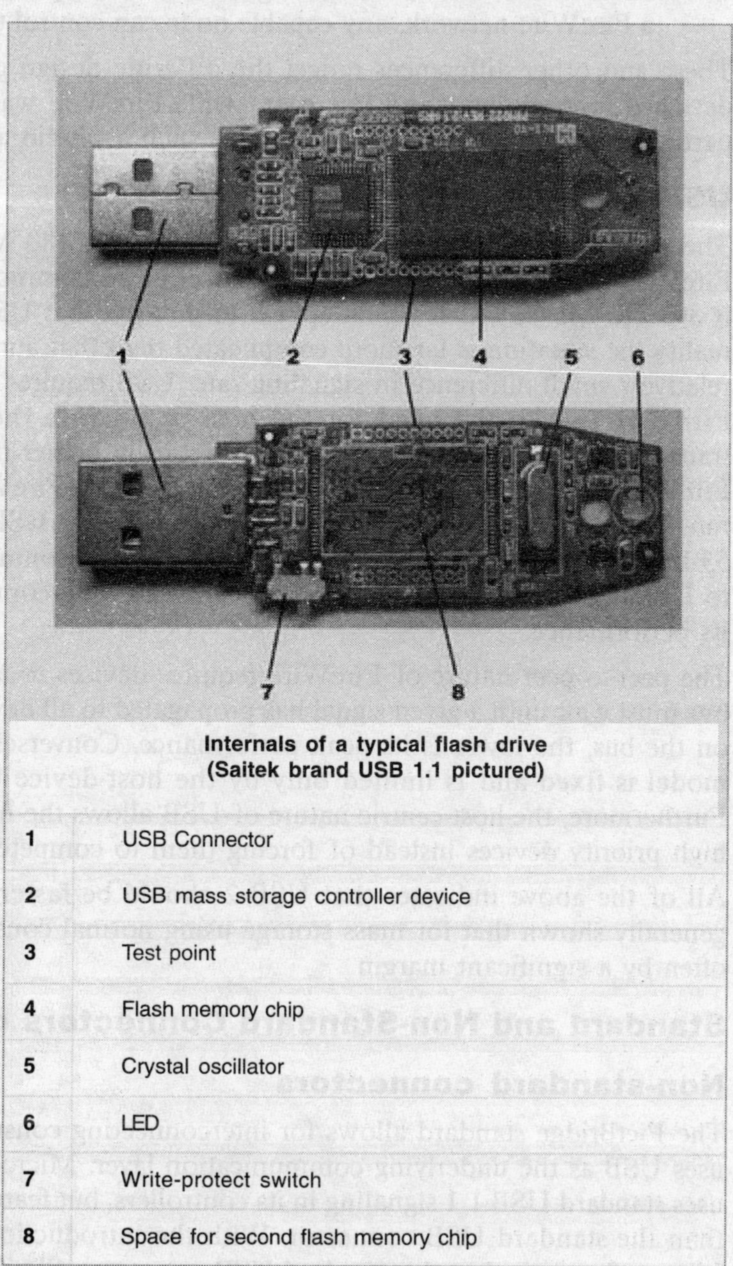

Internals of a typical flash drive (Saitek brand USB 1.1 pictured)

1	USB Connector
2	USB mass storage controller device
3	Test point
4	Flash memory chip
5	Crystal oscillator
6	LED
7	Write-protect switch
8	Space for second flash memory chip

Today, USB Hi-Speed is used in many consumer products. FireWire, however, retains its popularity in areas such as video and audio production.

Technical differences

The most significant technical differences between FireWire and USB include the following:

- USB networks use a tiered-star topology, while FireWire networks use a repeater-based topology.
- USB uses a "speak-when-spoken-to" protocol; peripherals cannot communicate with the host unless the host specifically requests communication. A FireWire device can communicate with any other node at any time, subject to network conditions.
- A USB network relies on a single host at the top of the tree to control the network. In a FireWire network, any capable node can control the network.

These and other differences reflect the differing design goals of the two buses: USB was designed for simplicity and low cost, while FireWire was designed for high performance, particularly in time-sensitive applications such as audio and video.

USB 2.0 Hi-Speed versus FireWire 400

The signaling rate of USB 2.0 Hi-Speed mode is 480 Mb/s, while the signaling rate of FireWire 400 (IEEE 1394a, the slower, yet more common variant of firewire as of 2007) is 393.216 Mb/s, which would appear to indicate that USB should be slightly faster, but in reality the situation is far more complicated than that and other design factors can dwarf a relatively small difference in signaling rate. USB requires more host processing power than FireWire due to the need for the host to provide the arbitration and scheduling of transactions. USB transfer rates are theoretically higher than FireWire due to the need for FireWire devices to arbitrate for bus access. A single FireWire device may achieve a transfer rate for FireWire 400 as high as 41 MB/s, while for USB 2.0 the rate can theoretically be 55 MB/s (for a single device). In a multi-device environment FireWire rapidly loses ground to USB: FireWire's mixed speed networks and long connection chains dramatically affect its performance.

The peer-to-peer nature of FireWire requires devices to arbitrate, which means a FireWire bus must wait until a given signal has propagated to all devices on the bus. The more devices on the bus, the lower is its peak performance. Conversely, for USB the maximum timing model is fixed and is limited only by the host-device branch (not the entire network). Furthermore, the host-centric nature of USB allows the host to allocate more bandwidth to high priority devices instead of forcing them to compete for bandwidth as in FireWire.

All of the above indicates that USB 2 should be faster than firewire 400 but tests have generally shown that for mass storage using normal consumer equipment firewire is faster often by a significant margin.

Standard and Non-Standard Connectors of USB

Non-standard connectors

The PictBridge standard allows for interconnecting consumer imaging devices. It typically uses USB as the underlying communication layer. Microsoft's original Xbox game console uses standard USB 1.1 signaling in its controllers, but features a proprietary connector rather than the standard USB connector. With the introduction of the newer Xbox 360 model, Microsoft switched to the standard USB connector. Similarly, IBM UltraPort uses standard USB signaling, but via a proprietary connection format.

The USB Implementers Forum is working on a wireless networking standard based on the USB protocol. Wireless USB is intended as a cable-replacement technology, and will use Ultra-Wideband wireless technology for data rates of up to 480 Mbit/s. Wireless USB is well suited to wireless connection of PC centric devices, just as Bluetooth is now widely used for mobile phone centric personal networks (at much lower data rates).

Non-standard power

A number of devices use the 5v power supply without participating in a proper USB network. The typical example is a USB-powered reading light; fans, mug heaters, battery chargers (particularly for mobile telephones) and even miniature vacuum cleaners are also available. In most cases, these items contain no digitally based circuitry, and thus are not proper USB devices at all. This can cause problems with some computers—the USB specification requires that devices connect in a low-power mode (100 mA maximum) and state how much current they need, before switching, with the host's permission, into high-power mode. An additional concern is that in addition to limiting the total average power used by the device, the USB specification limits the inrush current (to charge decoupling and bulk capacitors) when the device is first connected; otherwise, connecting a device could cause glitches in the host's internal power.

There are also devices at the host end that are dumb devices that don't support negotiation. A number of companies make battery packs that can power USB powered devices; some provide power, while others pass through the data lines to a host PC. There are also USB AC adapters and DC adapters that can be used to power or charge USB powered devices. Some of these devices can supply up to 1A of power. Without negotiation, the powered USB device is unable to inquire if it is allowed to draw 100mA, 500mA, or 1A. Powered USB uses standard USB signaling with the addition of extra power lines for point-of-sale terminals. It uses 4 additional pins to supply up to 6A at either 5V, 12V, or 24V (depending on keying) to peripheral devices. The wires and contacts on the USB portion have also been upgraded to support higher amperage on the 5V line, as well. This is commonly used in Point of Sale applications and provides enough power to operate stationary barcode scanners, printers, pin pads, and signature capture devices, etc. This standard was developed by IBM, NCR, and FCI/Berg. It is essentially two connectors stacked such that the bottom connector accepts a standard USB plug and the top connector takes a power connector.

Revision

1. USB, Universal Serial Bus, is a protocol that allows two way communcation between peripheral devices and a host computer.
2. A USB cable has four wires: power, ground, D+ and D–.
3. The USB mouse uses the Universal serial bus interface to communicate with computer.
4. USB mouses are of three types: mechanical, optomechanical, and optical.
5. USB keyboards are compatible with Windows computers.
6. USB keyboard may hold a hub, so other USB units are conneted.
7. The mechanical mouse has a small hard rubber ball underneath that moves against two rollers.
8. An optomechnical mouse works on the same principal, the rollers have wheels on the end of them with evenly spaced holes.

9. An optical mouse is more accurate or precise and has no moving parts.

Multiple Choice Questions

1. USB is a _______ device.
   (a) Input (b) Output
   (c) Both
2. USB cable has __ wires:
   (a) 3 (b) 4
   (c) 5
3. USB keyboards are compatible with:
   (a) Windows (b) Linux
   (c) DOS
4. A mechanical mouse has a _____ ball under it:
   (a) rock (b) rubber
   (c) glass
5. Pen drive is based upon:
   (a) Optical technology. (b) Magnetic Storage Technology.
   (c) Semi conductor technology. (d) None of these.

True/False Questions

1. A USB cable has four wires: power, ground, D+ and D–.
2. The USB mouse uses the Universal serial bus interface to communicate with computer.
3. USB keyboards are not compatible with Windows computers.
4. The mechanical mouse has a small hard rubber ball underneath that moves against two rollers.
5. An optical mouse is more accurate or precise and has no moving parts.

Descriptive Questions

1. What is a USB device?
2. What is USB cable made of?
3. How does USB handle software?
4. Which computer devices are available with USB?
5. Describe the working of USB mouse.
6. Describe the various types of USB mouses.
7. What is difference between a normal keyboard and a USB keyboard?

Answers to Objective Type Questions

Multiple Choice Questions

1. c	2. b	3. a	4. b
5. a			

True False Questions

1. T	2. T	3. F	4. T
5. T			

T Model Test Papers

Max. Marks 100

Time: 2.30 Hrs

Model Test Paper 1

PC Architecture and Peripherals - 1

Q.1 Fill in the blanks (1 marks x 10)

1. AZERTY is a .... format
2. CMOS stands for ....
3. DVD stands for ....
4. EPROM stands for ....
5. IDE is ....
6. Mechanical mouse uses ....
7. Optomechanical mouse uses ....
8. RAM stands for ....
9. SCSI is ....
10. USB 2.0 is a ....

(Hardware, Random Access Memory, Rubber Ball, Digital Video Disc, Hard Disk, Complimentary Metal Oxide Semiconductors, Keyboard, Integrated Drive Electronics, Erasable Programable Read Only Memory, Optical sensor, Small Computer System Interface, Software, Read Only Memory)

Q.2 T/F write correct answer in Bracket [] (1 marks x 10)

1. ROM is Read Over Memory. [ ]
2. Laptop computers are also very popular these days. [ ]
3. Display card generates and sends sound to a output. [ ]
4. A magneto-optical disk has the high-volume capacity of an optical disk but can be written over as a magnetic disk. [ ]
5. Computers have a few built in interfaces called ports. [ ]
6. On a band printer, several similar sets of fully formed characters are embossed on a horizontal band that is continuously moving in front of the print hammers. [ ]
7. RAM is Random Access Memory . [ ]
8. There are seven generation of computers. [ ]

9. NLX. known as New Low Profile Extended, motherboard has been a form factor in use with desktops for quite some time. [ ]
10. Optical disk technology is still emerging and has yet to stabilize; however at present there are three different types of optical disks in common use: read-only, recordable, and erasable. [ ]

Q.3 Multiple Choice Questions (1 marks x 10)

1. CPU contains Primary Storage, Arithmetic Logic Unit and
   (a) Control Unit (b) Data Unit
   (c) Alpha Unit
2. The three main units of computer are: Keyboard, Central Processing Unit and :
   (a) Monitor (b) Mouse
   (c) Motherboard
3. PC XT ran on Intel ____ processor.
   (a) 8086 (b) 80286
   (c) 8088
4. Every new floppy disk has to be _______.
   (a) stored (b) formatted
   (c) labelled
5. Magnetic tapes are used in:
   (a) Personal Computers (b) Mainframe Computers
   (c) Laptops
6. Mouse can be used by clicking, double-clicking and :
   (a) biting (b) eating
   (c) dragging
7. Line printers print a at a time.
   (a) character (b) dot
   (c) line
8. Which of the following does not belong to the Intel's Processor's series:
   (a) 8086 (b) 80186
   (c) 80486 (d) 8051
9. Pen drive is based upon:
   (a) Optical technology. (b) Magnetic Storage Technology.
   (c) Semi conductor technology. (d) None of these.
10. Zip drive is used for:
   (a) Storage (b) Input
   (b) Output

Q.4 Short answer type questions (2 marks x 10)

1. What is Random Access Memory? Explain its construction.
2. What is BIOS?

3. Describe the personal computer.
4. Which are the main parts of computers?
5. What is Central Processing Unit?
6. What is POST?
7. What all POST checks?
8. How the storage capacity is calulated of magnetic media?
9. Why SCSI hard disk is costly than IDE hard disk?
10. Draw back panel of CD ROM drive.

Do any five of the following

Q.5 Answer the following: (5 x 2 Marks)

(a) Which are the main parts of computers?

(b) Describe the various generations of computers.

Q.6 Answer the following: (5 x 2 Marks)

(a) How did PC XT worked?

(b) What do the following cards do: Display card, Sound card, Network card, TV Tuner card, and IDE card?

Q.7 Answer the following: (5 x 2 Marks)

(a) How the data is written on the floppy disks?

(b) Describe the working of Magnetic Tape.

Q.8 Answer the following: (5 x 2 Marks)

(a) How mouse works?

(b) Describe the various types of ports.

Q.9 Answer the following: (5 x 2 Marks)

(a) Describe the working of Daisywheel printers.

(b) Which are the different type of scanners?

Q.10 Answer the following: (5 x 2 Marks)

(a) What changes have been brought about in computer over the ages?

(b) What is Central Processing Unit?

Q.11 Answer the following: (5 x 2 Marks)

(a) Describe the various uses of the motherboard.

(b) Describe the following: ATX, LPX and NLX motherboards.

Q.12 Answer the following: (5 x 2 Marks)

(a) What do you understand by Access Time?

(b) Describe the working of DVD.

Answers to Objective Type Questions

Fill in the blanks

1. Keyboard
2. Complimentary Metal Oxide Semiconductor
3. Digital Video Disc
4. Erasable Programable Read Only Memory
5. Integrated Drive Electronics
6. Rubber Ball
7. Optical sensor
8. Random Access Memory
9. Small Computer System Interface
10. Software

True False Questions

1. T	2. T	3. F	4. T
5. T	6. T	7. T	8. F
9. T	10. T		

Multiple Choice Questions

1. a	2. a	3. a	4. b
5. b	6. c	7. c	8. d
9. a	10. a		

Max. Marks 100

Time: 2.30 Hrs

Model Test Paper 2

PC Architecture and Peripherals - 1

Q.1 Fill in the blanks (1 marks x 10)

1. .... is used to protect a floppy
2. CD ROM stands for ....
3. Dot Matrix Printers use .... to print
4. EEPROM stands for ....
5. FM stands for ....
6. Line printers print a ....
7. Optical mouse uses ....
8. PROM stand for ....
9. ROM stands for ....
10. Total number of bytes/sector is ....

(Line, Dots, Write Protect Notch, 512 bytes, Compact Disc Read Only Memory, Optical Sensor, Electronically Erasable Programmable Read Only Memory, Parallel, Frequency Module, Programmable Read Only Memory, Read Only Memory, Hard disk, USB)

Q.2 T/F write correct answer in Bracket [] (1 marks x 10)

1. The main keys on the keyboard are: Alphabetic keys, Numeric keys, Function keys, and Arrow keys. [ ]
2. Chain printer is a high-speed printer in which the type are carried by the links of a revolving chain. [ ]
3. An optical mouse is more accurate or precise and has no moving parts. [ ]
4. There are various types of memories which are used by computers. [ ]
5. The development of computers have been classified in the form of generations. [ ]
6. ATX motherboard had better cooling capacity. [ ]
7. POST card is used to diagnose the cards of the computer. [ ]
8. New floppy disk need not be formatted. [ ]
9. Keyboard is the main ouput device of the computer. [ ]
10. Daisy Wheel Printers are faster than dot-matrix printers, and they produce a high-resolution output. [ ]

Q.3 Multiple Choice Questions (1 marks x 10)

1. USB keyboards are compatible with:

   (a) Windows (b) Linux

   (c) DOS

2. RAM consists of binary numbers 1s and :
   (a) 0s (b) 2s
   (c) 3s
3. Computers are classified into ______ generations:
   (a) 7 (b) 3
   (c) 5
4. PC-ATs full form of:
   (a) Personal Computer Area Technology
   (b) Personal Computer Advanced Technology
   (c) Personal Computer Advanced Techniques
5. Program which checks for errors on the various cards is called:
   (a) POST (b) POP
   (c) MAIL
6. There are two types of floppies 5¼ and ____:
   (a) 3½ (b) 3¼
   (c) 5½
7. FM stand for:
   (a) Frequent Module (b) Frequency Module
   (c) Frequency Modulation
8. Video Output for monitor is obtained from .... card.
   (a) Sound card (b) Network card
   (c) Display card
9. Which one is optical storage media:
   (a) HDD (b) Floppy disk
   (c) Pen drive (d) DVD.
10. DMP stands for:
   (a) Dot Matrix Printer (b) Dot Multiple Printer
   (c) Dual Matrix Printer

Q.4 Short answer type questions (2 marks x 10)

1. What is access time of hard disk?
2. What is SCSI hard disk?
3. What is multimedia keyboard?
4. Describe the various types of mouse.
5. Describe the various type of keys on the keyboard.
6. How would you install a keyboard?
7. Describe the various type of printers.
8. Which are Electrostatic Printers?

9. Describe the working of Flat-bed scanner.
10. What is Random Access Memory? Explain its construction.

Do any five of the following

Q.5 Answer the following: **(5 x 2 Marks)**

(a) Describe the various types of mouse.
(b) How would you install a keyboard?

Q.6 Answer the following: **(5 x 2 Marks)**

(a) What are the advantages and disadvantages of Dot Matrix Printers?
(b) Which are Electrostatic Printers?

Q.7 Answer the following: **(5 x 2 Marks)**

(a) Describe the personal computer.
(b) Describe the various peripherals used in PC, PC-XT and PC-AT.

Q.8 Answer the following: **(5 x 2 Marks)**

(a) Describe the various components inside the main computer system.
(b) Describe the working of PC AT.

Q.9 Answer the following: **(5 x 2 Marks)**

(a) Describe the working of Hard Disk.
(b) Why are CD-ROM preferred over the floppy disks?

Q.10 Answer the following: **(5 x 2 Marks)**

(a) What is mouse used for?
(b) Describe the process of troubleshooting the mouse.

Q.11 Answer the following: **(5 x 2 Marks)**

(a) Describe the various type of printers.
(b) What are Chain, Band and Drum printers?

Q.12 Answer the following: **(5 x 2 Marks)**

(a) Which type of memories are used by personal computers?
(b) Describe the various classifications of computers.

Answers to Objective Type Questions

Fill in the blanks

1. Write Protect Notch
2. Compact Disc Read Only Memory
3. Dots
4. Electronically Erasable Programmable Read Only Memory
5. Frequency Module
6. Line
7. Optical Sensor
8. Programmable Read Only Memory
9. Read Only Memory
10. 512 bytes

True False Questions

1. T 2. T 3. T 4. T
5. T 6. T 7. T 8. F
9. F 10. F

Multiple Choice Questions

1. a 2. a 3. c 4. b
5. a 6. a 7. b 8. c
9. d 10. a

Max. Marks 100

Time: 2.30 Hrs

Model Test Paper 3

PC Architecture and Peripherals - 1

Q.1 Fill in the blanks (1 marks x 10)

1. .... card is used to give video output
2. BIOS stands for ....
3. Disk Access Time is part of ....
4. DVORAK is a .... format
5. ESDI is ....
6. Laser printer uses .... to print
7. MFM stands for ....
8. Plotter is used for ....
9. RIMM is ....
10. Seek time is used in ....

(Serial, Keyboard, Display, Laser beam, Basic Input Output System, Enhanced Small Device Interface, Rambus Inline Memory Module, 1 GB, Parallel, Hard Disk, Plotting, Modified Frequency Modulation, Hard Disk, Platter)

Q.2 T/F write correct answer in Bracket [] (1 marks x 10)

1. The mechanical mouse has a small hard rubber ball underneath that moves against two rollers. [ ]
2. Over the years personal computers have gone through various changes and have been named as XT, AT, etc. [ ]
3. The Central Processing Unit has: Primary Storage Unit, Arithmetic Logic Unit, Control Unit and Output Unit. [ ]
4. It supported 16 MB of memory at the most. [ ]
5. A TV Tuner card is a computer component that allows television signals to be received by a computer. [ ]
6. The 3.5 inch size floppy disk come in three capacities: double density, high density and very high density. [ ]
7. SCSI drive is a fast bus that can be connected to lot of drives to a computer at the same time. [ ]
8. Mouse can be used by clicking, double-clicking and dragging. [ ]
9. Dot-matrix printers are also called serial printers. [ ]
10. There are two types of scanners, Hand-held scanner and Flat-bed scanner. [ ]

Q.3 Multiple Choice Questions (1 marks x 10)

1. The mouse which is now commonly used is:

   (a) Optical (b) Optomechanical

(c) Mechanical

2. Dot matrix printers are so called because they print characters in terms of :

(a) Squares (b) Dots

(c) Circles

3. USB cable has __ wires:

(a) 3 (b) 4

(c) 5

4. RAM stands for:

(a) Random Allowed Memory (b) Ready Access Memory

(c) Random Access Memory

5. Data stored in ROM cannot be changed:

(a) Yes (b) No

6. LPX stands for:

(a) Low Profile Extended (b) Low Period Extended

(c) Low Profile Extra

7. Maximum memory in PC AT could be ___ MB:

(a) 8 (b) 16

(c) 32

8. Formatting is the process of arranging:

(a) Tracks (b) Sectors

(c) Both (a) and (b) (d) None of these.

9. Serial connector is of .... pins.

(a) 9 pin (b) 16 pin

(c) 20 pin

10. A modem performs

(a) Modulation (b) Demodulation

(c) Analog to digital and digital to analog conversion

(d) All of these.

Q.4 Short answer type questions (2 marks x 10)

1. What is BIOS?
2. Describe the personal computer.
3. Which are the main parts of computers?
4. What is Central Processing Unit?
5. What is POST?
6. What all POST checks?
7. How the storage capacity is calulated of magnetic media?
8. Why SCSI hard disk is costly than IDE hard disk?
9. Draw back panel of CD ROM drive.

10. What is access time of hard disk?

Do any five of the following

Q.5 Answer the following: **(5 x 2 Marks)**

(a) What all was there on PC AT motherboard?

(b) What is POST?

Q.6 Answer the following: **(5 x 2 Marks)**

(a) What are Optical Disks?

(b) What do you understand by FM and MFM?

Q.7 Answer the following: **(5 x 2 Marks)**

(a) Describe the various type of keys on the keyboard.

(b) How a modem works?

Q.8 Answer the following: **(5 x 2 Marks)**

(a) What are the advantages and disadvantages of using Ink-jet printers?

(b) Describe the working of Flat-bed scanner.

Q.9 Answer the following: **(5 x 2 Marks)**

(a) What all POST checks?

(b) Give the difference between RAM and ROM.

Q.10 Answer the following: **(5 x 2 Marks)**

(a) Write a short note on various types of storage devices.

(b) Explain the types of HDD available in the market along with the difference.

Q.11 Answer the following: **(5 x 2 Marks)**

(a) What is microprocessor? Explain its working.

(b) Explain the working of FDD.

Q.12 Answer the following: **(5 x 2 Marks)**

(a) Explain the working of a Keyboard.

(b) Explain the construction of various print heads of DMP printer.

Answers to Objective Type Questions

Fill in the blanks

1. Display
2. Basic Input Output System
3. Hard Disk
4. Keyboard
5. Enhanced Small Device Interface
6. Laser beam
7. Modified Frequency Modulation
8. Plotting
9. Rambus Inline Memory Module
10. Hard Disk

True False Questions

1. T	2. T	3. T	4. T
5. T	6. T	7. T	8. T
9. T	10. T		

Multiple Choice Questions

1. b	2. b	3. b	4. c
5. a	6. a	7. b	8. c
9. b	10. d		

Max. Marks 100

Time: 2.30 Hrs

Model Test Paper 4

PC Architecture and Peripherals - 1

Q.1 Fill in the blanks (1 marks x 10).

1. .... is used to protect a floppy
2. BIOS stands for ....
3. CMOS stands for ....
4. Dot Matrix Printers print ....
5. DVORAK is a .... format
6. EPROM stands for ....
7. FM stands for ....
8. Laser printer uses .... to print
9. Mechanical mouse uses ....
10. Optical mouse uses ....

(Complimentary Metal Oxide Semiconductors, Frequency Modulation, Write Protect Notch, Rubber ball, Dot Matrix Printer, Dots, Basic Input Output System, Keyboard, Laser beam, Optical sensor, Erasable Programable Read Only Memory,)

Q.2 T/F write correct answer in Bracket [] (1 marks x 10)

1. USB keyboards are not compatible with Windows computers. [ ]
2. The block diagram shows all the parts of the computer. [ ]
3. Personal computers are known for their speed, reliability and accuracy. [ ]
4. PC/AT, known as Advanced Technology of Personal Computer, used Intel 8088 microprocessor. [ ]
5. A Network card allows computers to communicate over a computer network. [ ]
6. There are two kinds of floppies, 3¼" and 5½" in sizes. [ ]
7. Zip disks are slightly larger than conventional floppy disks. [ ]
8. There are three basic types of Mouse: Mechanical Mouse, Optomechanical Mouse and Optical Mouse. [ ]
9. The modem is a device which allows you to connect your computer to any other computer, anywhere else in the world using a telephone line. [ ]
10. There are two main types of printers: Impact and Non impact printers. [ ]

Q.3 Multiple Choice Questions (1 marks x 10)

1. Hard disk is a _______ device.

   (a) Storage (b) Display

   (c) Removable

2. DVD stands for:
   (a) Direct Video Disc (b) Data Video Disc
   (c) Digital Video Disc
3. Mouse is a _______ device.
   (a) Input (b) Pointing
   (c) Output
4. The main keys of the Keyboard are Alphabetic, Arrows, Numeric and :
   (a) Function (b) Future
   (c) Faulty
5. Printer is a _______ device.
   (a) Input (b) Pointing
   (c) Output
6. Full form of LASER is:
   (a) Light Amplification by Stimulate Emission of Radiation
   (b) Low Amplification by Stimulate Emission of Radiation
   (c) Light Around by Stimulate Emission of Radiation
7. USB is a _______ device.
   (a) Input (b) Output
   (c) Both
8. Fastest communication port available is ....
   (a) Parallel (b) Serial
   (c) USB
9. Which of the following is not print-head standard:
   (a) 9 pin (b) 18 pin.
   (c) 24 pin. (d) 16 pin.
10. Formatting is the process of arranging:
   (a) Tracks (b) Sectors
   (c) Both (a) and (b) (d) None of these.

Q.4 Short answer type questions (2 marks x 10)

1. What is SCSI hard disk?
2. What is multimedia keyboard?
3. Describe the various types of mouse.
4. Describe the various type of keys on the keyboard.
5. How would you install a keyboard?
6. Describe the various type of printers.
7. Which are Electrostatic Printers?
8. Describe the working of Flat-bed scanner.
9. What is Random Access Memory? Explain its construction.

10. What is BIOS?

Do any five of the following

Q.5 Answer the following: (5 x 2 Marks)

(a) Describe the various generations of computers.

(b) What do the following cards do: Display card, Sound card, Network card, TV Tuner card, and IDE card?

Q.6 Answer the following: (5 x 2 Marks)

(a) Describe the working of Magnetic Tape.

(b) Describe the various types of ports.

Q.7 Answer the following: (5 x 2 Marks)

(a) Which are the different type of scanners?

(b) What is Central Processing Unit?

Q.8 Answer the following: (5 x 2 Marks)

(a) Describe the following: ATX, LPX and NLX motherboards.

(b) Describe the working of DVD.

Q.9 Answer the following: (5 x 2 Marks)

(a) How would you install a keyboard?

(b) Which are Electrostatic Printers?

Q.10 Answer the following: (5 x 2 Marks)

(a) Describe the various peripherals used in PC, PC-XT and PC-AT.

(b) Describe the working of PC AT.

Q.11 Answer the following: (5 x 2 Marks)

(a) Why are CD-ROM preferred over the floppy disks?

(b) Describe the process of troubleshooting the mouse.

Q.12 Answer the following: (5 x 2 Marks)

(a) What are Chain, Band and Drum printers?

(b) Describe the various classifications of computers.

Answers to Objective Type Questions

Fill in the blanks

1. Write Protect Notch
2. Basic Input Output System
3. Complimentary Metal Oxide Semiconductors
4. Dots
5. Keyboard
6. Erasable Programable Read Only Memory
7. Frequency Modulation
8. Laser beam
9. Rubber ball
10. Optical sensor

True False Questions

1. F	2. T	3. T	4. F
5. T	6. F	7. T	8. T
9. T	10. T		

Multiple Choice Questions

1. a	2. c	3. b	4. a
5. c	6. a	7. c	8. c
9. b	10. c		

Max. Marks 100

Time: 2.30 Hrs

Model Test Paper 5

PC Architecture and Peripherals - 1

Q.1 Fill in the blanks (1 marks x 10)

1. Plotter is used for ....
2. RAM stands for ....
3. ROM stands for ....
4. Seek time is used in ....
5. USB 2.0 is a ....
6. USB stands for ....
7. Zip drives are used for ....
8. IDE is ....
9. FM stands for ....
10. ESDI is ....

(Software, Hard Disk, Plotting, Universal Serial Bus, Random Access Memory, Storing data, Read Only Memory, Frequency Modulation, Integrated Drive Electronics, Enhanced Small Device Interface, Hard disk, Floppy drive)

Q.2 T/F write correct answer in Bracket [] (1 marks x 10)

1. Electrostatic printers are devices in which the parts of paper which are to be printed are electrostatically charged, and attract a fine dust which is then fused to the paper by the application of heat. [ ]
2. The USB mouse uses the Universal serial bus interface to communicate with computer. [ ]
3. The main parts of the computer are: Mouse, Central Processing Unit and Keyboard. [ ]
4. ROM can be of the type: PROM, EPROM, and EEPROM. [ ]
5. The original PC/XT used an Intel 8088 processor running at a speed of 4.77 MHz. [ ]
6. A Sound card can input and output sound under control of computer programs. [ ]
7. Access time is the interval between the instant a computer makes a request for transfer of data from a disk-storage device to RAM and the instant this operation is completed. [ ]
8. Magnetic tape units are used with laptop computers. [ ]
9. Mouse is an input device. [ ]
10. A 25-pin or 9-pin D-shell subminiature male connector is used on the system as connector for the serial interface. [ ]

Q.3 Multiple Choice Questions (1 marks x 10)

1. A mechanical mouse has a ____ ball under it:

   (a) rock (b) rubber

(c) glass

2. A copy of the current instruction is stored in:

(a) Instruction Register (b) Working Register
(c) General Register

3. Display card generates:

(a) Text (b) Sound
(c) Graphics

4. CD-ROM stand for:

(a) Current Disk Read Only Memory (b) Compact Disk Read Only Memory
(c) Close Disk Read Only Memory

5. A male connector for the serial interface can have 9 or __ pin:

(a) 30 (b) 20
(c) 25

6. The two scanners known are Hand held and :

(a) mouse held (b) Flat bed
(c) print bed

7. Printer is a

(a) Communcation equipment (b) Input device.
(c) Output device. (d) Processing device.

8. LASER printer's drum is charged with:

(a) –300 V (b) +300 V
(c) –600 V (d) +600 V

9. Which of the following does not belong to the Intel's Processor's series:

(a) 8086 (b) 80186
(c) 80486 (d) 8051

10. Which one is optical storage media:

(a) HDD (b) Floppy disk
(c) Pen drive (d) DVD.

Q.4 Short answer type questions (2 marks x 10)

1. Which are the main parts of computers?
2. What is Central Processing Unit?
3. What all POST checks?
4. How the storage capacity is calulated of magnetic media?
5. Draw back panel of CD ROM drive.
6. What is access time of hard disk?
7. What is multimedia keyboard?
8. Describe the various types of mouse.
9. How would you install a keyboard?

10. Describe the various type of printers.

Do any five of the following

Q.5 Answer the following: (5 x 2 Marks)

(a) What is POST?

(b) What do you understand by FM and MFM?

Q.6 Answer the following: (5 x 2 Marks)

(a) How a modem works?

(b) Describe the working of Flat-bed scanner.

Q.7 Answer the following: (5 x 2 Marks)

(a) How the data is written on the floppy disks?

(b) Describe the working of Magnetic Tape.

Q.8 Answer the following: (5 x 2 Marks)

(a) What do you understand by Access Time?

(b) Describe the working of DVD.

Q.9 Answer the following: (5 x 2 Marks)

(a) Describe the working of Hard Disk.

(b) Why are CD-ROM preferred over the floppy disks?

Q.10 Answer the following: (5 x 2 Marks)

(a) What are the advantages and disadvantages of Dot Matrix Printers?

(b) Which are Electrostatic Printers?

Q.11 Answer the following: (5 x 2 Marks)

(a) What are Optical Disks?

(b) What do you understand by FM and MFM?

Q.12 Answer the following: (5 x 2 Marks)

(a) Describe the following: ATX, LPX and NLX motherboards.

(b) Describe the working of DVD.

Answers to Objective Type Questions

Fill in the blanks

1. Plotting
2. Random Access Memory
3. Read Only Memory
4. Hard Disk
5. Software
6. Universal Serial Bus
7. Storing data
8. Integrated Drive Electronics
9. Frequency Modulation
10. Enhanced Small Device Interface

True False Questions

1. T	2. T	3. F	4. T
5. T	6. T	7. T	8. F
9. F	10. T		

Multiple Choice Questions

1. b	2. a	3. c	4. b
5. b	6. b	7. c	8. d
9. d	10. d		

FIREWALL MEDIA

(An imprint of Laxmi Publications Pvt. Ltd.)

Computer Books *for School, BCA, MCA, IGNOU, DOEACC and Engineering Students and Professionals*

ISBN	TITLE	AUTHOR	PRICE	PAGES
	.NET			
8170087155	**Building Business Intelligence Applications with .Net**	Robert Ericsson	Rs. 295.00	404
8170083567	**Learning VB.Net Through Applications**	Clayton Crooks	Rs. 295.00	450
8131800865	**Magic of C# with .Net Frame Work**	Shibi Panikkar, Kumar Sanjeev	Rs. 495.00	950
8170082471	**Magic of ASP.Net with C#**	Shibi Panikkar, Kumar Sanjeev	Rs. 395.00	828
8170089662	**ASP.Net Interview Questions and Answers**	J. Rajaram	Rs. 95.00	175
	A TO Z SERIES			
8170083214	**Access 2002 from A to Z**	Julia Kelly, Stephen L. Nelson	Rs. 75.00	185
8170083222	**Excel 2002 from A to Z**	Stephen L. Nelson	Rs. 75.00	193
8170083230	**Front Page 2002 from A to Z**	Heather Williamson	Rs. 85.00	219
8170083249	**Outlook 2002 from A to Z**	Stephen L. Nelson	Rs. 75.00	202
8170083257	**Page Maker 7 from A to Z**	Marc Campbell	Rs. 75.00	202
8170083265	**PowerPoint 2002 from A to Z**	Stephen L. Nelson	Rs. 75.00	202
8170083273	**Windows XP from A to Z**	Pat Coleman	Rs. 95.00	249
8170083281	**Word 2002 from A to Z**	Stephen L. Nelson	Rs. 75.00	199
817008329X	**XML from A to Z**	Heather Williamson	Rs. 75.00	200
8170083303	**Dreamweaver 4 from A to Z**	Heather Williamson	Rs. 85.00	215
	BEGINNERS & GENERAL INTEREST			
817008248X	**Shortcuts to Success in Computing**	Dheeraj Mehrotra	Rs. 55.00	110
8170083311	**Pictorial Computer Dictionary**	Dheeraj Mehrotra	Rs. 45.00	156
8170083486	**Pocket Net Browser**	Dheeraj Mehrotra	Rs. 95.00	302
8170084261	**1000 IT Quizzes**	Dheeraj Mehrotra	Rs. 75.00	120
8131800679	**Information Technology Bible**	Remesh Bangia	Rs. 295.00	567
8131800377	**Fundamentals of Information Technology Including MS Office**	Dinesh Maidasani, Jai Narayan Yadav	Rs. 175.00	356
813180089X	**Fundamentals of Information Technology Including MS Office (Hindi Medium)**	Dinesh Maidasani, Jai Narayan Yadav	Rs. 175.00	425
8170089719	**Foundations of Computer Science**	Ashok Arora	Rs. 250.00	386

Please write for a free color Firewall Media Catalog for details on the above books.

ISBN	TITLE	AUTHOR	PRICE	PAGES
	CALL CENTERS			
8170082196	Call Centers Made Easy	Stephen Medcroft	Rs. 195.00	310
	CISCO			
8170087481	Enabling IP Routing with Cisco Routers	R. Das, K. Chakrabarty	Rs. 295.00	486
817008749X	Designing Networks with Cisco	H. Pasricha, D. Jagu	Rs. 195.00	316
8170087503	Cisco IP Routing Protocols: Troubleshooting Techniques	V. Anand, K. Chakrabarty	Rs. 295.00	409
	DATABASES			
8170089530	DBMS—Complete Practical Approach	Sharad Maheshwari, Ruchin Jain	Rs. 350.00	656
8170082404	Learn to Program Visual Basic-Examples	John Smiley	Rs. 295.00	482
8170082412	Learn to Program Visual Basic-Databases	John Smiley	Rs. 325.00	653
8170082420	Learn to Program Visual Basic-Objects	John Smiley	Rs. 325.00	670
817008475X	IT Resources-Access 2002 VBA Programming Access	Michele Amelot	Rs. 195.00	424
8170084512	The Power of Oracle 9i	Rajiv Parida, Vinod Sharma	Rs. 475.00	1035
8170088518	Principles and Implementation of Data Warehousing	Rajiv A. Parida	Rs. 295.00	487
817008864X	DBA Study Guide OCP Prep Guide	Nazar Abdul	Rs. 295.00	474
8170088658	Oracle 11i—The Complete Reference	Rashmi Anandi	Rs. 495.00	975
8131800067	Toxonomy of Database Management System	Aditya Kumar Gupta	Rs. 75.00	146
8131800385	Introduction to SQL and PL/SQL	Sharad Maheshwari, Ruchin Jain	Rs. 200.00	389
	DOEACC 'O' LEVEL			
8170088089	DOEACC 'O' Level Model Test Papers	Ramesh Bangia	Rs. 175.00	296
8170089115	DOEACC 'O' & 'A' Level Programming & Problem Solving Through 'C' Language (Model Test Paper with Solutions)	Mukesh Sharma	Rs. 95.00	213
8170089069	DOEACC 'O' & 'A' Level Business Systems (Model Test Paper with Solutions)	Mukesh Sharma	Rs. 100.00	252
8170085640	Programming and Problem Solving Through "C" Language	Harsha Priya, R. Ranjeet	Rs. 95.00	306

Please write for a free color Firewall Media Catalog for details on the above books.

ISBN	TITLE	AUTHOR	PRICE	PAGES
8170084474	**IT Tools and Applications**	Ramesh Bangia	Rs. 145.00	370
8170085594	**Business Systems**	Ramesh Bangia	Rs. 175.00	452
8170089514	**Internet & Web Design**	Ramesh Bangia	Rs. 150.00	300

ELECTRONIC COMMERCE

ISBN	TITLE	AUTHOR	PRICE	PAGES
8170085497	**Electronic Commerce**	Pete Loshin, John Vacca	Rs. 295.00	472
817008119X	**E-Commerce**	Mamta Bhusry	Rs. 95.00	215
8170083524	**Marketing in the Cyber Age**	Kurt Rohner	Rs. 295.00	223

HARDWARE/EMBEDDED SYSTEMS

ISBN	TITLE	AUTHOR	PRICE	PAGES
8170087473	**Essential Electronics for PC Technicians**	John W. Farber	Rs. 295.00	546
8170086264	**Grid Computing: A Practical Guide to Technology and Applications**	Ahmar Abbas	Rs. 295.00	408
8170088186	**CD Cracking Uncovered Protection Against Unsanctioned CD Copy**	Kris Kaspersky	Rs. 295.00	422
8170083435	**Practical Linux Programming: Device Drivers, Embedded Systems and the Internet**	Ashfaq A. Khan	Rs. 295.00	420
8170083575	**TCP/IP Application Layer Protocols for Embedded Systems**	M. Tim Jones	Rs. 295.00	460
8131800520	**PC Repair and Maintenance : A Practical Guide**	Joel Rosenthal, Kevin Irwin	Rs. 195.00	362
8131800768	**The A+ Certification and PC Repair Handbook**	Christopher A Crayton, Joel Z. Rosenthal	Rs. 495.00	888

INTERNET & WEB TECHNOLOGY

ISBN	TITLE	AUTHOR	PRICE	PAGES
8170083206	**The Internet Handbook for Writers, Students and Teachers**	Mary McGuire, Linda Stilborne	Rs. 195.00	276
8170084776	**Way in-Internet Getting Started**	Elizabeth Bramire	Rs. 95.00	165
8170088976	**Web Technology**	Ramesh Bangia	Rs. 250.00	560
8170087163	**Web Design with Macromedia Studio MX 2004**	Eric Hunley	Rs. 295.00	558
8170083400	**Professional Web Design (Techniques and Templates)**	Clint Eccher	Rs. 295.00	425
8170088046	**HTML, XHTML, CSS and XML**	Teodoru Gugoiu	Rs. 195.00	355
8170083583	**FrontPage 2000 for Visual Learners**	Chris Charuhas	Rs. 95.00	200
8170083591	**HTML & Java Script for Visual Learners**	Chris Charuhas	Rs. 95.00	200

ISBN	TITLE	AUTHOR	PRICE	PAGES
8170083605	**The Visual Learners Guide to Managing Web Projects**	Chris Charuhas	Rs. 95.00	130
8170083613	**Dreamweaver 4 for Visual Learners**	Chris Charuhas	Rs. 95.00	200
8170084768	**IT Resource-Implementing XML: Managing and Formatting Data**	Johhny Brochard	Rs. 125.00	279
8170089476	**Design Your Web World**	Sunil Jalota	Rs. 75.00	146

KEEPING AHEAD SERIES

ISBN	TITLE	AUTHOR	PRICE	PAGES
8170084652	**Keeping Ahead-Exchange 2000 Server**	Philippe Levesque	Rs. 145.00	285
8170084660	**Keeping Ahead-Windows 2000 Professional**	Jose Dardoigne	Rs. 175.00	388
8170084679	**Keeping Ahead-Windows 2000 Server**	Philippe Mathon	Rs. 175.00	360
8170084687	**Keeping Ahead-Linux Administration Kernel Version 2.0 to 2.2**	Bruno Guèrin	Rs. 125.00	240
8170084695	**Keeping Ahead-Using Linux Kernel Version 2.0 to 2.2**	Bruno Guèrin	Rs. 125.00	258
8170084709	**Keeping Ahead-Java 2**	Benjamin Aumaille	Rs. 145.00	284
8170084717	**Keeping Ahead-SQL Server 7**	Joelle Mosset	Rs. 145.00	329
8170084725	**Keeping Ahead-JavaScript and VBScript**	Benjamin Aumaille	Rs. 145.00	313
8170084733	**Keeping Ahead-C++ Programming Language**	Bruno Dubois	Rs. 125.00	234
8170084741	**Keeping Ahead-TCP/IP in the NT Environment**	Bruno Ferec	Rs. 125.00	230

MCSE

ISBN	TITLE	AUTHOR	PRICE	PAGES
817008489X	**MCSE-Administering SQL Server 7.0**	Jerome Gabillaud	Rs. 295.00	580
8170084903	**MCSE-Networking Essentials**	Jose Dordoigne	Rs. 245.00	453
8170084911	**MCSE-Windows 2000 Professional**	Jose Dordoigne	Rs. 325.00	665
817008492X	**MCSE-Windows 2000 Server**	Phillippe Mathon	Rs. 345.00	712

MULTIMEDIA AND ANIMATION

ISBN	TITLE	AUTHOR	PRICE	PAGES
8170088208	**3DS Max 6 Animation with Character Studio 4 and Plug-Ins**	Boris Kulagin, Dmitry Morozov	Rs. 175.00	216

Please write for a free color Firewall Media Catalog for details on the above books.

ISBN	TITLE	AUTHOR	PRICE	PAGES
8170088216	**Adobe Audition: Soundtracks for Digital Video**	Roman Petelin, Yury Petelin	Rs. 195.00	278
8170086205	**Building A Digital Human**	Ken Brilliant	Rs. 295.00	380
8170086213	**Making Digital Videos**	Ben Long	Rs. 295.00	284
8170087171	**Illustrating with Macromedia Flash ™ MX2004**	Robert Firbaugh	Rs. 245.00	366
8170082439	**Multimedia Basics-Technology (Vol. I)**	Andreas Holzinger	Rs. 195.00	312
8170082447	**Multimedia Basics-Learning (Vol. II)**	Andreas Holzinger	Rs. 195.00	326
8170082455	**Multimedia Basics-Design (Vol. III)**	Andreas Holzinger	Rs. 195.00	280
8170083532	**Maya Feature Creature Creations**	Todd Palamar	Rs. 295.00	376
8170083540	**Sound Forge Power**	Scott R. Garrigus	Rs. 195.00	344
8131800288	**Multimedia and Web Technology**	Ramesh Bangia	Rs. 395.00	878
813180044X	**Photoshop CS**	Shruti Lal	Rs. 195.00	434

NETWORKING

ISBN	TITLE	AUTHOR	PRICE	PAGES
817008721X	**Networking Essentials**	Jose Dordoigne	Rs. 195.00	453
8170089328	**TCP/IP Distributed System**	Vivek Acharya	Rs. 250.00	474
8170087023	**Computer Networks**	Ajit Kumar Singh	Rs. 95.00	181
8131800148	**The Real—world Network Troubleshooting Manual**	Alan Sugano	Rs. 295.00	396
817008203X	**Telecom & Networking Glossary**	Robert Mastin	Rs. 300.00	250
8170082048	**Data Networking Made Easy**	Karen Patten	Rs. 360.00	350
8170082056	**Digital Convergence**	Andy Covell	Rs. 300.00	234

OFFICE AUTOMATION

ISBN	TITLE	AUTHOR	PRICE	PAGES
8170089891	**Desk Top Publishing**	Dinesh Maidasani	Rs. 150.00	311
8170087805	**Learning Computer Fundamentals, MS Office and Internet & Web Technology**	Dinesh Maidasani	Rs. 95.00	301
8170087686	**MS-Word 2000 Thumb-Rules and Details**	Snigdha Banerjee	Rs. 175.00	390
8170089239	**Computer Accounting with Tally 7.2**	Firewall Media	Rs. 195.00	330

ON YOUR SIDE SERIES

ISBN	TITLE	AUTHOR	PRICE	PAGES
8170084830	**On your Side-Powerpoint 2002**	Andrew Blackburn	Rs. 145.00	282
8170084849	**On your Side-Excel 2002**	Adrienne Tommy	Rs. 125.00	275

ISBN	TITLE	AUTHOR	PRICE	PAGES
8170084857	**On your Side-Word 2002**	Adrienne Tommy	Rs. 125.00	289
8170084865	**On your Side-Access 2002**	Adrienne Tommy	Rs. 125.00	303
8170084873	**On your Side-Frontpage 2002**	Andrew Blackburn	Rs. 95.00	245
8170084881	**On your Side-Windows XP**	Adrienne Tommy	Rs. 125.00	310

OPERATING SYSTEMS

ISBN	TITLE	AUTHOR	PRICE	PAGES
8170087236	**Linux—A Practical Approach**	B. Mohamed Ibrahim	Rs. 95.00	187
8170088623	**Red Hat Linux Study Guide**	Vijay Shekhar	Rs. 350.00	635
8170088631	**Red Hat Linux-The Complete Bible**	Vijay Shekhar	Rs. 545.00	1176
8170089581	**Unix and Shell Programming**	Archana Verma	Rs. 80.00	137
8170089131	**Operating System Concepts**	P.S. Gill	Rs. 95.00	181
8170083427	**The MS-Windows XP Professional Handbook**	Louis Columbus	Rs. 295.00	330
8170084784	**Way in-Windows XP Home Edition**	Andrew Blackburn	Rs. 95.00	183
8170086221	**Cyber Rookies—Operating System Fundamentals**	D. Irtegov	Rs. 295.00	498

PROGRAMMING

ISBN	TITLE	AUTHOR	PRICE	PAGES
8170087791	**The Art of Programming Through Flowcharts & Algorithms**	Anil Bikas Chaudhuri	Rs. 95.00	160
8170086248	**Preventative Programming Techniques: Avoid and Correct Common Mistakes**	Brian Hawkins	Rs. 295.00	322
8170083443	**Learning Computer Programming : It's not about Languages**	Mary Farrell	Rs. 295.00	375
8170086256	**Object-Oriented Programming: From Problem Solving to Java**	José M. Garrido	Rs. 295.00	360
817008931X	**Object-Oriented Programming-Concept and Implementation**	A. Rajesh	Rs. 95.00	182
8170089107	**Java: J2SE-5 A Practical Approach**	B. Mohammad Ibrahim	Rs. 175.00	332
8170089409	**Advance Java**	Gajendra Gupta	Rs. 175.00	305
8170088038	**Assembly Language Programming for Intel Processors Family**	Vasile Lungu	Rs. 295.00	577
8170088178	**The Assembly Programming Master Book**	Vlad Pirogov	Rs. 395.00	726
813180075X	**Java Messaging**	Eric Bruno	Rs. 295.00	480

Please write for a free color Firewall Media Catalog for details on the above books.

ISBN	TITLE	AUTHOR	PRICE	PAGES
	PROGRAMMING - C#, C, C++			
8170083702	**The Power of C#**	Rajiv Parida	Rs. 295.00	576
8170085632	**Mastering Graphics Programming in 'C'**	Sudhir Dawra	Rs. 145.00	286
8170088879	**Programming in C and Numerical Analysis**	J.B. Dixit	Rs. 350.00	355
8170087074	**Mastering C Programs**	J.B. Dixit	Rs. 195.00	434
8170081262	**Programming in C**	J.B. Dixit	Rs. 295.00	506
8170087619	**Unix and C Programming**	Ashok Arora, Shefali Bansal	Rs. 295.00	606
817008878X	**C Interview Questions and Answers**	J. Rajaram	Rs. 75.00	139
8170089034	**Pragmatic C**	R.K. Jangda	Rs. 150.00	258
8170086140	**Data Structure for 'C' Programming**	Ajay Kumar	Rs. 145.00	290
8170081270	**Programming in C++**	J.B. Dixit	Rs. 260.00	602
8170088194	**Hackish C++ Pranks & Tricks**	Michael Flenov	Rs. 245.00	326
8170082889	**Basics of C++ Programming**	Nishant Kundalia	Rs. 95.00	168
8170083648	**Mastering C++ Programs**	J.B. Dixit	Rs. 295.00	598
817008623X	**Cyber Rookies—C++ Programming Fundamentals**	Chuck Easttom	Rs. 295.00	417
8131800202	**Data Structure using C++**	N. Jayalakshmi	Rs. 65.00	126
8170089123	**C++ Made Easy**	T.D. Malhotra	Rs. 250.00	449
8131800393	**C++ & Introduction to C#**	T.D. Malhotra, Rajeev A. Parida, A. Rajesh	Rs. 200.00	440
8131800350	**OOPS with C++**	M. Jaya Prasad	Rs. 150.00	317
	SECURITY			
8170083419	**Computer Forensics : Computer Crime Scene Investigation**	John Vacca	Rs. 445.00	731
8131800156	**Computer Evidence (Collection and Preservation)**	Christopher L.T. Brown	Rs. 295.00	394
8170083494	**Firewall Architecture for the Enterprise**	Norbert Pohlmann, Tim Crothers	Rs. 295.00	480
8170086272	**Net Spies**	Andrew Gauntlett	Rs. 195.00	210
3826607546	**Firewall Systems**	Norbert Pohlmann	Rs. 1630.00	544
8131800504	**Homeland Security Techniques and Technologies**	Jesus Mena	Rs. 295.00	346

ISBN	TITLE	AUTHOR	PRICE	PAGES
	ENGINEERING AND TECHNOLOGY			
817008718X	**Human Aspects of Software Engineering**	James E. Tomayko, Orit Hazzan	Rs. 195.00	338
8131800032	**Management Information Systems**	Avdhesh Gupta, Anurag Malik	Rs. 195.00	400
8170087953	**Human Computer Interaction**	Rajendra Ranjan Kumar	Rs. 95.00	210
8170088097	**Structured System Analysis and Design**	Preeti Gupta	Rs. 125.00	192
817008802X	**Autocad 2005 for Engineers**	Ionel Simion	Rs. 175.00	271
8170088054	**Digital Signal Processing Fundamentals**	Ashfaq A. Khan	Rs. 295.00	391
8131800164	**Digital Communication System Using System VUE**	Dennis Silage	Rs. 295.00	365
8170089719	**Foundations of Computer Science**	Ashok Arora	Rs. 250.00	386
817008363X	**Practical Project Management**	Ivan Bayross	Rs. 195.00	342
8131800806	**Digital Signal Processing using MATLAB and Wavelets**	Michael Weeks	Rs. 350.00	452
8131800792	**Classical Electrodynamics**	Hans C. Dhanian	Rs. 395.00	620
8131800512	**The Software Vulnerability Guide**	Herbert H. Thompson, Scott G. Chase	Rs. 195.00	368
8131800776	**Robot Modelling and Kinematics**	Rachid Manseur	Rs. 295.00	380
8131800369	**System Software**	M. Joseph	Rs. 95.00	185
	STRAIGHT TO THE POINT SERIES			
8170084601	**STTP : Word 2002**	Corinne Hervo	Rs. 45.00	154
817008461X	**STTP : Excel 2002**	Corinne Hervo	Rs. 45.00	153
8170084628	**STTP : Dreamweaver 4**	Corinne Hervo	Rs. 45.00	135
8170084636	**STTP : Flash 5**	Corinne Hervo	Rs. 45.00	183
8170084644	**STTP : Photoshop 6**	Corinne Hervo	Rs. 45.00	152
817008881X	**STTP : MS Office 2000**	Dinesh Maidasani	Rs. 125.00	290
8170086100	**STTP : MS Office 2003**	Dinesh Maidasani	Rs. 145.00	288
8170087651	**STTP : MS Word 2003**	Firewall Media	Rs. 60.00	150
8170088011	**STTP : Photoshop CS**	Firewall Media	Rs. 60.00	150
8170088143	**STTP : MS Excel 2003**	Firewall Media	Rs. 60.00	150
8170088151	**STTP : CorelDraw 12**	Firewall Media	Rs. 60.00	150
8131800105	**STTP : 3ds MAX 7**	Dinesh Maidasani	Rs. 95.00	182
8131800083	**STTP : Auto CAD 2006**	Dinesh Maidasani	Rs. 95.00	190
8131800245	**STTP : CorelDraw X3**	Dinesh Maidasani	Rs. 75.00	188

Please write for a free color Firewall Media Catalog for details on the above books.

ISBN	TITLE	AUTHOR	PRICE	PAGES
8131800253	**STTP : Dreamweaver 8**	Dinesh Maidasani	Rs. 75.00	148
8131800237	**STTP : Photoshop CS2**	Dinesh Maidasani	Rs. 75.00	172
8170088380	**STTP : Tally 7.2**	Firewall Media	Rs. 175.00	322
8131800091	**STTP : Flash 8**	Dinesh Maidasani	Rs. 95.00	180
8131800407	**STTP : My SQL 5.0**	Dinesh Maidasani	Rs. 85.00	166
8131800458	**STTP : Microsoft Power Point 2003**	Dinesh Maidasani	Rs. 75.00	142

STUDIO FACTORY

ISBN	TITLE	AUTHOR	PRICE	PAGES
8170084792	**Studio Factory—Photoshop 6**	Christophe Aubry	Rs. 175.00	364
8170084806	**Studio Factory—Flash 5**	Sami Ben Yahiya	Rs. 145.00	314
8170084814	**Studio Factory—Dreamweaver Ultradev 4**	Phillippe Chatellier	Rs. 95.00	240
8170084822	**Studio Factory—Dreamweaver 4**	Christophe Aubry	Rs. 175.00	373
8170087643	**Studio Factory—Dreamweaver MX**	Christophe Aubry	Rs. 195.00	407
8170087627	**Studio Factory—Flash MX**	Arnaud Blanche	Rs. 145.00	337
817008766X	**Studio Factory—Photoshop 7**	Cyril Guerin	Rs. 195.00	420

LAXMI PUBLICATIONS (P) LTD

113, Golden House, Daryaganj, New Delhi-110002

Phone : **011 - 43 53 25 00**

Fax : **011 - 43 53 25 28**

EMAIL : info@laxmipublications.com

Website : www.laxmipublications.com

BRANCHES

- 129/1, IIIrd Main Road, IX Cross, Chamrajpet, **Bangalore** (*Phone* : 080-26 61 15 61)
- 26, Damodaran Street, T. Nagar, **Chennai** (*Phone* : 044-24 34 47 26)
- 43/1394D, St. Benedict's Road, Ernakulam North, **Cochin** (*Phone* : 0484-239 70 04)
- Pan Bazar, Rani Bari, **Guwahati** (*Phones* : 0361-254 36 69, 251 38 81)
- 4-2-453, Ist Floor, Ramkote, **Hyderabad** (*Phone* : 040-24 75 02 47)
- Adda Tanda Chowk, N.D. 365, **Jalandhar City** (*Phone* : 0181-222 12 72)
- 106/A, Ist Floor, S.N. Banerjee Road, **Kolkata** (*Phones* : 033-22 27 37 73, 22 27 52 47)
- 18, Madan Mohan Malviya Marg, **Lucknow** (*Phone* : 0522-220 95 78)
- 142-C, Victor House, Ground Floor, N.M. Joshi Marg, Lower Parel (W), **Mumbai** (*Phones* : 022-24 91 54 15, 24 92 78 69)
- Radha Govind Street, Tharpagna, **Ranchi** (*Phone* : 0651-230 77 64)